RACE AND CULTURE IN PSYCHIATRY

RACE AND CULTURE IN PSYCHIATRY

Suman Fernando

Tavistock/Routledge
London and New York

First published in 1988 by Croom Helm
Reprinted in 1989
by Routledge
11 New Fetter Lane,
London EC4P 4EE

29 West 35th Street,
New York, NY 10001

Printed in Great Britain by
Billing & Sons Ltd, Worcester

British Library Cataloguing in Publication Data

Fernando, Suman
   Race and culture in psychiatry.
   1. Medicine. Psychiatry. Cultural aspects
   I. Title
   362.2

Library of Congress Cataloging in Publication Data
Also available

ISBN 0-415-04737-4

Contents

To: Frances and Siri

Introduction

This is a book about psychiatry in a multicultural and multiracial setting. It is about the discipline of psychiatry—about the assumptions and ideologies that determine the ways in which psychiatry goes about its business in both developing theories and dealing with people. About the aims of the discipline — both explicit and implicit — and the methods used by people involved in that discipline; the pressures on them both as practitioners and as those at the receiving end of the practice. The book is also about psychiatry as an 'institution', an established order within our society that serves a particular function — or perhaps many functions. The book is not a treatise on Culture or Race or Psychiatry, nor indeed a comprehensive account of the connections between them. But it is an attempt to highlight some of the important issues about all three in connection with each other and, more importantly, in the context of British society. The notion of 'context' occurs time and time again throughout the book. Indeed the book itself must be seen in the context of where and when it is written — and by whom. Although there are references in the book to studies from all over the world, the main focus of interest is the British scene. It is written from a background of mainstream psychiatry rather than academic research; from psychiatry viewed from its professional grass roots rather than its ivory towers; from practical experience in many settings in and around London — from the hurly-burly of the inner city to the wastelands of the mental hospital; and last but not least, from reflections on the perceptions and feelings about culture and race based on personal experience of everyday psychiatry.

Since psychiatry has been developed in a Western (Judeo-Christian) cultural framework by (mainly) white people, the significance of cultural and racial considerations becomes obvious and important when the specialty is practised among people who do not conform to this culture and/or are identified as not being 'white'. Transcultural psychiatry developed as an interest arising from this encounter. At first the location of this encounter was identified (geographically) in Africa and Asia; the encounter in North America was largely ignored perhaps because, (a) there was a presumption that all voluntary (mainly white) immigrants to North America went into a cultural 'melting pot' (Herberg, 1960) to become 'American', (b) involuntary (black) immigrants were not perceived (by Whites) as having any culture, and (c) people indigenous to the American continent, disparagingly referred to as 'Red Indians', were disregarded altogether as not being 'American' at all. Hence, although racial attitudes towards Afro-Americans and indigenous Americans did develop within psychiatry, transcultural psychiatry did not emerge as an interest applicable to the American scene. One of the first books on transcultural psychiatry published in the United States (Kiev, 1972), as well as its fore-runner (Kiev, 1964), failed to mention American Blacks at all and merely made passing reference to indigenous North Americans. Differences between Whites and Blacks were seen as racial differences apparently devoid of a cultural content — and race was seen as a biological concept alone. For example, reports of higher rates of mental illness among Blacks compared to Whites were usually attributed to innate inferiority, too rapid acculturation, or striving for equality (Pasamanick, 1963), while reports of lower rates were ignored (Fischer, 1969). The tradition of ignoring the culture of American Blacks has persisted in American transcultural psychiatry. Thus, although transcultural psychiatry as a topic for study has progressed in the United States in terms of university posts (in the 'specialty' of transcultural psychiatry), research work and publications, the subject has remained largely a theoretical one as far as the black population is concerned.

However, it was at McGill University in Canada that interest in transcultural study developed in the 1950s stimulated by Eric Wittkower (Murphy, 1983). The development of the McGill group and the formation of the Transcultural Section of the World Psychiatric Association (WPA) have been described recently by Murphy (1986). Later, a base — as it were — for transcultural psychiatry as a research interest was established by Morris Carstairs at Edinburgh in Scotland.

Transcultural psychiatry arrived on the British scene in 1976 with the International Congress on Transcultural Psychiatry (1976) organised by Philip Rack with Morris Carstairs as the congress president. This meeting concentrated on diagnosis, migration, and drug therapy with sessions ranging from 'Cultural Variations in the Diagnosis and Classification of Mental Disorders' to 'Social and Emotional Stresses of Migrants and their Families'. However, there was a quick bite at possible racial issues in a session on 'Race Awareness, Prejudice and Discrimination'. The Transcultural Psychiatry Society (UK) came into being soon after this congress. As interest in the subject developed, the focus of attention of British workers in transcultural psychiatry shifted, partly as a result of attacks on them from community workers — as exemplified in an article by the Black Health Workers and Patients Group (1984) — and partly because of their own experience of racial discrimination. Racial issues surfaced strongly on the last day of a meeting of the British Transcultural Psychiatry Society held in April 1982. As a result of this, the annual meeting in the following year was devoted to the question 'Does racism cause Mental Illness?' Subsequent meetings — for example one on 'Women: Cultural Perspectives' (Fernando, 1985) — organised by the society have consistently examined aspects of both race and culture, and, in April 1985, the Society changed its constitution (Transcultural Psychiatry Society, 1985) to specify the following:

> The objects of the Society shall be the promotion of mental health and advancement of psychiatric knowledge for the public benefit irrespective of race class gender culture and in particular (but without in any way limiting the generality of the foregoing) to increase awareness and understanding of the effects of racism sexism and culture on health and illness and to encourage sensitivity to prejudiced attitudes, racist and sexist practices and cultural values among practitioners who are concerned with mental health.

For practical purposes, transcultural psychiatry in Britain is firmly embedded in ordinary clinical practice (Cox, 1986). It is a term used loosely to cover two interrelated topics namely, (a) cultural aspects of psychiatry — or 'cultural psychiatry' — and (b) psychiatry in non-Western cultures. Although the former can ignore race — and frequently does so — the latter cannot possibly do so.

Cultural psychiatry has been defined by Wittkower (1965) as a branch of social psychiatry which 'concerns itself with the cultural aspects of the aetiology, frequency and nature of mental illness and the care and aftercare of the mentally ill within the confines of a given cultural unit.' Cross-cultural studies are then means of examining and understanding cultural psychiatry. Transcultural psychiatry denotes a viewpoint which extends beyond the scope of any one cultural unit on to others (Wittkower, 1968). Since psychiatry itself is a part of Western culture, the transcultural perspective starts from the Western cultural base. Cross-cultural studies too make assumptions derived from a particular cultural base —

usually the Western. Hence, the terms cross-cultural and transcultural are usually used synonymously.

What is often referred to as transcultural psychiatry outside Britain is, in British terms, cultural psychiatry. Its scope and extent is interpreted in various ways: In the sixties it was seen by Wittkower (1965) 'as predominantly a field of research though there are also practical applications.' Later, for Yap (1974): 'Transcultural psychiatry, embracing many activities that are oriented towards action as well as theory, is an offshoot of the general art and science of psychiatry. Its academic content lies principally in its theoretical orientation and research interests.' Kleinman (1977) is very critical of what he calls 'traditional transcultural psychiatry' for its assumption 'that deviance can be studied in different societies independent of specific cultural norms and local patterns of normative behaviour.' He is particularly critical of the search by psychiatry for disease entities that are culture free, and sees one focus of cross-cultural study as the cultural shaping of illness phenomena. Questions about the effects of culture on the manifestation of psychiatric illness raises issues about the nature of illness itself; these lead on to other problems that are 'integral to the whole question of how culture might differentially affect perception, cognition and behavioural organisation more generally' (Fabrega, 1984).

There is no argument within main-line psychiatry that the cultural viewpoint is important in considering the role of psychiatry in non-Western cultures. But in doing so, various other aspects of human beings and their life experiences must be considered too. Geographical and/or biological factors may be important in some situations. Thus, certain personality attributes may be an advantage in certain climates: For example, the observation that schizophrenia is common in Northern Sweden (Book, 1953) may be explicable in terms of the advantage that schizoid people may have for living in the isolated conditions of that region. The genetic selecting-in of manic-depressive illness may lead to manic-depression being common in certain communities such as the Hutterites (Eaton and Weil, 1955). In some situations, the political ethos that is prevalent, or, an issue such as sexism or racism, may be an important consideration in evaluating what appears to be cross-cultural differences. The broad concept of schizophrenia in the Soviet Union (World Health Organisation, 1973) may be determined by the definition of mental health based upon political principles (Wing, 1978). The alleged preponderance of depression among Jewish minorities in Europe before the last war (Strecker, Appel, Eyman, Farr, Lamas, Falmer and Smith, 1931; Hes, 1960) may be largely to do with the under-mining of self-esteem by anti-semitism; the apparently high in-cidence of schizophrenic diagnoses among some ethnic minorities in British society (Bagley, 1971; Cochrane, 1977) may reflect atti-tudes (to people from these minorities) that are institutionalised within psychiatry or British society. The point is that, in studying the cultural dimension of what psychiatry identifies as mental dis-order, the impact of geographical, biological, political and social influences on mental disorder and on psychiatry itself must be taken into account. While it is relatively easy to allow for the first two groups of factors (i.e. geographical and biological), it is almost im-possible to separate political and social issues from specifically cul-tural influences. Therefore both dimensions — the sociocultural and the sociopolitical — must be considered at all levels of cross-cultural research and clinical practice in a multiracial and multicul-tural society.

In the field of psychiatric practice, transcultural psychiatry must recognise that social pressures and political issues impinge on people involved in psychiatry, as practitioners or patients, often in-teracting with cultural matters. Value judgements of culture further complicate the picture. And then there is race — or rather the cate-gorisation of people into different races and the judgements made about the people within those categories. Although there is no doubt about the reality of human variability, the distinction be-tween various groups based on a simple visual appraisal is scienti-fically faulty (Molnar, 1983) but real enough to those who are designated as racially inferior. Three facts should be noted here:

(a) Race identified by skin-colour does not correspond to genetic types (Jones, 1981).
(b) Genetic diversity of mankind, together with the unique genetic endowment of each person, gives a (genetic) potential that is vast and complex.
(c) Patterns of behaviour or psychological attributes are gener-ated by complicated interactions of factors that could not poss-ibly be limited to groups of genes inherited by races — however, race is defined (Spuhler and Lindzey, 1967; Fried, 1968).

Although race is a biological myth it is very much a social reality. In an introduction to a book on race in Britain, Charles Husband (1982) starts by quoting Banton and Harwood (1975) as follows: 'As a way of categorising people, race is based upon a delusion because popular ideas about racial classification lack scientific validity and are moulded by political pressures rather than by the evidence from biology.' Husband goes on to argue that one reason for the continuing validity of race (as a category) is that:

> Beneath its apparently simple reduction of complex individuals and societies to self-evidently basic units there lies a highly complex body of emotive ideas. There are ideas which reach out in their reference and significance beyond the immediate forms of racial categorisation as such. Rather they invoke a rich matrix of values and images referring to purity-pollution, Christianity-Heathen, national-alien, amongst others. 'Race', like 'love', is a word often used with innocent spontaneity, and yet it remains highly problematic to determine adequately the boundaries of its denotative and connotative meanings.

Since psychiatry is always practised in a social setting, it is inevitable that racial images and myths that are to hand (within society) would enter into its substance and affect all aspects of its work in a multi-racial society. Race would come into the picture — or rather is the canvas for the picture—whenever a psychiatric judgement is made, cross-cultural research is undertaken, or a deduction made about culture, especially if the people involved are from more than one racial category. Further, racial considerations, usually in the form of racism, affect theories of psychiatry through the perceptions of people who make these theories, the particular methodology that psychiatry uses, and through the traditions and history of psychiatry. Thus both race and culture are important aspects of psychiatric theory and practice. Although there has been a plethora of recent books on cultural aspects of psychiatry, there is a dearth of literature concerning race and psychiatry. It is the view of the author that issues concerning race and culture are so intertwined in a multi-racial and multi-cultural society that neither can be considered in isolation from the other in analysing the part they play in psychiatry.

In the course of this book it will be argued that psychiatry is not 'neutral', in the sense of being impartial or indifferent, to either culture or race. Therefore, a study of race and culture in psychiatry must examine the culture of psychiatry itself, i.e. the nature of the behaviour, beliefs and attitudes within the discipline and the social system of psychiatry. In order to understand its culture fully, one has to consider how psychiatry has been shaped by political and social forces and grasp the strength and nature of the ideologies that underpin its theory and practice. The book will therefore start by considering the culture of psychiatry in relation to the ideology of racism.

Although psychiatry has a background of theory, it is first and foremost a practical discipline. Current literature gives some indication of psychiatric practice but the proof of the pudding is in the eating. The second chapter of the book will analyse the current position of psychiatry on racial and cultural issues, examining its practice, trying to get as close to a feel of what psychiatry is like *now* : Its current theoretical concepts, ways of working and forms of service delivery will be considered from a racial and cultural viewpoint.

Cross-cultural psychiatric research is beset with immense methodological problems. These will be described in the third chapter when a few of the more useful studies in this field will be considered and these — and others less useful but more renowned — will be critically examined. Some conclusions of a general nature appertaining to transcultural psychiatry will be drawn, and the resistance of mainline psychiatry to incorporate these lessons will be discussed.

The cultural viewpoint in the practice of psychiatry will be discussed in the fourth chapter. It will be argued that incorporating culture in practical psychiatry means that the social realities of life that apply to people designated as belonging to cultural or ethnic groups must be taken on board. A 'socio-cultural psychiatry' will be formulated in the course of discussing the irrelevance of psychiatry when cultural and racial issues are not faced, and the perversity of some current diagnoses will be considered.

The fifth chapter will attempt to get to grips with the extent to which racism affects psychiatry, although this issue will also crop up in other parts of the book. The importance of considering the racist dimension in observations, evaluations and treatment of patients will be analysed and the racial and cultural connotations in the use of compulsory powers in a psychiatric context will be discussed. The interrelationship between racial and cultural issues in the practice of psychiatry is a central theme of the whole book but the sixth chapter will consider this in some detail and discuss ways of attempting to disentangle the issues in practice.

The final chapter will establish that psychiatry — both as an institution and a discipline — needs to free itself from the ideology of racism and incorporate the lessons of cross-cultural research into its theory and practice. An anti-racist approach must develop hand in hand with a culture-sensitive one. This may require fundamental changes in psychiatry as well as changes in society as a whole. But something can be done now; a start has to made. Although each chapter stands on its own with its own special emphasis, the seven chapters inevitably overlap and interrelate. The book as a whole is directed at the thinking public as well as professionals in the field of 'psychiatry'. It is presented both as a critique of psychiatric practice and as an aid to psychiatrists, social workers and others concerned professionally with mental health.

1

The Culture of Psychiatry

INTRODUCTION

The definition of the term 'culture' with reference to societies and people will be discussed in Chapter 3. In this chapter, however, the term 'culture' is used in a somewhat different sense. The sociological concept of culture is defined by Therborn (1980) as 'the ensemble of everyday activities and ideologies of a particular group or class, or as a more general inclusive concept for ideology, science and art and, possibly, other practices studied from the point of view of their production of meaning.' Psychiatry is both a professional discipline and a social system or institution (as described in the next paragraph); it is the 'culture of psychiatry' that gives meaning to its activities as a discipline and to its structure as an institution. Included within its culture are the ideologies and beliefs that determine the way psychiatry functions. Therborn describes an ideology as including both everyday notions and 'experience', as well as elaborate intellectual doctrines. In other words, an ideology includes common sense images within society as well as composite systems of belief. Although the terms 'culture' and 'ideology' are used in similar senses, the former covers a wider field than the latter does.

In a book based on the Reith Lectures broadcast on the BBC, Donald Schon (1971) described at some length the structure of social institutions or systems, the way they resist change, and the need to develop systems that are capable of adaptation. A social system is 'a complex of individuals which tend to maintain its boundaries and its patterns of internal relationships.' It contains a structure, theory and technology:

The structure is the set of roles and relations among individual members. The theory consists of the views held within the social system about its purposes, its operations, its environment and its future. Both reflect, and in turn influence, the prevailing technology of the system. The dimensions all hang together so that any change in one produces change in the others.

The structure within the social system of psychiatry consists of professional roles and relationships with attributes of status, commitment to particular theories and ways of working, and a set or sets of values. It is the culture of psychiatry that gives meaning to these values; the ideologies within it determine ways in which the institution functions. Theory within psychiatry is both formal, or official, and informal, or hidden. The former relates to ideals of service, professional codes, etc., and the latter includes notions of maintaining status within society and/or control over patients, as well as ways of seeing people. The technology of psychiatry as an institution is clearly identical with that of the discipline of psychiatry — ways of gathering information, methods of evaluating and examining people, and techniques of intervention in the form of physical, psychological and social treatment.

It is apparent that psychiatry as a discipline is connected with psychiatry as an institution both in its historical development and in its present state. This section is concerned mainly with a particular ideology within the culture of psychiatry, namely the ideology about race, and the extent to which this ideology is a part of the culture of psychiatry both as a discipline and as a social system or institution. The subject will be explored in the first place by considering the historical context in which psychiatry and the ideology about race have developed within Western culture.

HISTORY OF PSYCHIATRY

Any discussion of the history of psychiatry is faced with a need to define psychiatry itself. If considered primarily as a healing art, does it mean the practice of healing through the ages in all parts of the world (Veith, 1970), or should it be limited to modern — 'scientific' — psychiatry as a branch of medicine (Ellenberger, 1974) based on a Western medical model of illness? The approach here favours the latter view — with modifications.

Psychiatrists who view their discipline as essentially a healing art within the medical framework consider that 'scientific' psychiatry started at the middle of the nineteenth century (Mora, 1970). But medical interest in emotional disturbance and medical influence over the care of the insane goes back much further. *A Treatise of Melancholy* by Timothy Bright was published in 1586 and Robert Burton's *The Anatomy of Melancholy* in 1621. In practical terms, psychiatry may be envisaged as having started in 1632 when a medical governor was appointed to the Priory of St. Mary of Bethlem — an institution which had been taking in lunatics since 1403. However it was in the latter part of the eighteenth century that psychiatry became established as a field of medicine 'when a new attitude developed towards the mentally ill as a consequence of the new spirit of inner freedom brought about by The Enlightenment.' (Mora, 1961).

The establishment of asylums in the early part of the nineteenth century was accompanied by a rapid growth in specialisation and professional organisations of psychiatry. In his book *Museums of Madness* Scull (1979) describes how the building of physical — bricks and mortar — institutions in the early part of the nineteenth century enabled psychiatry to develop as a discipline dominating a social system dealing with the insane:

> Prior to the segregation of the mad into specialised institutions, medical interest in, and concern with, the mad was for the most part quite slight. In historical terms, of course, the idea that insanity was a disease was not without precedent. For many centuries, though, the medical approach to lunacy had either been ignored or been forced to compete with theological and demonological perspectives.

The new discipline of medical psychology (that developed into psychiatry) was installed in mental institutions and, in turn, formed the ideological rationale for the existence of the asylums (Donnelly, 1983). In Britain, a professional association, The Association of Medical Officers of Asylums and Hospitals for the Insane, was founded in 1841 and its *Asylum Journal of Mental Science* was published in 1853. The former became the Royal Medico-Psychological Association and finally the Royal College of Psychiatrists in 1971. The latter became the *Journal of Mental Science* and then the *British Journal of Psychiatry* in 1963. The American Psychiatric Association — originally called the Association of Medical Super-

3

intendents of American Institutions for the Insane — was established in 1844 (Mora, 1961) and the *American Journal of Insanity* started the same year (Amdur, 1944). The first comprehensive textbook on psychiatry for clinical training — *A Manual of Psychological Medicine* by John Bucknill and Daniel Hack Tuke — appeared in 1858. And a few years later, *The Physiology and Pathology of Mind* by Henry Maudsley (1867) was published — 'a turning point in English psychiatry' (Lewis, 1951). Thus, it could be said that the discipline of psychiatry started in the mid-seventeenth century and grew slowly over the years until it emerged, in the early nineteenth century, as a fully fledged (medical) discipline. From then onwards, psychiatry as an institution (linked to the discipline), became recognisable and respectable as a social entity.

In a book analysing perceptions of mental disorder in Western culture, Bennett Simon (1978) shows how modern psychiatry has precursors and analogues in what he terms 'ancient psychiatry' as represented in Greek poetry, philosophy and medicine. The West European cultural framework, within which psychiatry has developed, embodied several important notions which determined the path taken by the emerging discipline. In discussing the Cartesian view of a person as a dualism of mind and body which has dominated Western philosophy and scientific thinking for over three hundred years, Gold (1985) writes:

> The human body has been conceived as being a purely passive machine driven by mechanical causality. Thus, it is seen as an inanimate entity in itself, having no intentionality nor teleology (these latter properties Descartes attributes to God); in effect the body is seen: *'tout simple'* as a mere *' res extensa'*. The mind, on the other hand, has been understood as an incorporeal repository of intelligence, consciousness and motivation within the confines of the body i.e. the *' res cogitans'*.

The view of the body as a machine constructed from different parts has promoted the growth of biological sciences and physiology, thereby directing medical research into the investigation of bodily disorders. This has paid off tremendously in the development of medical science — at least as far as bodily illness is concerned. However the Cartesian view of nature has hindered the ability of science to tackle some biological problems that are concerned with psychic phenomena and the total functioning of human beings. According to Lewins and Lewontin (1985):

This great success of the Cartesian method and the Cartesian view of nature is in part a result of a historical path of least resistance. Those problems that yield to the attack are pursued most vigorously, precisely because the method works there. Other problems and other phenomena are left behind, walled off from understanding by the commitment to Cartesianism. The harder problems are not tackled, if for no other reason than that brilliant scientific careers are not built on persistent failure.

Although scientific medicine enabled physicians to gain detailed insights into intimate mechanisms of the human body and to develop complicated and sophisticated technologies for intervention at a mechanical level, the Cartesian concepts inherent in it had a dehumanising effect through its view of the person as a physiological mechanism (Gold, 1985).

As the medical speciality of psychiatry developed, it naturally took on a bio-medical view of illness; mental disorder was attributed to somatic causes; and a medical — as opposed to religious — dominance over madness was established (Scull, 1981):

This somatic emphasis is particularly unsurprising when we recall that to adopt a perspective which allowed disorders of the mind/soul to be the aetiological root of insanity threatened to call into question the soul's immortality and with it the very foundations of Christianity, or to lend substance to the notion that crazy people were possessed by Satan or the subjects of divine retribution — which, of course, made them better candidates for the ministrations of ecclesiastics than for those of physicians.

Thus, psychiatry took over the mind which — as the soul — had belonged to religion. Naturally there developed a growing acceptance that mind was a function of the brain. The German school of somatic psychiatry looked for the causes of mental illness in specific changes of bodily function or structure, to be understood in mechanistic terms. Since natural causation is implicit within the medical model of illness (Siegler and Osmond, 1974), aetiology was sought in natural events — injuries, defects, infections, etc — that happen to people rather than incidents that are caused by others. As psychological theories of the working of the mind were generated, the notion of psychopathology — pathological changes affecting the mind analogous with changes affecting the body —

developed. These psychological theories too were within the Cartesian framework but used concepts borrowed from Newtonian physics such as forces, energy and mechanisms. Altschule (1965) describes how 'ego-psychology' was developed by introspective psychology and the 'ego' given 'a real existence' when introduced into clinical psychiatry in the mid-nineteenth century. He quotes from a description of the 'ego' in a book by Griesinger (1845) which constitutes 'a landmark in psychiatric thinking':

> The solid, constant nucleus of individuality can be sought nowhere but in the strong complexes which have been combined to form *das Ich*. The nucleus may be shaken in the emotions but not destroyed; what else can be affected in the emotions than that group of ideas, *das Ich? Das Ich* can be detached and can disintegrate completely....

Although Descartes had suggested that the mind should be studied by introspection while the body was studied by methods of natural science, psychologists adopted both methods for studying the mind resulting in the two major schools of psychology — the structuralists (studying the structure of mind) and the behaviourists who analysed behaviour and ignored the mind as originally conceptualised.

The psychoanalytic theories of Freud had an enormous influence on psychiatry at the end of the nineteenth century and well into the twentieth. But these too did not break out of the mould set by the scientific thinking of the time. According to Capra (1982):

> As in Newtonian physics so also in psychoanalysis, the mechanistic view of reality implies a rigorous determinism. Every psychological event has a definite cause and gives rise to a finite effect, and the whole psychological state of an individual is uniquely determined by 'initial conditions' in early childhood. The 'genetic' approach of psychoanalysis consists of tracing symptoms and behaviour of a patient back to previous developmental stages along a linear chain of cause-and-effect relations... The strictly rational and mechanistic approach made it especially difficult for Freud to deal with religious, or mystical experiences... In the Freudian model there is no room for experiences of altered states of consciousness that challenge all the basic concepts of classical science. Consequently, experiences of this nature which occur spontaneously much more

frequently than is commonly believed, have often been labelled as psychotic symptoms by psychiatrists who do not incorporate them into their conceptual framework.

The work of the behaviourists affected psychiatry in the twentieth century. The mind, which other psychologists had conceptualised as a 'thing' analogous to the body, was denied by the behaviourists. The schools of behaviourism and psychoanalysis 'differed markedly in their methods and their views of consciousness but nevertheless adhered, basically, to the same Newtonian model of reality' (Capra, 1982).

Just as a mechanistic view of life and Newtonian physics determined the concepts used in Western psychology in the nineteenth century and the early part of the twentieth, the physical world became the model for understanding the social world (Shweder and Bourne, 1984): Physical metaphors (noted earlier) were used by social scientists to describe social events and systems. In the course of reviewing the history of psychiatry in Britain, Howells (1975) noted that 'materialism slowly but surely steered medicine away from psychopathology and left the psychiatrist in isolation, an alienist.' He reckoned that 'these three hundred years (i.e. from 1600 to 1900) deserve to be termed the dark age of psychiatry.'

Thus, by the early part of the nineteenth century, the 'culture of psychiatry' had been established: A mechanistic view of life, a materialistic concept of mind, a segmented approach to the individual, and a model of illness which assumed a bio-medical change and a natural causation. As neurology developed to take over the domain of brain disease, psychiatry, in keeping with the bio-medical approach to illness, looked for causes of illness within the individual psyche — in pathology of the psyche as opposed to pathology of the soma. The social context in which illness occurred was largely disregarded and the notion of illness being caused by relations within a social group did not become a part of psychiatric tradition (White and Marsella, 1984). Psychiatry took on Western thinking about normality; mental health was perceived as relating to psychological and behavioural qualities (Marsella, 1984) with a dualistic approach to the human person, rather than one that encompassed a harmony in relationships and a holism of somatic and psychological functioning. Materialism dominated over a spiritual approach to life.

Once established as an institution and a professional discipline, psychiatry developed in various ways. Physical restraint of earlier

7

years gave way in the early part of the nineteenth century to moral treatment. In the eighteenth century, theories of causation of insanity had been adopted for their metaphorical and visual aptness rather than on the basis of empirical facts (Skultans, 1979), but the approach changed at the turn of the century. The ideologist school in Paris held that scientific theory should be based on accumulative analyses of data (Rosen, 1946). Philippe Pinel (1809) allied himself with the ideologists and restricted his research to 'those symptoms and signs which are recognisable by the senses and which are not susceptible to vague reasoning' — thus preparing the way for modern psychiatry (Woods and Carlson, 1961). Moral treatment, as a means of manipulating the mind, developed side by side with physical treatment, as a means of acting on the brain, and thereby affecting mental processes. Various classifications of mental disorder (disease) appeared; psychological theories influenced the way they were conceptualised but classifications were based primarily on empirical observations. And then in the mid-twentieth century, the social sciences brought to bear on psychiatry its considerable body of theory and information, latterly questioning the concept of 'mental disease' itself. However, the diagnosis of 'illness' and the nosology of mental disorder has remained a central feature of psychiatric theory and practice.

In analysing the situation in the nineteenth century, Robert Castel (1985), Professor of Sociology at the University of Paris, states:

> To say that nineteenth century psychiatric knowledge is uncertain of its foundations signifies that it possesses only a weak autonomy in relation to other systems of interpretation, and hence that it is *permeable to non-medical norms,* and ready to interpret within the framework of an extra-medical synthesis, representations which have no theoretical relation with medically founded knowledge.

Thus, social values and ideologies present in the society at large permeated into psychiatry to influence its development in various ways. Cultural ideas about 'proper' feminine behaviour have shaped the definition and treatment of female insanity (Showalter, 1987). According to Skultans (1979), 'throughout two centuries female sexuality was seen as an ambiguous and dangerous force predisposing women to insanity.' But this was a dynamic situation that must be seen in the context of social events and social pressures: 'Thus the emphasis on female vulnerability and pathology increased with increasing articulateness of women and their demand for emancipation. By the turn of the century an explicit association was made between the education of women and increased risk of insanity.' However, cultural ideas on gender formed only one of the ideologies that permeated into psychiatry during its development. Ideas about race determined another — perhaps stronger — ideology that fed into psychiatry.

IDEOLOGY ABOUT RACE IN WESTERN CULTURE

Two major historical pursuits brought Europeans into contact with people living in Africa, Asia, and the Americas — slavery and colonialism. In 1492 Columbus landed in the Bahamas. After exploring the region with the help of the native people, he went back to Spain and returned with gangs of adventurers to colonise the area (Bethlehem, 1985). The occupation spread to the American mainland both North and South. As the 'American Indians' were enslaved, exploited and exterminated a classic controversy developed in Spain about their 'natural inferiority' to white people (Nash, 1972). In 1577 the first African slaves were shipped across the Atlantic to work on the Spanish colony of Hispaniola (Parkinson, 1978). Although slavery and colonialism played an important part in promoting European ideas on race (Institute of Race Relations, 1982a, 1982b), this was not the whole story.

In a comprehensive book on the history of black people in Britain, Fryer (1984) traces the growth of racial prejudice and then the dogma of racism in Britain. In arguing that race prejudice is particularly prone to take root in communities that are 'ethnically homogeneous, geographically isolated, technologically backward, or socially conservative', he suggests that England in the sixteenth and seventeenth centuries was a classic instance of such a community; further, the conceptual background in Britain provided a fertile ground for the growth of racism as a dogma:

> The English happened to have a very old and very convenient pigeon-hole for black Africans. If their skin was black, what else could they be but devils? The Ethiopian as devil can be found in *La Chanson de Roland* an early version of which is supposed to have been sung by Taillefer at the battle of Hastings. But the idea was much older. The so-called *Epistle of Barnabas* composed in the second century AD, termed the devil 'The Black One', and

9

in the fourth century St Jerome said: 'Born of the Devil, we are black.' By the seventeenth century this equation was a commonplace of English literature.

New information about Africa reaching Britain in the fifteenth and sixteenth centuries was fitted into the 'steamy mass of ancient folklore' about black people. Tales from travellers about the abnormal sexual behaviour of black people, their alleged barbarity and perceived ugliness were woven into a myth with religious backing — the curse of Ham theory based on the old testament or the notion of the separate creation of black people as intermediate between white people and apes (Fryer, 1984).

As slavery flourished in the sixteenth and seventeenth centuries, Britain became the foremost slave trading nation in the world. As a corollary of this, black people became a visible minority in British cities by the last decade of the sixteenth century. This fact was seized upon by the English official mind when social crisis occurred and there were calls for expulsion of blacks (Hall, 1978) — perhaps a foretaste of the twentieth century. In recommending 'that those kind of people be sent forth from the land', Queen Elizabeth I wrote to the Lord Mayors of major cities that 'there are of late divers blackamores brought into the realm, of which kind of people there are already here to manie ...' (Walwin, 1973). Slavery thrived on greed and in turn fuelled racism — 'it was their drive for profit that led English merchant capitalists to traffic in Africans. There was money in it. The theory came later.' (Fryer, 1984). The theory was summarised by David Hume in a footnote added in 1753 to an essay written in 1748 and quoted by Fryer:

I am apt to suspect the negroes, and in general all the other species of men (for there are four or five different kinds) to be naturally inferior to the whites. There never was a civilized nation of any complexion than white, nor even any individual eminent either in action or speculation. No ingenious manufacture amongst them, no arts, no sciences. On the other hand, the most rude and barbarous of the white, such as the ancient GERMANS, the present TARTARS, have still something eminent about them, in their valour, form of government, or some other particular.

With the abolition of the slave trade in 1807, racism became a crucial ingredient of colonialism. In his classic book *Asia and Western*

Dominance, Panikkar (1959) traces the progress of European imperialism in Asia. Trade in the sixteenth century led to conquest in the eighteenth century and, finally, to Empire in the nineteenth. European nations originally arrived in Asia in search of spices. As slavery and the plunder of America resulted in economic prosperity in Europe, the demand for superior goods from the advanced economies of the East increased. But 'Europe at the time had little to offer to the Asian economy', and trade was mainly one way. A new method of payment — namely opium — was discovered by the Portuguese and in 1773 Warren Hastings made the sale of opium a monopoly of the East India Company in India. The Company used 'this trade both for filling its coffers in India and as a payment for its trade with China.' Later, the 'opium wars' were fought by Britain to force the Chinese to allow opium into their country. Then, in conjunction with French, Americans and Portuguese a series of further wars with 'acts of unparalleled vandalism' such as the burning of the Summer Palace in Peking by Lord Elgin, led to the imposition of unequal treaties, finally leaving China in a state of 'subordination to and dependence on Western powers'. Meanwhile, the East India Company (with the backing of the British Government) used the dissension between rival states in India to take power into its hands. Taking over Bengal in 1764, 'the whole power of the organised state was directed to a single purpose — plunder.' The colonial administration was essentially 'a robber state' that impoverished the people and made huge profits. Famine followed in Bengal but the wealth acquired by the colonial power enabled the industrial revolution to take off in Britain. The rest of India was subjugated by a combination of deceit and superior armaments, the ease of conquest feeding into ideas of racial superiority. The last sovereign state in India, the Kingdom of Punjab, was conquered and annexed in 1846-8.

Once India was colonised, its industry was suppressed and destroyed in order to protect British manufactured goods. India was changed from an exporter of manufactured goods to a producer of raw materials and a market for British goods. The initial respect for the civilisation and economy of India changed to racist views of white superiority. From the late eighteenth century onwards, racism and colonialism reinforced each other in India as it did in other parts of Asia. The exploitation of the Asian colonies was justified as imperial trusteeship for backward people unable to rule themselves. Christian missionaries started going to India about 1813 supporting a view of the superiority of Europe over Asia. According to

Geoffrey Moorhouse (1983), William Wilberforce, a leader of the fight against the slave-trade, considered that the conversion of India to Christianity was a cause greater than the abolition of slavery:

> He told the House of Commons in 1813, in the debate which preceded the new India Act, that he saw the subcontinent as a place which would 'exchange its dark and bloody superstition for the genial influence of Christian light and truth', the gods of the Hindus being 'absolute monsters of lust, injustice, wickedness and cruelty. In short, their religion is one grand abomination.'

The British proceeded to 'civilise' India by suppressing its social and religious practices, re-organising its land tenure, reforming educational and legal systems — often with disastrous social and economic consequences. 'The driving force behind this "civilizing" zeal remained the inherent belief prevalent in mid-Victorian England that the British were culturally and racially superior to the mass of their subjects in India and elsewhere in the Empire.' (Visram, 1986).

While colonial exploitation and plunder was in full swing, 'scientific' justification for racism had emerged: Linnaeus (1758-9) classified human beings in a hierarchy based on skin colour — with whites at the top; physical anthropology developed 'methods' for classifying skulls to indicate levels of intelligence and the criteria they used invariably placed Europeans at the top (Jordan, 1968); anatomists, physicians and biologists joined in to 'prove' the superiority of the white race over all other races. The crude notions of white racial superiority that had developed during slavery was refined and confirmed into a lasting dogma — an ideology that was to endure.

In a recent book, *Black Athena*, exploring the Afroasiatic roots of classical (Greek) civilisation, Martin Bernal (1987) has shown how racism affected the writing of history in the nineteenth century: 'The paradigm of "races" that were intrinsically unequal in physical and mental endowment was applied to all human studies, but especially to history.' European estimation of China had declined as the balance of trade between China and Europe shifted in favour of the latter; European nations mounted attacks on the country and the Chinese were forced to accept opium. The image of China was changed 'from one of a refined and enlightened civilization to one of a society filled with drugs, dirt, corruption and torture.' Similarly, 'ancient Egypt, which in the eighteenth century had been seen as a very close parallel to China, suffered from the same effects from the need to justify the increasing European expansion into other continents and maltreatment of their indigenous people. Both were flung into prehistory to serve as a solid and inert basis for the dynamic development of the superior races, the Aryans and the Semites.' But the racial position of the Egyptians on the black–white classification presented a problem for historians:

> If it had been scientifically 'proved' that Blacks were biologically incapable of civilization, how could one explain ancient Egypt — which was inconveniently placed on the African continent? There were two, or rather, three solutions. The first was to deny that the Ancient Egyptians were black; the second was to deny that the Ancient Egyptians had created a 'true' civilization; the third was to make doubly sure by denying both. The last has been preferred by most 19th- and 20th- century historians.

Until the early nineteenth century, the conventional view had been that Greek culture had arisen as a result of colonisation, around 1500 BC, by Egyptians and Phoenicians who had civilised the native inhabitants. But to nineteenth-century historians 'it became increasingly intolerable that Greece — which was seen by the Romantics not merely as the epitome of Europe but also as its pure childhood — could be the result of the mixture of native Europeans and colonising Africans and Semites.' The view developed of an invasion of Greece from the north; 'European thinkers were concerned to keep black Africans as far as possible from European civilization.'

By the mid-nineteenth century the 'natural' superiority of Europe — seen in racial terms — became an article of faith and the term 'primitive' was applied indiscriminately to 'coloured' people all over the world (Worsley, 1972). The histories and achievements of African, American and Asian cultures were discredited. Although highly developed systems of social organisation had flourished in Africa for many centuries before the European invasion Davidson, 1974), the historian Trevor-Roper (1963) argued, in a talk on British Television, that African history before imperial rule was non-existent: 'There is only the history of the Europeans in Africa. The rest is darkness, like the history of pre-European, pre-Columbian America. And darkness is not a subject of history.' The great civilisation of Egypt was somehow presented as 'white' while Egyptians themselves were seen as 'black'; the civilisations of the American continent were written off (Institute of Race Relations, 1982a); the once respected cultures of the East were seen as inferior to European culture (Worsley, 1972). Billig (1982) has noted that a 'dramatic indication of the way in which racial presuppositions were spreading in the nineteenth century is provided by the admiration of both Engels and Darwin for the biological writings of Ernst Haeckel', identified as 'one of the most important forerunners of nazism.' According to Billig, Haeckel's *The History of Creation* (1876) was praised by Engels and his *The Riddle of the Universe* (Haeckel, 1901) was similarly praised by Lenin. Both books argued for the inequality of races; the latter, developing notions of 'Aryan' superiority, claimed that Caucasians have 'from time immemorial been placed at the head of all races of men, as the most highly developed and perfect'. Darwin (1871) in *The Descent of Man* argued against the 'races of man' being 'distinct species' but clearly supported the view of white superiority: 'When civilized nations come into contact with barbarians the struggle is short, except where a deadly climate gives its aid to the native race'. The application of Darwin's theory of evolution to psychological issues by his cousin, Francis Galton, led to the eugenic movement, which in turn provided the dogma for European fascism in the 1930s.

Social sciences that developed in the nineteenth century reflected the division of the world into the civilised white people of Western Europe and the savage races native to Asia, Africa and America. Sociologists studied white people while anthropologists studied 'primitive races'. In tracing European myths of the Orient, Rana Kabbani (1986) has observed that 'nineteenth-century anthropology was predominantly a system for the hierarchical classification of race' :

As such, it was inextricably linked to the functionings of empire. Indeed, there can be no dispute that it emerged as a distinctive discipline at the beginning of the colonial era, that it became a flourishing academic profession towards its close, and that throughout its history its efforts were chiefly devoted to a description and analysis — carried out by Europeans, for a European audience — of non-European societies dominated by the West. It was the colonial cataloguing of goods; the anchoring of imperial possessions into discourse.

Even the total extermination of 'inferior' races was justified as being a way of improving the human stock — by no less a person than a professor of London University and a Fellow of The Royal Society, Karl Pearson (1901). 'Virtually every scientist and intellectual in nineteenth-century Britain took it for granted that only people with white skin were capable of thinking and governing.' (Fryer, 1984).

In the mid-nineteenth century began the final onslaught on Africa. First came the missionary drive following on the explorers. Then came European coastal traders. In 1861 the British seized Lagos Island and proclaimed it a colony. Step-by-step invasion of the mainland of Africa followed. The historian Basil Davidson (1984) writes:

> From the very first encounter, the Europeans established as a principle their superiority over the black race. They affirmed it by a profound contempt for the inferior race. And soon enough, using their force, they reduced Africans to slavery, justifying this by the right of the strong, asserting their moral supremacy. The missionary cause had become a racist cause.

The 'scramble for Africa' was agreed to by European powers at the Berlin conference in 1884/5 but not completed until about 1920. The nations of Africa, which had been as distinct as those of Europe before the nineteenth century, were destroyed and tribalism encouraged in the interests of cheap colonial rule (Davidson, 1984). Two types of colony emerged — those with European settlers and those without. In the former 'labour was extracted from otherwise self-sufficient farmers by force or taxation'; in the latter, 'large trading companies were formed... to promote African production of crops for export, and to buy this produce at prices fixed by themselves for sale abroad. In return they imported manufactured goods from Europe and sold these to Africans, once again at prices fixed by themselves.' In spite of vast profits being made, education and responsibility were withheld from blacks 'for it was generally held by the masters of colonial rule that blacks were incapable of growing up.' In this way, racism was used to maintain colonial rule and prevent economic, cultural and political development. But as African communities were wrecked, poverty spread and crises developed. With Asian colonies becoming independent after the war, the winds of change reached Africa. Political liberation in Africa started with the independence of Ghana in 1957 and, in 1988, threatens the white regime of South Africa. But the economic plunder of African resources by Western nations continues (Mazrui, 1986).

Thus, through its history of slavery and colonialism, on a background of myth and superstition supported by missionaries, capitalists and educationalists, European culture has absorbed into itself an ideology about race which, in the words of Fanon (1964) 'bloats and disfigures the face of the culture that practises it. Literature, the plastic arts, songs for shop-girls, proverbs, habits, patterns, whether they set out to attack it or vulgarize it, restore racism.' While becoming deeply embedded in all aspects of European culture racism has been integrated into the psyche of the European person, black or white. Again, to quote Fanon (1952), a black psychiatrist who was educated in France:

> *In Europe, the black man is the symbol of Evil.* ... In the remotest depths of the European unconscious an inordinately black hollow has been made in which the most immoral impulses, the most shameful desires lie dormant. And as every man climbs up towards whiteness and light, the European has tried to repudiate this uncivilized self, which has attempted to defend itself. When European civilization came into contact with the black world, with those savage peoples, everyone agreed: Those Negroes were the principle of evil. ... In the collective unconscious of *homo occidentalis* the Negro — or, if one prefers, the color black — symbolizes evil, sin, wretchedness, death, war, famine.

Just as the wealth extracted by slavery and colonialism has enriched all social classes in Britain (Hall, 1978), racist ideology has, over the years, pervaded all political and social systems. Hall (1978) argues that post-war, indigenous British racism is different to that of the slavery-colonial era since it assumes a specific form 'which arises from the present — not the past — conditions and organisation of society', but he accepts that it draws on 'cultural and ideological traces which are deposited in a society by previous historical phases'. Therefore, the ideology of racism in British culture is an essential background for considering the place of psychiatry in a multiracial and multicultural society.

HISTORY OF RACISM IN PSYCHIATRY

Psychiatry prides itself on having a background of basic sciences upon which to draw. To start with, these were Anatomy and Physiology, but more recently, Psychology and Sociology have come to the fore. Historically speaking, two important sets of ideas came into psychiatry from the basic sciences. First, the view that black people are born with inferior brains and limited capacity for growth; and secondly, that their personalities tend to be abnormal or deviant because of nature (genetic endowment) and/or nurture (upbringing). The influence of these themes on psychiatric theory and practice was overt in the nineteenth century and early part of the twentieth century, but, although less obvious since the war, shows a tenacious persistence into the present. However, racism within psychiatry does not come just from the basic sciences. Since psychiatry developed in a Western culture with a strong ideology of racism, it was hardly surprising that racism has seeped into — or more correctly been actively absorbed into — the theory and practice of the discipline and become integrated into its institutional practices.

Psychiatry is affected by racism in various ways. In the field of research and observation, racist thinking often underlies, or even determines, the methods used, the analysis of results, and the interpretation of the findings. Stereotypes based on racist assumptions derived from the traditions of Western culture or the 'common sense' of European thinking and values are often taken over by both practitioners and researchers. These assumptions are incorporated into practice or research in such a way that they become self-fulfilling prophecies that serve to reinforce the original (false) assumptions. Further, psychiatry has grown, and continues to function, in a context from which popular ideas and beliefs permeate into it to a greater or lesser extent. Psychiatry, taking into itself ordinary words in order to use them in a technical sense, often absorbs the prevailing confusion about their meanings or the double meanings they carry. Thus in British society today, pairs of words such as 'culture' and 'race', 'primitive' and 'under-developed', 'advanced' and 'Western', 'alien' and 'inferior', 'immigrant' and 'black', etc. are often confounded or used purposefully to obscure racist contentions. Further, racial images are raised in references to 'muggers', 'inner city decay', 'alien cultures' etc. All this is taken into psychiatry. A habit has developed in Britain to refer to those who are considered inferior as 'black and ethnic minorities'. Psychiatry has no option but to go along with this — for example in the paper by the author in the recent book edited by John Cox (1986). A problem arises when an objective definition about an ethnic minority is deemed to cover 'white' people such as British Jews or London Irish: white professionals tend to argue that Jews and Irish cannot possibly be 'ethnic'.

The following discussion of some aspects of racism in psychiatry must be considered in the context described above. In particular, it must be noted that psychiatry is ultimately rooted in the 'common sense' of the society in which it functions. Ideas about race are very strong in Britain and it is this ideology which pervades psychiatry. In Western terms, race is to do with colour of skin — but not just that. As early as the eighteenth century, according to Sypher (1942) quoted by Lawrence (1982a), the British were in the 'habit of calling yellow, brown or red people "black"'. It seems that the 'noble African' was not distinguished from the 'noble Indian' even by anti-slavery writers. European racist ideologies were not just organised around skin colour but extended to views about religious and cultural practices of people who were seen as 'black'.

Contributions from the Basic Sciences

The anthropological and medical tradition that brains of black people were inferior to those of Whites was supported by dubious research in the nineteenth century and early part of the twentieth. An example of this sort of claim is an article in 1906 by Robert Bean, then Professor of Anatomy at the Johns Hopkins University (Bean, 1906). Bean examined 103 brains from American Negroes and forty nine from white Americans. In discussing his findings that the former were on the average smaller than the latter, Bean starts off by stating: 'So many factors enter into brain weight that it is questionable whether discussion of the subject is profitable here.' Then, without describing these factors at all and clearly making no allowance for their effects on what he observed, Bean analysed the differences between the brains of Negroes and Whites, to state dogmatically:

> From the deduced differences between the functions of the anterior and posterior association centres and from the known characteristics of the two races the conclusion is that the Negro is more objective and the Caucasian more subjective. The Negro

has lower mental faculties (smell, sight, handcraftmanship, body-sense, melody) well developed, the Caucasian the higher (self-control, will-power, ethical and aesthetic senses and reason).

Although there were dissenting voices (e.g. Mall, 1909), reports on the alleged inferiority of the brains of black people continued into the 1940s. Significantly, reports that did not support the ethos of white superiority, such as the report that brains of Eskimos were larger than those of the average white person (Connolly, 1950), were ignored. In summarising the literature on this topic, Cobb (1942) concluded that the brain of the Negro 'is slightly smaller than that of the comparable white.'

In the field of psychology too, a racist ideology was often evident. Nineteenth century study of facial expression and the emotions attached great importance to blushing as a particularly human characteristic. In his classic *The Expression of the Emotions in Man and Animals*, Charles Darwin (1872) devoted a whole chapter to it. Blushing and conscience were thought to be related; the debate that ensued about the capacity of Negroes to blush was 'not so much a physiological one, as one about moral development.' (Skultans,1979). Francis Galton (1865), in an article entitled *Hereditary Talent and Character*, which is 'commonly held to mark the start of modern British psychology' (Billig, 1982), claimed that European 'civilised races' alone possessed the 'instinct of continuous steady labour' while non-European 'savages' showed an innate 'wild untameable restlessness'. Stanley Hall, founder of the *American Journal of Psychology*, in a classic text on adolescence published in 1904 and widely accepted in the profession, described the inhabitants of 'colonies and dependencies of the world, that are in a relation of greater or less subjection to a few civilized nations' as members of 'adolescent races'; he saw Africans, Indians and North American 'Aborigines' as immature children who 'live a life of feeling, emotion and impulse,' where the 'individual is always merged in the tribe, and only the chief, and often not even he, can give pledges or make bargains.' Instinct theories to explain natural characteristics of human beings were popular during the early part of the twentieth century; McDougall (1921), (who wrote the standard textbook on social psychology (McDougall, 1908) which went into several editions), formulated the concept of national minds, or 'group minds', which were dependent on racial homogeneity; he described Nordics showing a propensity for scientific work,

Mediterraneans for architecture and oratory, and Negroes an 'instinct for submission'. Thomas (1904), a sociologist of the University of Chicago, legitimised racism by claiming that racial prejudice was 'an instinct originating in the tribal stage of society', i.e. a natural characteristic of human psychology.

In the 1920s, Carl Jung postulated that the Negro 'has probably a whole historical layer less' in the brain (Thomas and Sillen, 1972). Jung considered himself to be a specialist on 'primitive' people. In speculating on a supposed (psychological) danger to white people of living in close proximity to black people, Jung (1930) deduced the theory of 'racial infection' as 'a very serious mental and moral problem whenever a primitive race outnumbers the white man.' He explained his theory thus:

> Now what is more contagious than to live side by side with a rather primitive people? Go to Africa and see what happens...The inferior man exercises a tremendous pull upon civilised beings who are forced to live with him, because he fascinates the inferior layers of our psyche, which has lived through untold ages of similar conditions.

Jung proceeded to analyse the behaviour characteristics of white Americans in terms of the degree of 'racial infection' that they had assimilated from the black population around them. However, Jung (1945) may have changed his views somewhat as a result of the events in Germany in the 1940s:

> The terrible things that have happened in Germany, and the moral downfall of a 'nation of eighty millions,' are a blow aimed at all Europeans. (We used to be able to relegate such things to 'Asia'.) The fact that one member of the European family could sink to the level of the concentration camp throws a dubious light on all others.

But Jung's position was not clear even then. In that same article he referred to his own alleged 'close relationships with non-Europeans' and to 'the crimes committed against the coloured races' by Whites; he concluded that 'for the first time since the dawn of history we have succeeded in swallowing the whole of primitive animism into ourselves.' Back, it seems, to the 'racial infection' theory.

In an influential book *The Measurement of Intelligence*, Lewis Terman (1916), the eminent psychologist from Stanford University, claimed that Negroes, Spanish-Indians and Mexicans were of low intelligence because of their race. He was part of a 'racist IQ movement' (Thomas and Sillen, 1972) which gathered momentum after the first world war with support from army data published by the National Academy of Sciences under the editorship of Robert Yerkes (1921). This led to considerable discussion on the value of psychometric testing and the reasons for differences in test results between racial groups. The outcome was summarised in a book by Ruth Benedict first published in 1942:

> The intelligence testers at the present time, therefore, regard their data as indicating achievement and primarily scholastic achievement. For this both innate aptitude and specific training are necessary; in other words both heredity and environment play their parts. The problem is whether the hereditary factor is a *racial constant*. The results of racial tests are believed today to show that hereditary aptitude is not distributed by races and that when environmental conditions for different groups become similar, average achievement also becomes similar.

The controversy over racial inferiority in intelligence seemed settled until Arthur Jensen (1969), Professor of Educational Psychology at the University of California, Berkeley, wrote a paper in the *Harvard Educational Review* that attracted world-wide attention. Jensen offered a genetic explanation for differences in IQ ratings between black and white Americans and suggested that intensive educational efforts, which were being made at the time to raise the intellectual achievements of low IQ scorers (mainly Blacks), were wasteful. Jensen went further to argue that the 'profile or pattern of scores was distinctly different' for different racial groups. He identified two broad categories of mental ability — abstract reasoning ability, which Jensen called intelligence, and, associative learning ability, — for example memory span or rote learning — that 'appear to be distributed differently between various social classes and racial groups.' These differences were seen as a reflection of genetic difference. According to Jensen, Blacks had inherited a type of cognitive ability — rote learning — different to the intelligence of Whites. Although there was widespread criticism of Jensen's racist interpretations of observations on how people scored on IQ tests, H. J. Eysenck (1971, 1973), Professor of Psychology at the

Institute of Psychiatry in London, supported Jensen's viewpoint. Apart from the inherent racist nature of their conclusions, the arguments of Jensen and Eysenck have been shown to be of dubious validity (Stott, 1983; Kamin, 1974). Moreover they relied heavily on the classic work of Sir Cyril Burt, the credibility of which is now in considerable doubt; after analysing Burt's work in some detail, Kamin (1974) concluded:

> The absence of procedural description in Burt's reports vitiates their scientific utility. The frequent arithmetical inconsistencies and mutually contradictory descriptions cast doubt upon the entire body of his later work. The marvelous inconsistency of his data supporting the hereditarian position often taxes credibility; and on analysis, the data are found to contain implausible effects consistent with an effort to prove the hereditarian case. The conclusion cannot be avoided: The numbers left behind by Professor Burt are simply not worthy of our current scientific attention.

The genetic explanation for IQ differences between Blacks and Whites presented by Jensen and Eysenck 'represented a reversal of post-war trends in psychological theory' (Billig, 1979); it was strongly opposed by many psychologists (for example, Kamin (1974) in the United States and Watson (1973b) in England) but is far from dead; for example, Jensen (1984) defends his position in a commentary to a recent book by Scarr (1984). Gillie (1976) believes that the Jensen-Eysenck theory of race is a social danger because it 'points an accusing finger at all black people in the United States and by implication at black people everywhere.' Gillie writes:

> The terrible consequence of this type of theory is that it can be self-fulfilling. When failure is expected it often comes. Whether the theory is true or not, if sufficient people believe in it, it might become true. The energetic promotion of this theory has already held up the provision of better teaching for blacks and other minority groups in the United States and has provided a convenient theoretical bolster for repressive educational policies in South Africa. The consequence is that coloured people are being robbed of the opportunity to develop their brains. Other minority groups such as Mexicans and Puerto Ricans in the United States and Irish and West Indians in Britain are similarly categorized

and robbed of opportunity, although these minority groups have been much less well studied.

Although overt racism was not popular in scientific circles after the last war, the arguments of Jensen and Eysenck may have helped the revival of a 'scientific racism' of the type that thrived in Germany in the 1930s. In an important booklet *Psychology, Racism and Fascism* Billig (1979) analysed the connections between the psychological theories of race that grew up in the 1970s and the postwar rise of fascism. He recalls that in the thirties 'respectable scientists (principally geneticists, biologists, physical anthropologists and psychologists) contributed to the growth of *Rassenkunde* (literally 'Race-science')' which supported the rise of Nazism. Billig notes that the editor of the journal *Mankind Quarterly* (established in 1960) is Professor R. Gayre, a physical anthropologist with fascist connections. From its earliest issues, this journal 'has provided a platform for former colleagues and present heirs of Nazi racial theorist Hans Gunther' and has published various articles supporting racism all over the world. Billig quotes the evidence given by Gayre in defence of members of the Racial Preservation Society who were charged with an offence under the Race Relations Act in 1968: In his evidence as an 'expert' witness, Gayre maintained that blacks 'prefer their leisure to the dynamism which the white and yellow races show'. Among several eminent scientists involved in *Mankind Quarterly* are Robert Kuttner an American biochemist, Professor Henry Garrett, a past president of the American Psychological Association and author of well-known books, and Professor H. J. Eysenck.

Contributions from American Psychiatry

The observations of psychiatrists in the United States during the times of slavery left little doubt that psychiatry colluded with racism in reinforcing and justifying slavery. 'The black man, it was repeatedly claimed, was uniquely fitted for bondage by his primitive psychological organisation. For him, mental health was contentment with his subservient lot, while protest was an infallible symptom of derangement.' (Thomas and Sillen, 1972). Since slavery was seen as the natural condition for blacks, a deviation from this 'norm' was identified as 'disease'. Daniel Tuke (1858) quotes a report in the *Medical Times and Gazette* of November 8th

1856: 'Dr Cartwright describes a form of disease called "Drapeto-mania", which, like a malady that cats are liable to, manifests itself by an irrestrainable propensity to run away.' Clearly, any treatment would be designed to return the 'patient' to his/her 'normal' state of slavery. Another such 'disease' of black slaves 'Dysoesthesia oethiopeca' was characterised by a person 'paying no attention to the rights of property' and therefore destroying things, 'breaking the tools he works with', carelessness when 'driven to work by the compulsive power of the white man', self-indulgence leading to 'idleness and sloth', and other features on these lines. 'The term rascality given to this disease by overseers, is founded on an erroneous hypothesis, and leads to an incorrect empirical treatment which seldom or never cures it.' (Cartwright quoted by Tuke, 1858).

The psychiatrisation of black protest against oppression was only one way in which psychiatry played a part in legitimising slavery in America. Many psychiatrists held that black people benefited from slavery by receiving special care and supervision (Babcock, 1895; Powell, 1896; O'Malley, 1914). Epidemiological studies which seemed to show that the rate of insanity among Negroes was lower in the slave states than in the free states were used to argue that slavery protected Blacks from mental disorder and to justify the extension of slavery (for example) to the state of Texas; statistical evidence was again used later by reputable psychiatrists to argue that freedom resulting from emancipation caused an increase in the rate of mental disorder among Blacks (Thomas and Sillen, 1972). Mental illness among black people after the abolition of slavery was attributed to the residual effects of their African heritage (Evarts, 1916) or their inherent sense of inferiority (Lind, 1914). Dr W. M. Bevis, a physician from a hospital in Washington DC, read a paper on psychological traits of Negroes to the Society for Nervous and Mental Diseases. His paper, as published in the *American Journal of Psychiatry*, (Bevis, 1921) introduced the subject thus:

Less than three hundred years ago the alien ancestors of most of the families of this race were savages or cannibals in the jungles of Central Africa. From this very primitive level they were unwillingly brought to these shores and into an environment of higher civilisation for which the biological development of the race had not made adequate preparation. In later years, citizenship with its novel privileges (possibly with a greater transition than the first) was thrust upon the race finding it poorly prepared, intellectually, for adjustment to this new social order.

Bevis described the Negro as cunning, superstitious, promiscuous, lacking initiative and living only in the present — stereotypes taken over from society at large and established as scientific 'fact' by the way they were presented.

General Contributions

In the mid-nineteenth century, psychiatrists, like others around them, had very definite ideas on who was civilised and who was not. A paper in the *Journal of Mental Science* (Foote, 1858) by a former Physician Superintendent of Norfolk County Asylum who was working in Turkey referred to that land as 'a country which forms the link between civilization and barbarism'. In the same journal, Tuke (1858) a lecturer in Medicine at the York School of Medicine denoted Esquimaux, Chinese, Egyptians and American Blacks as 'uncivilised' people, contrasting them with Europeans and American Whites referred to as 'civilised' people, but with a grudging reference to China as 'in some respects decidedly civilized'. The black person in the British Empire was generally seen as cunning and infantile but faithful and superstitious and insensitive to pain (Street, 1975). It is against this background that the large body of psychiatric observations of black people — especially those in conditions of colonialism or slavery — must be viewed. So-called cross-cultural studies in India where black soldiers were compared to white soldiers (Williams, 1950; Abse, 1966) fall into this category. The context in which illness was presented and diagnosed was ignored in such studies although clearly it was very different for the two groups considered. In the study by Williams (1950), 30 per cent of Indians as opposed to less than 8 per cent of British soldiers were diagnosed as suffering from hysteria — a bald 'fact' that has been quoted many times, most recently by Leff (1986a), as evidence of the inability of Indians to present illness in a 'sophisticated' (Western) fashion.

Overt racial generalisations were not so evident in scientific journals after the last war. But Carothers (1951), a psychiatrist and prison medical officer analysing his observations in Kenya and the descriptions of personality traits of Africans given by various Europeans, postulated a 'resemblance between the African and the leucotomized European' and concluded that the African does not use the frontal lobes of his brain. Carothers (1953) went on to write a monograph for the World Health Organisation called *The African Mind in Health and Disease* and to repeat his remarks about the African brain in a much later publication (Carothers, 1972). In the WHO monograph, Carothers reviewed many of the claims of inferior brain function of black people equating (for this purpose) American and African Blacks. Vint (1934) concluded from histological cell counts on European and African brains that the 'cerebral development reached by the average native is that of the average European boy of between seven and eight years of age', and Carothers argued against criticisms levelled at Vint deploring that 'this fine piece of pioneer research did not inspire something more than criticism.'

The apparent rarity of depression among Blacks in the American South was discussed by the clinical director of Georgia State Sanatarium (Green, 1914):

> It appears that the negro mind does not dwell upon unpleasant subjects; he is irresponsible, unthinking, easily aroused to happiness, and his unhappiness is transitory, disappearing as a child's when other interests attract his attention... Depression is rarely encountered even under circumstances in which a white person would be overwhelmed by it.

Carothers (1953) was one of the foremost among many (white) psychiatrists who claimed that depression was rare among (black) Africans. He was in tune with the general tenor of the time in attributing his alleged observation to 'the absence of a sense of responsibility' (among Blacks). In reviewing the reports on depression from Africa, Prince (1968) has recently noted that, although this condition was quoted as being uncommon among Africans well into the 1950s, since 1957 (the year of Ghana's independence) papers have appeared reporting that depression was not rare but common among Africans. He believes that 'the climate of opinion' about Africans determined the observations made by psychiatrists and continues to do so. In other words, it is likely that Carothers found depression to be rare in Africans because he saw them as lacking a sense of responsibility, rather than vice versa. The author recalls being taught that mental illness in people from Asia and the West Indies often presented as an undifferentiated 'primitive psychosis' — and that was in the nineteen sixties in London.

CULTURE OF PRESENT-DAY PSYCHIATRY

Social science studies after the war focus on the effects of discrimination and social conditions on the personalities of black people in the United States. A renowned study of this type is that by Kardiner and Ovesey (1951) published as the book *The Mark of Oppression*. The book is based on a psychodynamic assessment of twenty-five case records of black people considered against a background of the history and oppression of Blacks in American society. The authors argue that the original (African) culture of black people in America was 'smashed, be it by design or accident.' Black slaves are seen as having participated vicariously in the 'extrinsic culture' of their white masters, with a special status for the female black 'through her value as a sexual object and as a mother surrogate.' Since, (for Kardiner and Ovesey) 'no *culture* can arise under these limitations' (of slavery), Blacks are seen as people living in a sort of cultural vacuum, with a personal adaptation 'by a process of passivity... and vicarious participation through identification with the master.' The family life of Blacks after emancipation is viewed as having suffered 'a great deal of disorganisation.' The dominance of the female is seen as disturbing 'family cohesion'; high standards of behaviour are said to be expected from children 'without the affectionate background that can act as an incentive to the child.' Racial discrimination is assumed to result in a 'depressed self esteem' and 'self-hatred' within the black personality, partly dealt with by being 'projected' as aggression and anxiety. Thus cultural deprivation, lack of family cohesion and social disorganisation compounded by racial discrimination are seen as being 'integrated into the life of the individual' so that: 'There is not one personality trait of the Negro the source of which cannot be traced to his difficult living conditions. There are no exceptions to this rule. The final result is a wretched internal life.'

The line of argument exemplified in the book by Kardiner and Ovesey is as racist in its conclusions as earlier views on genetically determined inferiority of black brains. The arguments themselves are based on a naive view of human development where negative experiences are assumed to lead to personality defects. The lack of cohesion of black family life and the passivity of black people are clearly the deductions made by Whites. Black experience is looked at from the outside — through the (mis)perceptions of white people; the fact that oppression may uplift as well as depress self-worth and may promote as well as destroy communal cohesion is not considered. After all, if this argument is applied to the Jewish people, generations of persecution should have left them incapable of any leadership quite apart from being able to establish a political state after the war. But this line of argument has not been applied to white communities in America or anywhere else. The sociological approach that transfers the focus of emphasis from the oppression — racist oppression — in American society on to the oppressed black population, has the effect of pathologising and stigmatising the oppressed.

The alleged inferiority of the black person's brain, personality and intelligence has been gradually supplemented in the sixties by 'culturalist' theories quoting defective family and kinship systems, marital arrangements and child-rearing practices of black communities (Lawrence, 1982b). The focus on black families has taken the form of 'dissecting the culturally bizarre' (Brittan and Maynard, 1984), the theme being that deviant behaviour and personality traits in black people can be traced back to family structures — or the lack of structure — in black families. The alleged matrifocal character of black American families is seen by some researchers (e.g. Rainwater, 1968) as pathological and detrimental to the personality development of black children, while others (e.g. Bernard, 1966) suggest that the matrifocal family is an outgrowth of the failure of black men to fulfil their paternal roles. In reviewing the research on these themes, Dodson (1981) writes:

Implicit in the dichotomous conceptualization of functional versus dysfunctional capacities of black families is an assumption regarding normative model families. The belief that a statistical model of the American family can be identified and used to ascertain the character of the families of all American cultural groups is mythical at best.

The body of 'research' on black family life gathered together in an important report by Moynihan (1965) has been integrated into American social policy and into the thinking of psychologists and sociologists, as the focus of interest in these sciences shifted in the late sixties on to families and culture. According to Lawrence (1982b), writing for the 'Centre for Contemporary Cultural Studies':

Daniel Moynihan, using statistics — which were apparently 'rigged' — to support his case, argued that the experience and deprivations of slavery had 'forced' the Afro-American community into a 'matriarchal' structure. Basically his argument was that black women were too dominant, were more likely to be able to find work, and were therefore too independent. The outcome of this was the 'emasculation' of the black male. This, he felt, retarded the progress of the community as a whole, since it was contrary to the family structure of the rest of 'American society'.

In fact, it is the black family alone, and not the families of other cultural groups in America, that are subjected to the sort of analysis that ignores its functional integrity.

In Britain, too, negative images have developed about Afro-Caribbean and Asian families. The approach to black family life which characterises the Moynihan report is evident in British research (Lawrence, 1982b). Afro-Caribbeans in Britain are seen as having suffered 'cultural stripping' during slavery, leaving them with a 'weak' version of European culture (Pryce, 1979). British Asian communities are seen as having a culture which has remained intact for many generations, and, by failing to comment upon the effects of British imperialism in Asia, British sociologists collude with the commonly held view that the rigidity of Asian culture has resulted in the poverty and underdevelopment of Asia. Lawrence (1982b) shows how recent books on sociology vilify both Afro-Caribbean and Asian cultures of British people: Afro-Caribbean family life in contemporary Britain is seen as weak and unstable, with the lack of a sense of paternal responsibility towards children (Pryce, 1979), a failure by the family to apply adequate social control over its youth (Cashmore, 1979), and a negative (personal) self-image. In contrast, the Asian family is seen as strong — 'but the very strength of Asian culture is seen to be a source of both actual and potential weaknesses.' The hierarchical family structure is said to produce 'stress-ridden relationships'; Asian women are seen as isolated because of their traditional customs and views of the world; and the failure by Asians to take up the 'services' provided by statutory agencies is attributed to their lack of skills in Western life-styles (Saifullah Khan, 1979). These are then the images and models (of family life) that come into psychiatry. The cultural stereotypes are inevitably confounded with racial categories so that (cultural) assumptions are made about people identified on the basis of colour.

Clearly, the concepts that have been developed about black families and black culture in the USA (and transferred to Britain) are as racist as those earlier ones about black brains and black personalities. The 'Moynihan Report' (Moynihan, 1965) in the USA calls the black American family 'a tangle of pathology'. The 'Select Committee on Race Relations' (1977) in the UK follows the American lead in reporting a connection between the problems of Afro-Caribbean British families and family life in the Caribbean which is seen in similar terms to that of American Blacks. However, publications have begun to appear in America attempting to put the record straight. To quote the preface to a recent American book edited by McAdoo (1981):

> The demythologization of the negative images about the Black family is an ongoing process that will probably continue for generations, for the ethnocentric concepts held by the mainstream social science literature about black families will persist. The one main change that has occurred is that fewer writers are able to make blatant conjectures about black families and remain unchallenged. Publishers and editors of professional journals, the 'gate keepers' of much of the literature on Blacks, have become more sensitized to these issues.

Britain, however, lags behind. The report by Lord Scarman (1981) on *The Brixton Disorders 10-12 April 1981* repeats some of the usual negative stereotypes of black family life imported from America, applying them to Afro-Caribbean families in Brixton. But, for once, this report does not attribute the real problems of black and ethnic minorities to defects in their family life alone. Books such as *The Empire Strikes Back* (Centre for Contemporary Cultural Studies, 1983) and *Sexism, Racism and Oppression* (Brittan and Maynard, 1984) are attempting to correct the sociological perspective, while Stone (1981) has challenged their implications for education.

The culture of present-day psychiatry in Britain need not be entirely dependent on its inheritance from the basic sciences and the traditions derived from the days of colonialism and slavery. Perhaps one could argue that the ideas of American psychiatrists have not influenced psychiatric thinking in Britain; that writings of colonial psychiatrists like Carothers has had no real impact on psychiatric tradition in Britain. One may insist that the ideas within the theory and practice of psychiatry in Britain are not dependent on American literature and viewpoints, and think — hope — that British psychiatry is immune from the influence of racist ideas currently prevailing in British society and in British sociological literature. It is therefore useful to examine the present position in British psychiatry itself in some detail.

Clearly, psychiatric literature — especially papers published in well-established learned journals — and the views of eminent British researchers in the field have a strong influence on the current culture of psychiatry and hence on its practice. A recent textbook *The Scientific Basis of Psychiatry* (Weller, 1983) has a chapter by Fitzpatrick (1983) in which he states: 'Many non-Western societies lack a vocabulary whereby mental feeling states can be expressed.' Since this 'scientific fact' (!) is based on Leff's theory of emotional differentiation developed over the past thirteen years, the background is worth considering in some detail. A paper 'Culture and the Differentiation of Emotional States' (Leff, 1973) attracted some attention and has been quoted in many publications. This paper developed an argument, using data from the International Pilot Study of Schizophrenia (IPSS) (World Health Organisation, 1973), to conclude that people from 'developed countries show a greater differentiation of emotions' than do people from 'developing countries'. (The WHO study is critically considered in Chapter 3.) Although there are serious objections to this study because, (a) it draws conclusions about emotional expression in various cultural settings from data based on a method of examination constructed in London, and (b) it equates emotional expression to actual experience of emotions, the point to note here is the way in which Leff's theory has been formulated and strengthened over the years. To the alleged cultural differences which were deduced from a complex statistical study of some of the IPSS data, has been added diverse observations about so-called 'somatisation' of emotional difficulties in non-Western people (Leff, 1977) and the alleged 'disappearance of conversion hysteria in the West whereas it persists as a common form of neurosis in the Third World.' (Leff, 1986a). On a theoretical basis, fully described by Leff (1973), which related linguistic factors to culturally determined ways of expressing emotion, a theory was constructed that there has been 'a progressive differentiation of the vocabulary of emotion' as a 'historical process', so that 'in many cultures today emotional distress is still communicated through a rich variety of somatic symptoms.' (Leff, 1986a). The 'shift in focus from the bodily expression of distress to its communication through language, with a consequent progressive differentiation of the vocabulary of emotion' is seen as an 'evolutionary process' — as stated in a review by Leff (1977).

There is the clear implication that, eventually, the non-Western world will evolve languages as 'advanced' as those within Western culture. In more direct terms and returning to Leff's original data, the theory states that people from (industrially) less-developed countries show less differentiation of emotions when compared to people from (industrially) developed countries.

The ways of thinking that have influenced the development of a (supposedly) scientific theory is noteworthy. In the original paper (Leff, 1973) the argument was on the basis of language — basically the Indo-European group of languages vs others — but the grouping (of countries) for analysis of IPSS data was made on the basis of industrialisation. The comparison between developed and under-developed countries was supplemented by a study using data from the US:UK study (Cooper, Kendall, Garland, Sharpe, Copeland and Simon, 1972) comparing black Americans and white Americans. The reason for choosing to study black people living in a predomi-nantly white society is stated as follows: 'It was thought that con-tact with a culture in which emotions were relatively well-differentiated might have an educative effect.' In this study, the black group was found to be similar to people from (indus-trially) less-developed countries in terms of 'emotional differentia-tion'. Clearly countries could have been grouped together quite differently in analysing the IPSS data especially if the linguistic ar-gument was followed through. The way the analysis was conducted and the reasoning given for the black — white study showed a very clear racial orientation. Thus it is not surprising that the theory it-self came very close indeed to being a racial one, not too far from the ideas of Carothers. The overall conclusion was that cultures of 'developed countries' were different from those of 'developing countries' (Leff, 1973) — with a definite thrust as to which was su-perior and who needed to be 'educated' in emotional expression. Perhaps it was a significant reflection on the power of language that the division of the world into (industrially) developed and under-developed — 'third-world' — nations was being confounded with their cultural status. Industrial underdevelopment was equated with linguistic underdevelopment and cultural underdevelopment in an overall racial division of the world into ('inferior') black and ('su-perior') white people.

A recent survey of what is called the *'Epidemiology of De-pressive Disorder'* by Bebbington (1978) is another good example of the assumptions within Western culture that distort scientific ob-jectivity. The problem of defining the concept of 'depression' across cultures will be discussed in Chapter 3, but the point to note here is the approach of an eminent reviewer of the topic: In discussing the need for an agreed basis for diagnosing depression, Bebbington argues for a 'provisional syndromal definition of depression as used by a consensus of Western psychiatrists against which cross-cultural anomalies can be tested.' Although the validity of taking such a position is very dubious, it may be one way of proceeding since it enabled Bebbington to write his review. However, in referring (in his review) to 'primitive cultures' as synonymous with non-Western cultures, Bebbington clearly indicates the value judgement given to his 'provisional definition'. His 'primitive' cultures are expected to evolve their illness concepts as their cultures become less 'primitive', i.e. Westernised. The racial implication in dividing the world into primitive non-Western and advanced Western cultures is obvious.

One of the few British studies in which a black group was compared with white groups was reported as a study of *Psychiatric Disorder among Selected Immigrant groups in Camberwell* (Bebbington, Hurry and Tennant, 1981). The researchers from the Institute of Psychiatry of London University studied the incidence of mental disorders in a district of London, comparing people of (black) West Indian origin with those of Irish origin and indigenous British-born people. Ignoring, for the present, serious faults in the methodology in terms of the assumptions made about diagnostic reliability etc., the way in which the findings were interpreted as conclusions are striking:

The differences in the pattern of disorder between the West Indians and Irish immigrants and the British born in Camberwell seem to be real ones. They are in rough agreement with the national figures. It is difficult to explain the findings in West Indians in terms either of selection or of the stress of immigration. The establishment of accurate psychiatric hospital statistics in the West Indies could do much to clarify the issue. In interviewing British West Indians in the community we were left with a distinct and persistent clinical impression that they respond to adversity with cheery denial. We speculate that it might be possible to explain the apparent proneness of West Indians to major psychiatric disorder and their relative immunity to minor disorder in terms of this cultural characteristic — the Irish citizens of Camberwell seemed much more readily aware when things were going badly.

The researchers were explaining a lower incidence of depression and anxiety among black people by postulating a (pathological) 'cheery denial'. The ethos which determined such a conclusion seems little different to that of a study conducted nearly a hundred years ago in the United States and quoted by Thomas and Sillen (1972):

> A contributor to the 'Psychological Review' in 1895 compared the speed of sensory perception in a group of 12 whites, 11 Indians and 11 Blacks. When the white subjects proved to have the slowest reactions, this was taken as proof that they were the superior group. Their reactions were slower because they belonged to a more deliberate and reflective race than did the members of the other two groups.

It must be stated that there are attempts by British psychiatrists to address the problems of race and culture in psychiatric theory and practice in a realistic and constructive way. However, these are few and far between — at least as far as the main psychiatric journals are concerned — and as Shelley and Cohen (1986) have pointed out, 'publication in scientific journals is the method that is accepted for the creation of scientific facts.' (The reality is that so-called 'ethical committees' can prevent research projects being carried out — and do so for non-ethical reasons — and that publication in the prestigious journals, being dependent on approval by establishment figures, is related to power within the psychiatric establishment.) Although racial theories are not stated overtly, current psychiatric literature in Britain tends to reflect the racist ethos which is evident in society at large. The assumptions underlying research methodology and interpretation of data reveal a lack of objectivity (to say the least) when it concerns race — often referred to as 'culture'. Racism inherent in references to 'primitive' cultures (usually meaning black races) is not too difficult to identify; but racist assumptions in research method are not so easy to detect: For example in referring to the use of the 'Present State Examination' (Wing, Cooper and Sartorius, 1974) — an interview schedule devised in England for data collection in the IPSS, it is assumed (without even a discussion) that as 'English has an extensive vocabulary for unpleasant emotional states, the translation should not have given rise to any difficulties ...' (Leff, 1974). Such an assumption about a language identified with black people — Yoruba or Urdu for example — would be considered unscientific but not so in the

Figure 1.1: Historical context of psychiatry

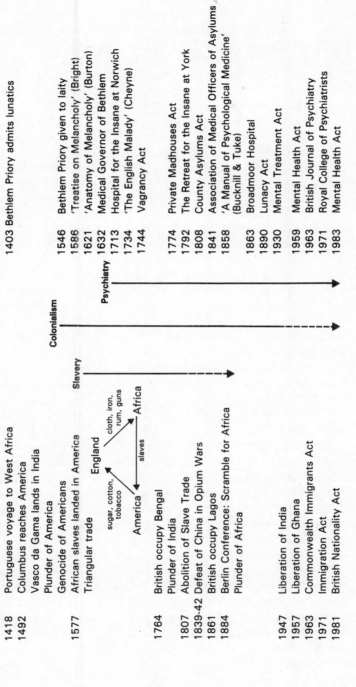

Historical Events

1418 Portuguese voyage to West Africa
1492 Columbus reaches America
     Vasco da Gama lands in India
     Plunder of America
     Genocide of Americans
1577 African slaves landed in America
     Triangular trade

1764 British occupy Bengal
     Plunder of India
1807 Abolition of Slave Trade
1839-42 Defeat of China in Opium Wars
1861 British occupy Lagos
1884 Berlin Conference: Scramble for Africa
     Plunder of Africa

1947 Liberation of India
1957 Liberation of Ghana
1963 Commonwealth Immigrants Act
1971 Immigration Act
1981 British Nationality Act

Growth of Psychiatry

1403 Bethlem Priory admits lunatics

1546 Bethlem Priory given to laity
1586 'Treatise on Melancholy' (Bright)
1621 'Anatomy of Melancholy' (Burton)
1632 Medical Governor of Bethlem
1713 Hospital for the Insane at Norwich
1734 'The English Malady' (Cheyne)
1744 Vagrancy Act

1774 Private Madhouses Act
1792 The Retreat for the Insane at York
1808 County Asylums Act
1841 Association of Medical Officers of Asylums
1858 'A Manual of Psychological Medicine' (Bucknill & Tuke)
1863 Broadmoor Hospital
1890 Lunacy Act
1930 Mental Treatment Act
1959 Mental Health Act
1963 British Journal of Psychiatry
1971 Royal College of Psychiatrists
1983 Mental Health Act

Figure 1.2: Racist heritage of psychiatry

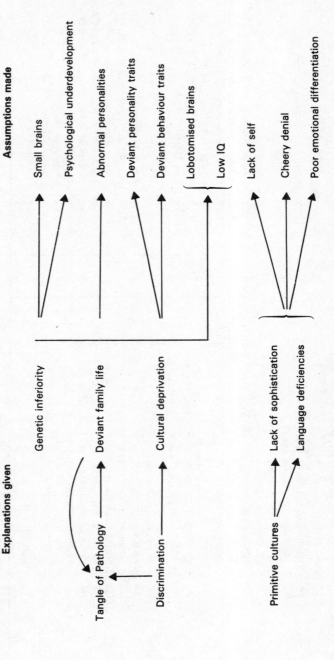

Explanations given   Assumptions made

Genetic inferiority   Small brains
                                  Psychological underdevelopment

Deviant family life   Abnormal personalities
                                  Deviant personality traits
                                  Deviant behaviour traits

Cultural deprivation   Lobotomised brains
                                  Low IQ

Tangle of Pathology

Discrimination

Primitive cultures   Lack of self
                                  Cheery denial
                                  Poor emotional differentiation

Lack of sophistication
Language deficiencies

case of a 'white' language. It is not surprising that findings of international studies are analysed in terms of the differences between countries grouped essentially on racial lines.

SUMMARY

Although myths and prejudice about black people prevailed in England long before the English met people whose skins were black, it was during the times of slavery that these ideas became 'woven into a more or less coherent racist ideology; a mythology of race.' (Fryer, 1984). Slavery and colonialism, on the one hand, and racism, on the other, reinforced each other in a context of economic gain for Europeans (in particular the English) during the seventeenth and eighteenth centuries, leaving European culture with an ideology of racism based on skin colour — an ideology that persists to the present day. The growth of psychiatry in the seventeenth and eighteenth centuries, its acceptance as a scientific discipline in the mid-nineteenth century and its assumption in the twentieth of a position of some power in society, must be seen in the context of historical events that punctuated the rise of racism (Figure 1.1). As psychiatry flourished, various racist ideas were incorporated into it. These included views about the (alleged) inferiority of black people with regard to their brain-size (Bean, 1906), psychological maturity (Hall, 1904) and emotional functioning (Jung, 1930). And the process continues: current concepts which are used to denote or imply (alleged) inferiority of people viewed as 'underdeveloped' or 'coloured', i.e. 'black' in a political sense (Donovan, 1984), include personality deviancy (Kardiner and Ovesey, 1951), brain quality (Carothers, 1951), low IQ (Jensen, 1969), poor emotional differentiation (Leff, 1973) and 'cheery denial' (Bebbington et al., 1981). The racist tradition of psychiatry, composed of its inheritance from the past and from its present day literature, is summarised in Figure 1.2. The reasons for the continuation of racism in psychiatry is analysed in Chapter 2; in doing so the 'manufacture' of psychiatry is described as illustrated by Figure 2.1 encompassing the influences that impinge upon the growth of the subject. The effect of this racism on psychiatric practice in Britain is considered in Chapter 5; the way forward for psychiatry to break away from its racist culture is discussed in Chapter 7.

2

Current Psychiatry

INTRODUCTION

Psychiatry is not an exact science. At best it is a healing art based on a body of knowledge about people, built on a framework of hypotheses and information. The hypotheses are to do with brain-function and so-called psychological processes. Information comes from the basic sciences and from observations of people referred to as 'patients', i.e. clinical observations. The basic sciences were, at first, anatomy and physiology but psychology began to influence psychiatry towards the end of the nineteenth and into the twentieth century. More recently, anthropology and sociology as well as biochemistry have all come into the picture as the official 'scientific background' to psychiatry. The unofficial background, namely the social and political forces that underpin psychiatry, was described in the last chapter, where it was also shown that, very early in its history, psychiatry took over from medicine the concept of mental disease as an entity seen essentially as a disorder within an individual. Although the methods of observation in psychiatry have never been very objective and the ideal of a precise classification of disease entities still remains largely illusory, the identification (diagnosis) and classification of 'diseases' is fundamental to psychiatry both as a discipline and as an institution performing a social function in society.

Systems of classification (of mental diseases) should, in general, reflect the (current) state of knowledge within psychiatry. But this begs several important questions such as those posed by Malt (1986) in commenting on a system of classification in current use — the DSM-III (American Psychiatric Association, 1980): 'What is knowledge? How is consensus about state of knowledge reached?

What kind of data should form the basis of knowledge? What does it mean to understand mental disorder?' Malt goes on to suggest that 'the DSM-III system has presupposed an answer to these questions' by devising a classification system allegedly based on 'knowledge and data' with the aim to 'understand mental disorders'. Malt (1986) identifies two main approaches to knowledge that are evident in Western thinking over the past 400 – 500 years.

One approach (labelled empiricism, positivism or analytic philosophy) emphasizes observation and formal logic: only phenomena that can in some definite sense be empirically and intersubjectively observed and described are considered scientifically valid and only sentences that can be tested empirically are considered meaningful. The hypothetical-deductive method is the method of obtaining knowledge. Questions which can only be answered by intuition or reflection (reason) — like metaphysical questions — are considered to be outside the scope of science.

The second approach to knowledge is that of reason — with the implied existence of 'some kind of basic truth, rule or ideal independent of observation (the synthetic *a priori*).'

Current systems of classification of diseases, such as the ICD-9 (World Health Organisation, 1978) or the DSM-III (American Psychiatric Association, 1980) are based primarily on empirical observations that emphasise 'pathology' in thinking and behaviour of an individual 'patient', although concepts based on reason are used sometimes to separate disorders. Apart from missing out the social and political dimensions of what constitutes 'illness', they fail to take into account an important dimension for understanding mental disorder at a personal level — 'the metaphysical dimension' (Malt, 1986). 'This dimension may be defined as a cosmic view of life where man is part of a greater meaning beyond rational thoughts. Humility towards life and man may be key words describing this attitude.' The author agrees with Malt that 'current concepts and understanding in psychiatry' will be very different 'if this approach to comprehension of man and life' is incorporated into psychiatry.

During and following the last world war, interest in the social environment of hospitals led to a consideration of the social aspects of mental disorder. Social psychiatry today denotes the study of the impingment of social phenomena upon the genesis and manifestations of mental and physical illness, and the utilisation of social forces in the treatment of mental and emotional disturbances (Arthur, 1973). More recently, transcultural psychiatry has developed as an interest and is now gradually emerging into its own with the rise of multi-cultural populations in the West. Meanwhile, techniques of family therapy have grown rapidly during the last few years, often with scant recognition of cultural differences in family structure.

To add to the apparent 'ideological chaos within psychiatry' (Clare, 1976), the 'anti-psychiatry' movement sprang up in the 1960s and 1970s to challenge the very existence of the discipline. The reaction to this from the traditionalists has been to tighten up the criteria for diagnosis and to return to an increasingly biological approach to the concept of illness. In spite of the complex issues within psychiatry and the variability in the specifics of its practice, there is little doubt that the discipline has, on the whole, a way of working which is recognisable. It is, moreover, an important part of the total social system we live in. Therefore, whether mental illness is perceived as a myth (Szasz, 1960) where psychiatry serves functions which are non-medical in nature, or, as a bio-medical disorder of individuals who require intervention from psychiatry in the form of physical, psychological or social treatment, psychiatry as a social process is a reality.

The last chapter discussed in some detail how the ideology of racism (as a social and political norm in society) has become embedded in psychiatry through its historical roots in (racist) Western culture. Further, it was argued that racism within the theory and practice of psychiatry persists into the present. In discussing the development of psychiatry itself, Professor Castel (1985) makes an important point:

> One of the fundamental reasons for the permeability of nine-teenth-century psychiatry to the social and political norms of the time resides in the impossibility for practitioners at the time of grounding their intervention on the basis of a corpus of theoretically articulated knowledge.

He goes on to argue that, since such a body of knowledge does now exist, contemporary psychiatry should be 'capable of breaking with dominant ideology and even developing, if its own analyses happened to lead in that direction, a theory that was subversive of that ideology.' The question whether this applies to the ideology of racism within psychiatry will now be considered.

Resistance to Change within Psychiatry

An important consideration is the capacity of psychiatry, as a discipline, to face up to the ideology of racism that is a part of its inheritance. In order to do this, psychiatry has to recognise the ideology (of racism) for what it is, and, to appreciate the effects of racism in both psychiatric practice — that is dealing with 'patients' — and practices within the institution of psychiatry, such as recruitment and training of professional staff. Further, at a personal level, psychiatrists need to be subjectively aware of racist practices that they are involved in — wittingly or unwittingly — as well as prejudiced attitudes within themselves towards both patients and their colleagues in their own and other related disciplines such as nursing, psychology and social work. British psychiatry fails on both counts.

First, there is no evidence that the existence of racism is recognised by the 'establishment' in the discipline as reflected in its approach to psychiatric practice, research, or training. If racism is perceived as a significant factor in determining psychiatric practice, one would expect the topic to find a place in the field of 'social psychiatry', now an important branch of main-stream psychiatry in Britain. The main research body that sets current trends in British social psychiatry is the Social Psychiatry Research Unit at the Institute of Psychiatry in London. This unit has ignored — or perhaps avoided — the topic of racism completely. But worse than that, its tentative forays into 'cultural' research (e.g. Bebbington *et al.*, 1981) are highly suspect. Individuals from this Unit have played a significant role in designing and supervising the International Pilot Study of Schizophrenia (World Health Organisation, 1973, 1979) — a study that imposes Western concepts with little regard for the cultures of the non-Western people it studies — bringing to psychiatric research and planning a colour-blind approach in a colour-conscious world, and, thereby revealing a serious bias against facing up to the history of racism in Western Psychiatry. (The IPSS is quoted many times in this book because it exemplifies much of what is wrong with psychiatry at present while attracting considerable attention and becoming accepted by the psychiatric

41

establishment as a sort of standard for international and cross-cultural investigation.)

The Royal College of Psychiatrists supervises the training of psychiatrists in Britain and has a voice in appointments to psychiatric posts at a senior level. A survey done in 1986 of psychiatrists who had passed the membership examination of the College in 1981– 2, showed that four times as many overseas than UK graduates were still in junior posts (Bhate, Sagovsky and Cox, 1986). The authors report that their questionnaire 'attempted to elicit information about whether or not discrimination had been experienced by the overseas graduates, but doctors were reluctant to commit themselves on this controversial topic. Indeed several people had implied that they feared their response to the questionnaire might have adverse repercussions when applying for posts in the future, and could not be reassured about the confidentiality of a college-sponsored research undertaking.' There is no indication that the Education Committee of the Royal College of Psychiatrists is prepared to take this matter any further, apparently preferring not to recognise their own racism or the racism that is institutionalised in the procedure for psychiatric (medical) appointments. Although its representatives to appointments committees are instructed on the need to keep within the laws against racial discrimination, the college has refused to allow any outside body such as the Commission for Racial Equality to examine its records on appointments and has no specific advisor on race relations. Even when a member of the college was found by an Industrial Tribunal to have suffered from racial discrimination at an appointments committee in Cambridge (Anwar and Ali, 1987), the President of the Royal College of Psychiatrists observed that he did not think that any major changes were necessary in the part played by college representatives at such committees (Hospital Doctor, 1985).

It is difficult to gauge accurately the extent of the personal awareness among psychiatrists of their own racism and the racist practices that they participate in within the institution of psychiatry. Anecdotal evidence collected by the author points to a remarkable resistance by individual psychiatrists against examining this aspect of their practice. Sometimes, it seems that racist stereotyping is the bedrock of psychiatric practice among people seen as 'black'. The rejection of black patients as potential candidates for psychotherapy, and possibly for informal treatment in general, is exemplified by a comment made to the author by a colleague: 'The trouble with Cypriots is that they only want to talk about physical symptoms'.

This comment, which could apply to any person perceived as 'black', was made about people in an area where a community psychiatric service was being planned for a population of which 20 per cent are Cypriot, without including a single Cypriot person on the staff. The impression among the staff was that Cypriots cannot benefit from psychotherapy. Meanwhile research conducted in the area concerned has shown that the Cypriot population view the professionals within the service as being disinterested in psychological problems and 'only interested in physical symptoms' (Andreou, 1986). Although it is evident that 'somatisation' reflects a dissonance of communication and is accepted as a challenge by most psychotherapists, it is generally held to reflect inaccessibility of the patient to the expertise of the therapist when the patient is seen as culturally inferior — and cultural inferiority is usually judged on the basis of racial typing.

Another common situation where racism plays havoc with the 'expertise' of medical and nursing staff in the psychiatric service involves the assessment of dangerousness. Although psychiatric assessments of dangerousness are notoriously unreliable (Steadman, 1983), psychiatrists continue to make them. Since an established body of knowledge on this subject does not exist, psychiatric assessment of dangerousness has to rest on 'common sense'. A powerful image in the society that determines this 'common sense' is that of the dangerous Black. Aggrey Burke (1986), an Afro-Caribbean British psychiatrist, believes that psychiatric reports for courts 'show an obsession with ideas of Blacks being bad, big Blacks somewhat worse, and big black males — particularly those who have had any contact with the police — as the most dangerous of all cases.' Thus, a black skin is a factor that identifies dangerousness — leading to the sort of observation made by Bolton (1984) in a study at Springfield Hospital in South London: Although similar proportions of 'aggressive' patients were transferred to a locked ward in all ethnic groups, in the case of 'uncooperative' patients, 87 per cent of West Indian and African as opposed to 36 per cent of (white) British patients were transferred to a locked ward. Although racist selectivity in assessments of psychotherapeutic potential and dangerousness may be a part of the racism institutionalised within psychiatry, rather than the effect of specific personal prejudices of psychiatrists, it is often difficult to separate one from the other in practice. Moreover, the result, as far as black patients are concerned, is identical whatever the reason for the racist practice.

However, it is in the field of recruitment that personal prejudice and institutionalised racism are very evident. Anecdotal reports of racism in appointments at all levels of (psychiatric) hospital staff are plentiful. In these circumstances, 'culture' or 'language ability' is usually used as a synonym for 'race' when objections are raised against a black candidate applying for a post. In situations where racism is less overt, racial stereotypes such as that of the 'passive Asian' are used to argue against candidates' suitability — even though, for example, the appointee may be destined to work with Asians. The need to appoint professional staff with particular language skills is often rejected on the basis of being 'discriminatory', while candidates whose first language is one other than English are often rejected on the basis of not having sufficient command of English — unless of course the candidate happens to be white. Further, there is strong pressure on people serving on selection committees to 'toe the line' of the establishment and appoint staff who are 'acceptable'. It should be noted that, although appointment committees convened by Regional Health Authorities (for senior medical staff) have a statutory format, those invited to serve are selected in devious ways. The author had the opportunity to serve several times on such committees some years ago but was suddenly dropped after he asked questions that alluded to racial issues.

The second consideration concerns the methodology of psychiatry as a discipline and the arrangements within it as an institution. If, supposing, there is a recognition of racism as a feature of psychiatric practice, one needs to consider how amenable psychiatry is to change — or allow change — to combat racism. This is dependent on the arrangements for day-to-day functioning within the discipline or institution of psychiatry, i.e. the internal organisation, or 'machinery', that determines its activities.

Manufacture of Psychiatry

The knowledge within psychiatry is produced and organised in the following way. Information based on some sort of common-sense is gathered and categorised. This information is then used to develop stereotypes of people in terms of their feelings, behaviour personalities etc. Both categories and stereotypes lead to generalisations — sometimes called 'typifications' (Schwartz and Wiggins, 1987) about people. This is the 'core' of the process, but it works in a context of a culture of psychiatry (described in Chapter 1) and the current ethos in society. Although traditional ideas, ongoing clinical observations, and knowledge from the basic sciences

Figure 2.1: Machinery of psychiatry in context

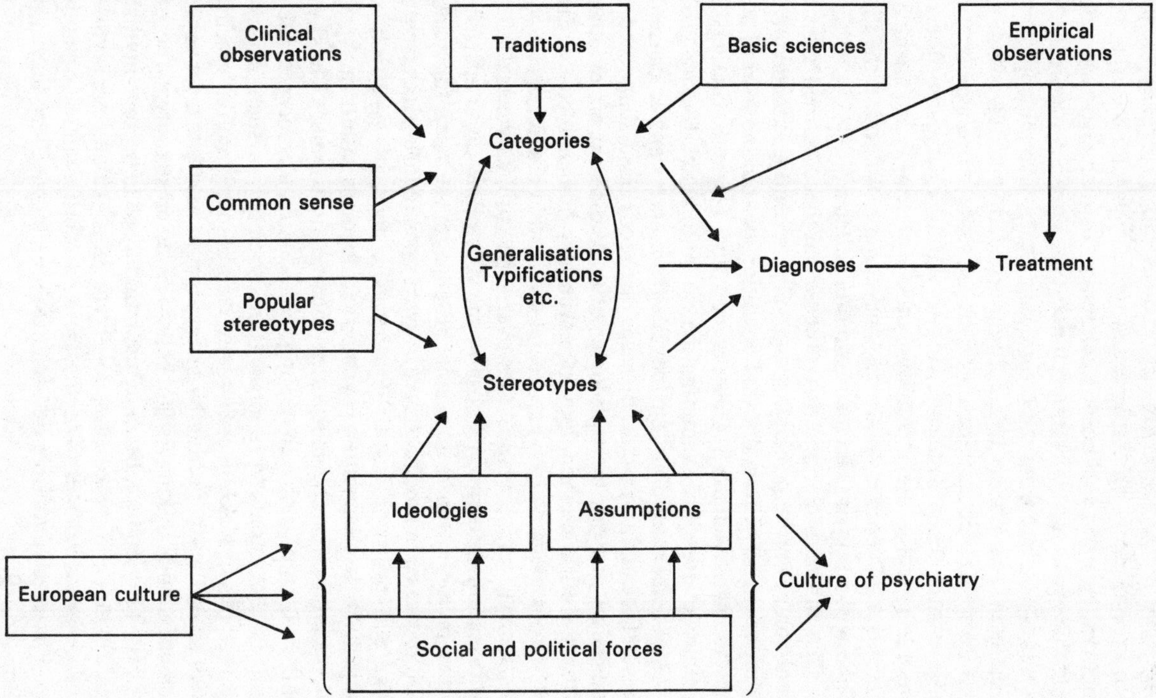

(anatomy and physiology in the nineteenth century, and physiology, psychology, biochemistry, and sociology currently) contribute to the body of information within psychiatry, the basic methodology of psychiatry is centred on its diagnostic procedure, and this works through its 'machinery' illustrated in Figure 2.1. Diagnoses emanate from the central core, but, since the approach to treatment in psychiatry is largely empirical, treatment methods may not do so. The understanding of the causation of (diagnosed) disease is sometimes wide, referring to various explanatory theories from chemical to social. Aetiology too may draw from outside this core. But this core is what *makes* psychiatry. Without it the discipline will disappear and the institution collapse.

The information-gathering process has been refined over the years on scientific principles, and, more recently, extended to encompass family life and social conditions within the overall aegis of 'social psychiatry'. Observations and research findings are usually analysed by examining the extent to which feelings, behaviour, social conditions, etc. deviate from norms and/or cause distress. It is in this way that 'diseases' are recognised, diagnosed and measured, and that the aetiologies of these diseases are evaluated. This scientific methodology of psychiatry has enabled the discipline to achieve a certain respectability within medicine and within society as a whole. However, the subjectiveness of the information-gathering process in the discipline, quite apart from other factors (such as resistance to change, the need for respectability and economic pressures), lays it open to influences from social and political forces. Further, the lack of precision and objectivity in designating psychiatric categories results in slippage of meaning whereby categories become stereotypes. Thus, psychiatry is comfortable in dealing with, and in, stereotypes; the result is that stereotypes present in society — such as racial stereotypes of black people — are incorporated into its 'machine' with no difficulty. Further by being incorporated into a supposedly scientific body of knowledge, beliefs based on stereotypes become 'facts'. They, in turn, become institutionalised to become myths. In reality, much of what passes for 'facts' in psychiatry are myths — and a major drawback of myths, from a scientific angle, is that they serve to close the circle that science has necessarily to leave open (Rendon, 1984).

It is evident from this discussion that a major problem in the machinery that manufactures psychiatry is that myths are confused with scientific facts and categories with stereotypes. Myths persist for both social and psychological reasons. Rendon (1984) notes that social forces opposing assimilation of human groups and equality of human beings, tend to present social facts, such as poverty, famine and oppression, as natural phenomena in order to stress the lack of equality and the alienness of certain human beings, designated as 'barbarian', 'primitive' or 'underdeveloped'. Psychological reasons for the persistence of myths is discussed by Wilkinson (1970) in analysing myths about black people that affect psychiatric practice in the United States:

> In a nation in which a series of myths has been built up with their bases rooted in a difference in skin color, one segment of the country, commonly termed 'the white majority', has a readily available source of beliefs that it may use to relieve anxiety. White Americans can thus use myths to buttress for themselves as valid their view of black Americans as being different and inferior. It is not uncommon both in daily life and in psychiatric practice to observe a direct relationship between degrees of belief in prejudices (and their accompanying myths) and fluctuations in levels of anxiety...Some of the myths underlying prejudices are that blacks are morally inferior to whites, who by implication become very moral, and that blacks are childish, irresponsible, and given to the pleasure of the moment; also, they are supposed to be sexually overresponsive.

Allport (1954) discusses the difference between categories and stereotypes, defined by Sykes (1982) as 'unduly fixed mental impressions':

> A stereotype is not identical with a category; it is rather a fixed idea that accompanies the category. For example, the category 'negro' can be held in mind simply as a neutral, factual nonevaluative concept, pertaining merely to a racial stock. Stereotype enters when and if, the initial category is freighted with 'pictures' and judgements of the Negro as musical, lazy, superstitious, or what not... They are sustained by selective perception and selective forgetting;... they aid people in simplifying their categories; they justify hostility; sometimes they serve as projection screens for our personal conflict. But there is an additional, and exceedingly important, reason for their existence. They are socially supported, continually revived and hammered in, by our

media of mass communication — by novels, short stories, newspaper items, movies, stage, radio, and television.

Thus, stereotypes and myths about black people persist within psychiatry because of the way in which psychiatry functions. Two points should be noted at this stage:

First, the permeation into psychiatry of ideologies in society is a constant and continuing process. It is possible that psychiatry will lose its racism if racially egalitarian — or anti-racist — ideas and beliefs permeate into it from society at large. But of course society is not like that. It is racism, not anti-racism, that continues to permeate into psychiatry. It is not merely a question of racism having become embedded in psychiatry in the nineteenth century continuing to influence it currently; racism in society at large actively affects the current development of psychiatry. This is particularly evident in terms of the stereotypes that psychiatry takes on. The image of the violent black male was referred to earlier; the docile Asian woman is another such stereotype. In fact, in these situations, as in many others in this society, race and culture are confounded and generalised: black male patients are seen as potentially violent and brown females as docile.

Secondly, the results of so-called scientific research are often permeated by racist ideology because psychiatry, by its very nature, is unable to filter off the (non-scientific) racially biased influences. Just as nineteenth century anatomists working in the context of overt racism came to racist conclusions about brain size — and psychiatry took this on — so today, racist findings of cross-cultural studies are taken over without much difficulty. For example, consider the study of 'Psychiatric Disorder among Selected Immigrant Groups in Camberwell' (Bebbington *et al.*, 1981). A conclusion of the researchers based on their 'clinical observation' is that West Indians deal with adversity by 'cheery denial'. This 'observation' is clearly determined by the racial stereotype of the happy-go-lucky Black normally present in Western society. If the people concerned had been white, they may well have been seen as showing a 'stiff upper lip'. Such stereotypes are derived from a racist ideology which acts 'functionally on men via a process that escapes them.' (Althusser, 1965). Ideology of this type is embodied in social institutions, influencing 'the social axes around which experience becomes organised' (Banton, Clifford, Frosh, Lousada and Rosenthal, 1985). The ideology of racism acts on researchers, black and white, in British society not (necessarily) because they (the researchers) are racist but because British society is racist.

Thus, the methodology of psychiatry, as a discipline, is so structured as to lay itself wide open to absorb current ideas in society about people, and incorporate them into its theory and practice. It is not naturally geared to provide a lead in breaking with an ideology that is dominant in society. Since, the ideology of racism is currently prevalent, psychiatry will continue to absorb it unless positive action is taken to prevent that happening. The fact is that psychiatry is not outside the society within which it functions any more than education or law. In many ways psychiatry is more integrated within society than either of these two institutions and reflects society's ideas all too fully. However, there are other aspects to the institution and discipline of psychiatry. Its theory — at least the formal and official theory — includes a humanitarian ideal and its technology aims at being scientific. A humane psychiatry should be anti-racist and a scientific discipline should be free of racist myths. So what stops it? Two groups of factors are considered here, the alliance between psychiatry and social control, and, the 'dynamic conservatism' (Schon, 1971) of the institution of psychiatry.

Psychiatry and Social Control

In considering the capacity of an institution (such as psychiatry) to change, Schon (1971) points out that 'social systems resist change with an energy roughly proportional to the radicalness of the change that is threatened.' A peripheral change without disruption of the system as a whole would be less resisted than a change which would shake the system to its roots. Further, any change in one part of the system effects changes in other parts. How central then is racism to psychiatry as an institution? Racism within the institution of psychiatry does not exist in isolation from racism in other institutions in society such as the judiciary and police. Therefore, the function of psychiatry in relation to other systems is crucial. It was shown in the last chapter that the rise of psychiatry as a social institution was directly related to the confinement of large numbers of people in physical institutions and the subsequent medicalisation of their care. The involvement of psychiatry in controlling people has always been as evident as its function of treating patients. Indeed one view of psychiatry (Ingelby, 1985) sees its treatment methods as forms of social control. In practice, it is not difficult to see psychiatry as one of the social systems that enforce the law — the others being forensic systems which include prisons and remand homes — although some writers see psychiatry as 'keeping people in line' in a much wider sense (Ingelby, 1985). If, then, racism within psychiatry is connected with racism within the other institutions that, together with psychiatry, are involved in social control, removing racism from psychiatry will involve destabilising the other systems too. What is seen in practice is that black people are over-represented in compulsory care in psychiatric institutes to a similar degree to which they are over-represented in prisons (Home Office Statistical Bulletin, 1986) and remand homes (Kettle, 1982). This indicates the likelihood that removing racism from the culture of psychiatry as an institution will meet strong resistance. To put it bluntly, if, as seems likely, psychiatry is involved in social control systems that keep black people 'in their place', i.e. within limits set by (white) society, racism within psychiatry is necessary for maintaining the status quo.

Dynamic Conservatism of Psychiatry

Schon (1971) has described the resistance to change of a social system as, not an 'inertia', but a 'dynamic conservatism — that is to say, a tendency to fight to remain the same.' He likens it to a living system where, according to Cannon (1963), 'any tendency toward change is automatically met by increased effectiveness of the factors which resist change.' The different parts of a social system 'all hang together so that any change in one produces change in others.' If there are external threats to its stability, energy is expended to hold the system as a whole stable.

Thus, psychiatry resists pressure (for example, from people wishing to see it respond to the needs of black people) to drop the ideology of racism because this ideology is important, if not central, to its culture, and to do so will destabilise psychiatry as an institution. What does this mean in practice? Suppose, for example, that racist stereotyping is excluded from psychiatric practice in some hard-to-imagine way. This would alter both its technology and its theory. The image of psychiatry as a 'sensible' profession with a 'scientific' basis would be threatened. Consequently psychiatry would lose social status as an institution that reflects the norms of society, and its reputation as a common-sensible discipline managed by a 'sane' profession rather than the 'mad doctors'

(Scull, 1981) of the early nineteenth century. Take for instance the following personal experience of the author:

> I was called to the Accident and Emergency Department of a hospital to see a black person brought there by the police under section 136 of the Mental Health Act (1983). The staff of the department, including doctors and nurses, reckoned that he was in need of further observation in hospital but too dangerous to be kept in a general hospital. I gathered that their assessment was based on three bits of psychiatric information obtained in the usual professional manner. Firstly, there was the police report that he had talked to strangers in the street in an abusive manner; secondly, it was observed that he would not speak to anyone in the Accident and Emergency Department; and finally, 'everyone' agreed that he 'looked' dangerous. It was normal in such circumstances to have the police present on interviewing a patient. My decision to dismiss the police and offer the patient a cup of tea generated alarm and suspicion of my credentials as a sensible psychiatrist. Clearly, I was letting down the side by showing up a dissonance between psychiatric judgement and common-sense.

This is not an isolated case. When the author made a similar judgement with regard to a black person on remand in Brixton Prison, the prison doctor decided to get another psychiatrist — one whose scientific credentials had been proven by being the editor of a book on scientific principles of the subject. If racism is dropped from the stereotyping system that often goes for psychiatric judgement, psychiatry would need to compensate for the consequent instability (in terms of loss of social status) by strengthening its image in some other way. But there are few ways open to psychiatry to do this.

Conclusions

Several ways in which psychiatry resists any pressure to change its racist ways of working have been outlined above. By far the most important in terms of the profession of psychiatry is its internal structure — its methodology and technology. However, the most serious observation, in terms of the people affected by psychiatry as an institution, is the alignment of psychiatry with social control. Dynamic conservatism is something that applies to many institutions, and therefore ways of shaking it may emerge. Despite these and other strong forces that keep racism going within psychiatry, there are people within the profession and, more importantly, in political circles that are concerned at the situation. Therein lies hope for the future.

THEORY AND PRACTICE

Current literature in the basic sciences that feed into psychiatry does not normally give space for overt racist views — at least not in Britain — but racist ideology does indeed come through in print often disguised as views about culture. This is possible because of an assumption, which is seldom made explicit but generally accepted, equating race and culture. This 'faulty logic' commonly found within social anthropology 'that if an individual is of a certain race, then he must exhibit certain cultural traits as well' (Burnham, 1972) is very much a part of the assumptions within British society generally. The designations of what are called 'cultural' groups, whether for research purposes or for service provision, are usually based on racial differentiation alone. This has the 'advantage' of avoiding the obvious implication of defining them as 'racial' groups: If defined as racial groups, any inter-group difference in psychopathology, consultation rates, hospital admission rates, diagnostic labelling, use of services, etc. has then to be recognised as relating to race rather than culture. And since biological differences are an insufficient, or unacceptable, explanation in many instances, the question of racism has to be faced. By quoting 'culture' instead of 'race' this ugly matter is avoided. For example, a study of general practice records (Brewin, 1980) found that the average number of annual consultations by Asians is not significantly different from that by English people, although the former have considerably lower rates of psychiatric hospitalisation when compared to indigenous people (Cochrane, 1977). The conclusion drawn by Brewin was that referral practices on the part of general practitioners were different for the two groups. Since the two groups — referred to in his paper as 'Asian' and 'white native-born' — were perceived as ethnic (meaning cultural) groups, the discussion of the difference in referral practices was pursued in terms of cultural factors alone. Questions about 'communication of information', 'cultural taboos against revealing certain symptoms' and 'lack of knowledge about patients' way of life' were delineated as possible reasons for the relative failure by general practitioners to refer their Asian patients to hospital, while racial discrimination by professionals, racism within the psychiatric service and similar factors were disregarded. In such situations, both racial and cultural considerations may be important and conclusions should be based on both groups of factors.

Although blatant racist ideas of the type put forward by Carothers (1951, 1953) and quoted in Chapter 1 are not evident in current psychiatric literature, ethnocentric arrogance amounting to racism is very close to the surface in many references to cross-cultural study. In a recent review of depression, Bebbington (1978) refers several times to 'primitive cultures' as synonymous with non-Western cultures. After quoting cross-cultural studies on depression, he makes this extraordinary statement:

> It is the argument of the author that issues arising from the cross-cultural and intracultural studies of depression are more likely to be classified if a precise definition of depression is accepted: we must measure the unknown by the yardstick of the known...The author therefore argues for a provisional syndromal definition of depression as used by a consensus of western psychiatrists against which cross-cultural anomalies can be tested.

The experiences of non-Western people are dismissed as 'anomalies' presumably because they are from 'primitive cultures'. 'Non-Western' in this context means 'non-white'; 'cross-cultural anomaly' is the modern version of 'racial inferiority'.

In the paper quoted above, Bebbington claims that his views on cross-cultural approaches to depression 'accords with the approach of the World Health Organisation'. A major study organised by the WHO and reported extensively in the psychiatric literature is the 'International Pilot Study of Schizophrenia' (World Health Organisation, 1973, 1979). It is described critically in Chapter 3. The use of Western diagnostic methods and interview techniques across five continents seems a foolish way of going about research. However, it may merely reflect the ethos of the WHO derived from the people who advise that body on psychiatric research. Just as colonial powers imposed imperial languages such as English, French, etc. as the medium of education in the colonies (partly) because they were thought to be superior to native languages, psychiatric nosology, which may be seen as a sort of language of psychiatry derived in Europe, is being imposed because of similar assumptions. A truly scientific approach is to examine nosology objectively and to devise a system that is valid for the particular population being studied. But commonsense dictates otherwise — and 'commonsense' in this case comprises the assumptions of people who make decisions and wield power in matters psychiatric.

Psychiatric research in Britain tends to ignore the social experiences of black and ethnic minorities or to marginalise it. Research based on these groups is perceived as being applicable to those groups alone, while research based on white people is incorporated into mainstream psychiatry as being applicable to everyone. Cross-cultural research in Britain seldom takes on racial issues but is itself sometimes almost explicitly racist. For example, consider the recent paper on psychiatric disorder in selected immigrant groups in Camberwell quoted in Chapter 1: in this paper, white researchers from the Medical Research Council's Social Psychiatry Unit (Bebbington *et al.*,1981) conclude that 'West Indians' have a relatively low rate of depression and anxiety because they (West Indians) give a 'clinical impression' of responding to adversity with 'cheery denial'. Not only is the lack of depression perceived as a pathological finding, but the observers make no allowance for the cultural and racial context within which they (the white researchers) observe black people. Here, as in other studies, when a black group is compared to a white group, characteristics of the latter are assumed to be the norm. Researchers working within the ethos of institutions that do not recognise the racism that is inherent within their ways of working, i.e. institutionalised racism, do not question the validity of their judgements of black people any more than did colonial civil servants in the time of the Empire.

In looking at the practice of British psychiatry today, it is striking that the discipline is failing to take the views and experiences of black people seriously, quite apart from trying to incorporate these into mainstream psychiatry. First, the practice of psychiatry applied to ethnic minorities tends to be seen as something special while, usually, denying the reality of racism. It is easy for well-meaning professionals to collude in this approach. Indeed the establishment of special services for black people may be a useful short-term strategy — so long as it is short-term — that can be used as a springboard for developing a service that is both appropriate and fair to everyone. The best known version of the special-service approach is the 'Transcultural Psychiatry Unit' at Lynfield Mount Hospital in Bradford, Yorkshire. The British psychiatrist who founded the unit describes it in an appendix to his book *Race, Cul-*

ture and Mental Disorder (Rack, 1982): the Unit was set up because 'it became apparent to the hospital staff that the mental health provision that they were making for these ethnic minorities was unsatisfactory, mainly because of language difficulties and lack of cultural understanding.' The approach of the unit is clearly aimed at remedying problems arising from cultural, rather than racial, differences between ethnic minorities and the indigenous population. This is commendable as a start towards recognising the need for any psychiatric service to be sensitive to the people it serves. However, if the unit is allowed to remain as a special unit for ethnic minorities that serves them but does not identify with them, for example by allowing the unit to be controlled by people who can represent them and take up issues which are important to them, it will merely reinforce the racist model which sees black people as requiring a psychiatry that would 'educate' them into white norms. Furthermore, if a service for ethnic minorities fails to recognise the reality of racism, the problems are seen as the need to understand the 'primitive' ways of black people and to develop an expertise in communicating with them (Brent Community Health Council, 1981).

Another way of marginalising the experience of black people and relegating it to an inferior position is to conceptualise it as an 'anthropological' issue. A recently established post at a London teaching hospital of a Senior Lecturer in Transcultural Psychiatry is designed to incorporate both anthropology and psychiatry. The 'job description' sees a background of anthropology as a necessary qualification for understanding psychiatric problems of 'ethnic subcultures in Britain' (personal knowledge of author) — an euphemism for black and ethnic minorities — but not for dealing with the white indigenous population. Since this is the first British psychiatric appointment at a senior level in Transcultural Psychiatry, and one agreed by the University of London and the Department of Health, it could be seen as a model for the future. Clearly, here too, a professional may unwittingly collude in a racist system, but could, if determined and committed, use such an appointment as a strategy for moving the system on to recognise that black people are not inferior to whites. However, this could not happen unless black people are appointed to key positions such as the post referred to — and that is at present unlikely to happen.

Secondly, the practice of psychiatry (as a discipline) as well as its institutions tend to adopt a 'colour-blind' approach in its dealings with both patients and its own members. This is sometimes taken to an absurd extent; for example, Crammer (1986) of

55

the Institute of Psychiatry gives this advice to trainee psychiatrists: 'In making a diagnosis, it does not matter whether the patient is 25, 35 or 45, yellow, white or brown, male, female or other. One should always put the most relevant matters first, particularly when time is short.' Questions about racism are seldom, if ever, raised at psychiatric case conferences. This may reflect the emphasis on organic considerations in British Psychiatry, but it is rare even for psychiatrists who claim to practise social psychiatry to consider racism either as a factor denoted under the rubric of 'life events', or, as a determinant of diagnostic labelling.

At an institutional level, The Royal College of Psychiatrists has singularly failed to establish a position on racism in Britain or even to consider having a policy on race, although it has been called upon to do this. This reflects the failure by that College to recognise the experiences of its own black members, and more importantly, to acknowledge that there is serious disquiet among black patients about the practice of psychiatry by members of the College. In the wider scene, the Royal College of Psychiatrists resists moves towards taking a public stand on racist psychiatric practices in South Africa, although a committee appointed by the American Psychiatric Association to visit South Africa condemned these several years ago (Stone, Pinderhughes, Spurlock and Weinberg, 1978).

Psychiatric practice today continues to reflect assumptions that come from the past or permeate into psychiatry from society at large. A report by the Brent Community Health Council (1981) states: 'In the National Health Service the mythology is that Afro-Caribbean women are feckless and irresponsible, while Asian women are compliant but stupid. West Indians are dubbed as having no culture, the problem for the Asians *is* their culture.' Case conferences frequently reflect the stereotype of the mother-centred Afro-Caribbean British family as being unstable, weak and disorganised. The Asian family is criticised for being 'too structured' and too authoritarian because it is father-centred and its women docile. As Brittan and Maynard (1984) observe, the Afro-Caribbean family 'creates individual and societal problems because of its lack of mechanisms for imposing restraint, the Asian family creates such difficulties for opposite reasons'. Professional views are often put forward to explain psychological disorders in British Blacks in terms of a family (such as the Asian family) being 'too close'; in the case of the Afro-Caribbean family it is not close enough. Such cultural arrogance which sees pathology in deviation from (assumed) white nuclear family structures is a reflection of racist ideology within psychiatry and allied social work.

In everyday practice, Asian families are said to be 'supportive' without any clear conception of what this really means; myths about Afro-Caribbeans lead to a view that they cannot 'use' help. In a situation where resources are limited, professionals often concentrate these on people who 'need' and can 'use' the sort of help that is available. The result is that professionals behave in a racist manner confirming the racist assumptions that led to their behaviour. In order to be non-racist, not only must professionals scrutinise their attitudes critically, but also examine their assumptions (about clients) closely, analyse the ways in which services are organised and delivered and explore the meaning of terms such as 'help', 'supportive families', etc. in the context of the pressures on black and ethnic minorities in contemporary British society.

Stereotypes of black violence lie behind many of the attitudes towards psychiatric patients and indeed people in general. An expectation of violence based on 'common-sense' catches black people — especially black men — in situations that result in violence leading to a self-fulfilling prophecy. The causes of justified anger are often not recognised because the black experience in society is not appreciated; or even if it is, a disease or criminal model is used to explain it because society (and possibly the needs of professionals working in the psychiatric and social services) promotes its use. Sometimes, psychiatric opinions seem to be very similar to police perceptions of black people. In the recent enquiry into the 'riots' in Handsworth, Birmingham, psychiatric evidence was given (Imlah, 1985) that consumption of cannabis was to blame for exciting black youth — in line with the 'common-sense' of the police which blamed 'drugs' for the conflict between the black population and the police. Psychiatric diagnoses of schizophrenia in adults or maladjustment in children (both of which are 'over-diagnosed' in black people and discussed later) may work in a similar way ,in other settings.

When black and ethnic minority people are admitted to hospital they usually find themselves in institutions where black staff may be present but are seldom in charge. Such an environment — reminiscent of colonial institutions of the bad old days — cannot instill a sense of security in black people. The powerlessness of black people and the discriminations they face in society play a considerable role in causing mental stress and breakdown. If the power structure of the hospital ward reflects their powerlessness in society at large, any therapeutic effect that the hospital environment may have is lost. In fact, the ambience of such a hospital ward may accentuate their problems (arising from powerlessness) by rendering them less able to cope in a hostile world. It is no wonder that black patients tend to 'abscond' from hospital more often than do whites. What is regrettable is that this very fact is used as a reason for suggesting that Blacks are unsuitable for open hospitals and/or cannot use treatment. Surely it is the hospital that is failing and the 'treatment' that is unsuitable. Furthermore, the norms of behaviour that black and ethnic minority patients have to adhere to in hospital add to the alienation they feel. They are made to feel ashamed of their eating habits, ways of talking (too loud or too soft) and hair styles — thus leaving them as outsiders to the ward community. If they try and keep to their own norms such as eating with their fingers or praying in a certain way, they are seen as deviant or even sick. Vicious circles develop and emotional disturbance induced by the situation may arise confirming the wrong assumptions made in the first place.

3

Cross-Cultural Research

INTRODUCTION

In the early part of this century, the German psychiatrist Kraepelin (1913) observed that patients in mental hospitals in Java were seldom depressed, and, that when they were depressed, rarely felt sinful. Kraepelin was comparing (his impression of) the patient population of Java with that of Germany — a cross-cultural observation. In attributing these and other cross-national differences to heredity, pre-natal damage and illness in early life (Kraepelin, 1920), he perceived the differences in terms of genetic and physical factors rather than culture. Meanwhile anthropologists were describing so-called culture-bound syndromes such as Amok (Ellis, 1893) and Latah (Van Brero, 1895), applying psychoanalytic theories to their studies (Wittkower and Dubreuil, 1971). In the mid-eighteenth century, the followers of Rousseau took the view that mental disorder was a product of 'civilisation' — Western civilisation — while others saw 'uncivilised' people as mentally degenerate (Lewis, 1965). Rousseau's concept of 'The Noble Savage', led to a belief that mental disorder was the result of the restrictions and stresses arising from a Western life-style — generally referred to as 'modern civilisation' — and thus would be rare in people who did not adhere to it — generally referred to as 'savages'. In the mid-nineteenth century, both Tuke (1858) and Maudsley (1867, 1879), thought that 'civilisation' was a cause of insanity and, hence, that non-Europeans were relatively immune to mental disorder — a way of thinking that can be traced through to Freud (1930) in his book *Civilization and its Discontents*. But other beliefs developed too: the German – British school of psychiatry with its biological approach to mental illness assumed that psychiatric disorders (in the classical sense of discrete disease entities) were prevalent in all cultures, i.e. the cultural invariance of mental disorder (or same disorders everywhere); social anthropologists, such as Benedict (1935), emphasised the importance of culture in determining the behaviour, thinking and emotions of individuals, leading to the concept of the cultural relativity of psychopathology — or each culture to its own disorders.

All these ideas developed within an overall ethos prevalent in Europe that some cultures were superior to others. Non-Western cultures were frequently referred to as 'primitive' with the implication that their ways of thinking, feeling and getting ill were less-developed forms of Western equivalents. Psychiatric literature continued to use the word 'civilisation' to denote an attribute of white people, for example, in the notable treatise on the history of insanity entitled *Madness and Civilization* by Foucault (1967). Freud's famous *Totem and Taboo* (Freud, 1950) suggested that (Western) neurotics regress to the kind of thinking that 'savages' have (as indicated by the subtitle to the original edition of the book – *Some Points of Agreement between the Mental Lives of Savages and Neurotics*). In the collection of works by Jung (1964), translated by Hull, the volume *Civilization in Transition* contained several articles in which Jung clearly placed non-Europeans outside the bounds of what he regarded as 'civilisation', although paradoxically, Jung drew a great deal on Asian culture and tradition for his own work. However, it was a British psychiatrist Carothers (1953), who, writing for the World Health Organisation, made explicit the sort of views that influenced, and emanated from, what was accepted as cross-cultural research among black or 'coloured' races. For example, in describing neuroses among Africans, he stated:

In general, it seems that the clear distinction that exists in Europeans between the 'conscious' and 'unconscious' elements of mind does not exist in rural Africans. The 'censor's' place is taken by the sorcerer, and 'splits' are vertical, not horizontal. Emotion easily dominates the entire mind ; and, when it does, the latter's tenuous grip on the world of 'things' is loosened, and frank confusion takes the place of misinterpretation. All the neuroses seen in European individuals are here, as a rule, resolved on social lines; and the structure of psychoses is so altered by the lack of conscious integration that these are apt to take amorphous or abortive forms.

Three models for understanding psychiatric disorder cross-culturally were evident within the sphere of interest that gradually developed in the 1950s into transcultural psychiatry. These models corresponded closely to the interpretive models used by Western anthropologists trying to make sense of the apparent diversity of human societies generally — *universalism, evolutionism,* and *relativism* (Shweder and Bourne, 1984):

Universalists are committed to the view that intellectual diversity is more apparent than real, that exotic idea systems, alien at first blush, are really more like our own than they initially appear.
Evolutionists are committed to the view that alien idea systems not only are truly different from our own, but are different in a special way; viz., other people's systems of ideas are really incipient and less adequate stages in the development of our own understandings.
Relativists, in contrast, are committed to the view that alien idea systems, while fundamentally different from our own, display an internal coherency which, on the one hand, can be understood but, on the other hand, cannot be judged.

The concepts of cultural invariance and cultural relativity (mentioned earlier) clearly correspond to those of universalism and relativism of anthropology. Evolutionist ideas in psychiatry tend to be an extension of universalist arguments that see idea systems and illness models that are alien to Western culture as primitive forms of those within Western culture. This approach is seen in the writings of influential workers in the transcultural field, for example, Carothers (1953) and Wittkower (1968), and in those of more recent workers such as Bebbington (1978) and Leff (1973, 1981, 1986a). Carothers, in particular, was explicit in his contention that he saw Africans as inferior to Europeans. The fact that he saw this as a matter of biological race — denoted by skin colour — was made clear when he quoted reports on American Blacks to argue his case. When, later in his monograph, he stated that the 'modes of thinking' of black people 'can be largely, if not entirely explained on cultural grounds', Carothers saw African cultures as being underdeveloped, i.e. 'concomitant of a certain stage of human social evolution', and needing 'less explaining than do the peculiarities of other cultures.' In line with the conceptual framework of culture-personality studies of the time (Frijda and Jahoda, 1966),

61

Carothers concluded that 'the peculiar features of European mentality derived from a total personal integration which the African does not achieve'. As in most discussions of this nature, race and culture were confounded, but the cultural theme in the WHO monograph written by Carothers was an evolutionary one with Blacks as less developed than Whites.

Contemporary theories and writings are not usually explicitly racist in the mode of Carothers, but the evolutionary approach, with implications of white superiority, are still recognisable in them. The ideas put forward by Leff on the effects of culture on the differentiation of emotional states and those of Bebbington on depression were described in Chapters 1 and 2.

Important consequences flow from the use made of these models by researchers. The universalist would consider it justifiable to use the psychiatric classification system developed in the West as a basis for identifying disorders anywhere in the world, in any cultural context. The evolutionist, working within the universalist model, would interpret cross-cultural difference as a reflection of (cultural) development or underdevelopment. This attitude lends itself to value judgements within the general assumption that a culture identified as 'Western' is superior to one identified as 'non-Western'. Since race and culture are so easily confused in such situations, the nett result is usually a racist interpretation of cultural worth.

The relativist, taking an 'emic' view of mental disorder (Marsella, 1984), would look at illness as a part of the total cultural pattern deriving its meaning from the culture concerned. The extreme relativist position may not get beyond describing culture-bound syndromes and constructing intracultural explanations; consequently the relativist may be unable to contribute very much to cross-cultural epidemiology of mental disorder or the application of (Western) psychiatry in non-Western cultures — and this is an important aspect of transcultural study. Even if, as Marsella (1978) suggests, a researcher starts off by determining disorder categories which are meaningful to the cultures under study — the 'emic' approach — the ethnoscience techniques used for this purpose are themselves grounded in particular ways of thinking about illness and may therefore distort the findings. For example, the assumption that symptoms are linked together to form illness categories is not applicable to all cultures (Good and Good, 1984); the features of an illness may refer to the social and moral characteristics of the person who is ill rather than symptoms (Fabrega, 1970). Even in Western psychiatry, the definition of illness is formed by a mixture of symptoms and aetiology — and the balance is likely to be culturally determined (Good and Good, 1984). Further, moral characteristics, such as antisocial behaviour, may be converted into (pseudo)symptoms as in the diagnostic category of psychopathy used in Western psychiatry. The models used in research for analysing emotions, identifying stress and evaluating psychological processes are often those developed in a Western context, used without any attempt to test their cross-cultural validity. The illness categories that emerge may well be artefacts of the research methodology of ethnoscience. Furthermore, in some cultures, thought and feeling are not distinguished (as in Western psychology) and emotional states, such as anger, work very differently to the way they function in the West (Rosaldo, 1984)

Although issues concerning the ethnocentricity of diagnostic categories and methods of cross-cultural investigation are a major problem of research in non-Western cultures, there are other difficulties too. Therefore, before discussing the lessons that may be drawn from cross-cultural research, a brief review of some other problems inherent in carrying it out must be considered.

PROBLEMS

The definition of the term culture can become a problem if it is not confronted early in a research project and made clear in reporting its findings. Theorising about culture has become a popular pastime that cuts across disciplines. In a preview to a recent book on *Culture Theory* (Shweder and LeVine, 1984), an anthropologist, D'Andrade, comments:

> When I was a graduate student, one imagined people *in* a culture; ten years later culture was all in their heads. The thing went from something out there and very large to something that got placed inside. Culture became a branch of cognitive psychology; it was the content of cognitive psychology.

Later on in that book, D'Andrade (1984) discusses technical definitions of culture used by anthropologists. First, culture as the accumulation of knowledge — about illness, building houses, the nature of the universe, and so on; secondly, culture may consist of 'conceptual structures' that determine the total reality of life within which people live and die; and finally, culture could be seen as almost the same as society, being made up of institutions such as the family, the village and so on.

In transcultural psychiatric research, the term culture must have a down-to-earth, practical meaning. In a broad sense, it is applied to all features of an individual's environment, but generally refers to its non-material aspects that the person holds in common with other individuals forming a social group — similar to D'Andrade's third technical definition. For example, it refers to child-rearing habits, family systems, and ethical values or attitudes common to a group — a mixture of behaviour and cognition (in a wide sense) arising from what Leighton and Hughes (1961) call 'shared patterns of belief, feeling and adaptation which people carry in their minds'. In similar vein, Linton (1956) defines culture as 'an organised group of ideas, habits and conditioned responses shared by members of a society'. Brody (1964) provides a short definition of culture as 'a pattern of shared behaviour characteristics of a society', and, Kluckholm (1944) an even shorter one, 'a blueprint for living'.

In actually carrying out research, a 'cultural unit' (Wittkower, 1965) has to be defined. In practice, criteria such as nationality of origin, religious affiliation, skin colour (generally referred to as race) or, more recently, self-definition of 'ethnicity', are used to denote membership of such a category. But the validity of such criteria to denote cultural group membership is arguable: Individuals belonging to a cultural group should resemble each other in certain (definable) ways of behaviour, belief, and attitudes representing (at least) ways of living, meanings given to important entities and an attitude to society at large. If membership of a group is based on a sense of belonging (to that group), the group is an ethnic group (Cashmore and Troyna, 1983). Cultural similarity may of course engender or even determine such a sense of belonging, but the latter may well arise for different reasons. For example, a sense of belonging that emerges in a racist society is likely to be based on race (as perceived by society at large) rather than culture (as experienced by the group members). However, culture, race and ethnicity are interrelated in complex ways depending on historical, political and social factors. For example, the experience of black people in the United States has shaped a black consciousness — a sense of belonging to a group — as well as a recognisable black culture (Richardson and Lambert, 1985). Black people who came to Britain from British colonies — or countries which, having obtained political independence, continued to suffer from economic dependence

— find themselves trapped under a system of internal colonialism within British cities (Pryce, 1979). And these 'internal colonies' have provided the material base for a cultural revival (Hall, Critcher, Jefferson, Clarke, and Roberts, 1978): 'First, of a "West Indian consciousness", no longer simply kept alive in the head or in memory, but visible on the street; second (in the wake of the black American rebellions), of a powerful and regenerated black consciousess.'

In a study where group comparisons are used, an operational definition of group boundaries is important. If a group boundary is defined by characteristics denoting race (however defined) or religion, the groups should be termed racial groups or religious groups. If ethnicity is used, the study is a cross-ethnic study. In a cross-cultural study, the individuals within each group must be culturally similar quite apart from their propensity to form an ethnic or racial group. In writing about units of society which are larger than discrete families, Kardiner (1939) states:

> Wherever we find these organised collections of human beings, we find some habitual regularity and organisation of inter-relations among various individuals; we find also organised ways of dealing with the outside world in order to derive from it satisfactions essential to life; furthermore we find organised ways of dealing with processes of birth, growth, development, maturity, decline and death, with due regard for differences in age and sex. Wherever there is a persistence or transmission of these organised methods, we have a culture.

Thus a cultural unit can be big or small, so long as it is larger than a discrete family unit.

Apart from the problem of definition of culture and the boundary of a cultural unit, there are various other difficulties in the field of cross-cultural research. Differences in services that are available and help-seeking practices of individuals often determine what is measured. Indeed the two may be interrelated and culturally determined. For example, Field (1958) found that most of the devotees attending a particular religious shrine in Ghana were suffering from psychotic depression in terms of Western nosology. And that study was done at a time when psychiatrists were reporting the apparent lack of depression among Africans. A community study in South India (Carstairs and Kapur, 1976) found that, although the consultation rates for people suffering from epileptic and psychotic symptoms were 100 per cent, all the former but less than 50 per cent of the latter sought help from Western-type doctors. Since most international studies, including those being done under the aegis of the WHO (World Health Organisation, 1973, 1979), use Western-type service provisions for collecting cases, their findings should be viewed with caution.

The problems of diagnosis are not just about the nosology used but are concerned with questions of recognition and delineation of symptoms across national and linguistic boundaries. As the US – UK diagnostic study (Cooper *et al*.,1972) has shown, there are considerable differences in diagnostic criteria and threshold for symptom-recognition between these two countries although the majority of people in both countries use the same basic language and adhere to a similar broad conceptual framework and culture. Diagnostic discrepancy is likely to be far greater between groups where cultural and semantic differences are wide.

The question of normality further compounds the problems of diagnosis. If the research method incorporates views of illness and symptomatology that are inconsistent with one or other of the cultural groups being studied, there is the problem of the cultural relativity of normality; what is normal in one culture may be abnormal from a different standpoint. For example, it has been shown in Sri Lanka that a combination of social withdrawal, lack of energy and feelings of sadness (commonly called 'depression' in Western societies) receives relatively little attention as an illness (Waxler, 1977). Refining the research method by improving reliability does not get over the basic problem of what Kleinman (1977) calls 'category fallacy', which he describes as follows with respect to studies on depression:

The depressive syndrome represents a small fraction of the entire field of depressive phenomena. It is a cultural category constructed by psychiatrists in the West to yield a homogeneous group of patients. By definition, it excludes most depressive phenomena even in the West because they fall outside its narrow boundaries. Applying such a category to analyse cross-cultural studies, or even in direct field research, is *not* a cross-cultural study of depression, because by definition it will *find* what is 'universal' and systematically *miss* what does not fit its tight parameters. The former is what is seen and therefore 'seen' by a Western cultural model; the latter, which is not so defined and therefore not 'seen', raises far more interesting questions for cross-cultural research.

Kleinman suggests that an ideal cross-cultural study should begin with phenomenological descriptions that are indigenous to each cultural group. He believes that researchers may then 'elicit and compare symptom terms and illness labels independent of a unified framework.'

The main problems of cross-cultural research can be illustrated by considering a well-known study conducted by the WHO — *The International Pilot Study of Schizophrenia* (World Health Organisation, 1973; 1979) — commonly called the IPSS. The diagnostic method used in this study was (Wing, 1978) 'a special technique of interviewing patients, known as the Present State Examination (PSE), which is simply a standardised form of the psychiatric diagnostic interview ordinarily used in Western Europe, based on a detailed glossary of differential definitions of symptoms.' It has been likened to a telescope (Wing, 1985) — 'within its specifications it can be used by trained people to look for a limited range of phenomena.' The IPSS assumed that the categorisation system developed within Europe (in a Western cultural setting) was applicable universally, and set out to establish a reliable method of diagnosing schizophrenia (in Western terms). Nine centres, namely Aarhus (Denmark), Agra (India), Cali (Colombia), Ibadan (Nigeria), London (United Kingdom), Moscow (USSR), Prague (Czechoslavakia), Taipeh (Taiwan) and Washington (USA), were used. The diagnosis was standardised in a medical framework so that a group of people deemed to suffer the 'disease' schizophrenia was identified at each centre.

The IPSS established reliability of the diagnosis of schizophrenia (World Health Organisation, 1979), but did not even attempt to establish cross-cultural validity of 'schizophrenia' — as measured by the PSE — as an illness, or even as a phenomenon, although it proceeded as if it did. In keeping with a bio-medical model of illness, the next step in the IPSS was to follow-up the patients who had been identified as 'schizophrenic' in order to determine their prognoses. On the whole, the outcome of patients from (industrially) underdeveloped countries was superior to that in the West although, of course, the patients in Western countries had more thorough psychiatric treatment, after-care, etc. than their counterparts in underdeveloped areas of the world.

The methodology of the IPSS, as a cross-cultural study, has been seriously criticised, notably by Kleinman (1977):

> Although that study is an important advance in our understanding of schizophrenia, it starts from a category fallacy which significantly limits its value as a study of cultural influences on mental illness. Its strength comes from reifying a narrowly defined syndrome affecting patients in nine separate cultural locations, but that is also its weakness. It is unable to systematically examine the impact of cultural factors on schizophrenia, since its methodology has ruled out the chief cultural determinants.

However, the basic tool of the IPSS — the PSE (Wing *et al.*, 1974) — has been used in several cultures (Orley and Wing, 1979; Okasha and Ashour, 1981; Swartz, Ben Arie and Teggin, 1985), regardless of its lack of cross-cultural validity.

In reviewing the literature on the topic of recovery from schizophrenia in the Third World, Warner (1983) has noted that the findings of the IPSS were supported by studies in Mauritius (Murphy and Raman, 1971), Sri Lanka (Waxler, 1979), and Hong Kong (Lo and Lo, 1977) but not by observations in Chandigarh, India (Kulhara and Wig, 1978) and among Blacks in South Africa (De Wet, 1957). The Chandigarh study was open to serious technical faults (i.e. only 100 of the 174 cases were actually followed up) and must be disregarded. Since the medical and psychiatric care for Blacks in South Africa is 'grossly inferior to that for Whites' (Stone *et al* ., 1978), it is not possible to give much credence to the study from that country. Therefore, the general thrust of the results of the IPSS (in which schizophrenia is considered as a medical illness) is that, if schizophrenia is indeed an illness recognisable by the methods developed in the West, treatment envisaged as being appropriate and even necessary does not lead to a better outcome. An alternative view, however, is that the initial samples of patients are different in different places — that calling someone a schizophrenic because he or she is perceived as thinking, behaving and feeling in certain ways does not mean the same thing everywhere and may not invariably denote a biological disease. There are of course other explanations for the findings. However, the IPSS, which deliberately imposed a disease-concept derived in the West, has actually raised questions about the very concept (of schizophrenia) or at least cast doubt on the validity of using it cross-culturally and, more importantly, the validity of treating people diagnosed as schizophrenic, in a culture-blind way. The lessons of the IPSS are clear enough but not really being taken into main-stream psychiatry.

The research involving the diagnostic category of depression has been described recently by the author (Fernando, 1986). Although Singer (1975) reckons that a 'core illness' (of depression) is universally recognised, the clinical picture varies so much cross-culturally that Marsella (1978) suggests that depression is a disorder of the Western world and is not universal. He argues that, if depression is essentially an experience, then a psychologically experienced 'depression' is different to one associated with somatic experience. It is conceivable that the recognition of a somato-psychic disturbance which includes 'depression' of Western psychiatry as well as other abnormal states may gradually evolve if the lessons of transcultural psychiatry influence the development of main-stream psychiatry.

STUDIES

The discussion so far indicates that methodological problems in cross-cultural research have not been overcome sufficiently to justify any modification of the view expressed by Kessel (1965) that international studies should be abandoned for the present. Carstairs (1965) has pointed out that there are great advantages in limiting cross-cultural study in such a way as to keep the groups compared within one national, linguistic, political and geographical framework. However, cross-cultural studies across subcultural groups may be complicated if the groups being studied are racially different and/or the researchers or their methods of study are racially biased. Thus any cross-cultural study must take into account the racial dimension, both in its methodology and in the analysis of findings. The racial and cultural status of the researcher(s) must be assumed to affect the quality of any observations or measurements dependent on interviews; racist or cultural bias in the techniques used in the study must be carefully evaluated; assumptions made about methodology and the value judgements of 'culture' based on racist considerations must be allowed for in assessing results and, in particular, the conclusions; the findings of research must be viewed in the context of differential pressures arising from racism as well as any cultural differences that are identified. Very few cross-cultural studies allow for racial bias, and earlier chapters have referred to some studies which are overtly racist. This latter type of study will not be discussed in this section. Cross-cultural studies which provide a background to, and cast some light on, the ways in which culture and race affect psychiatry in Britain fall into four groups:

(1) The study of subcultural groups within predominantly European culture.

(2) Studies in non-Western cultures (outside Europe) based on community surveys (rather than hospital settings) where some attempt is made to recognise the cultural context of the society and the effect of culture on the pattern of illness within the society.

(3) Observations on specific features of culture which have a bearing on psychiatry such as guilt and the so-called 'culture-bound syndromes'.

(4) Considerations of the meaning of 'treatment'.

Subcultural studies

This review is by no means comprehensive. Three studies are described and a general discussion of research in Britain at the present time is presented. Two studies have been picked out as examples of research within a European cultural context based on people perceived by society as 'white'; the third is one within the black community in the United States. All three studies used random samples where necessary and were carefully carried out.

A study carried out by the author (Fernando, 1975, 1978) examined relationships between certain cultural factors and some aspects of depressive illness using samples of British-born people living in a defined geographical area in the East End of London. In making the assumption (based on sociological observations) that Anglo-Jews as a group are culturally distinct from non-Jewish groups in British society, a Jewish group was demarcated on the basis of their self-identity (as Jews) while the rest of each sample was divided into Protestants and Roman Catholics on the basis of nominal (but acknowledged) religious affiliation. This was not an epidemiological study but one that sought to examine cross-cultural aspects of psychopathology as well as family and social dynamics of depressive illness. The findings have been summarised elsewhere (Fernando, 1978):

> First, Jewish and Protestant depressives were similar in many ways including illness rating, the incidence of family history of psychiatric illness, and outcome of illness. Secondly, depression in Jews (but not in Protestants) was associated with weak fathers in childhood, a loosening of ethnic links, and waning of religious conformity. Thirdly, Jewish depressives were different from Protestant depressives on certain aspects of hostility, although normal Jews and normal Protestants did not differ in this way. Fourthly, Jewish depressives showed a different distribution on a subgrouping of depression from that shown by Protestant depressives.

Another finding of the same study reported in the original thesis (Fernando, 1973) was that a sense of failure in socio-economic achievement was associated with depression among Jews but not among Protestants.

In interpreting the findings of the East End Jewish study, the author found support for a relationship between marginality and depression among Jews, repressed anger showing itself as extrapunitive hostility among Jewish depressives, and relatively high aspiration levels among Jews which were culturally determined and likely to cause depression if unfulfilled. Also, he noted the need for caution in applying a classificatory system cross-culturally. Thus, although British Jews and Protestants have a similar cultural and religious heritage, they were different when depressed. It is likely that bigger differences would be found between groups which are widely dissimilar culturally — if such studies could be carried out without the methodological problems noted earlier in this chapter.

Since the researcher in the East End study was racially and culturally 'neutral' — in the sense of not being Jewish, Protestant or Roman Catholic, and also being non-white — distortion of the observations by a 'halo' effect was discounted. Although all the groups studied were white, a 'racial' factor was present in that Jews had until recently been subjected to a type of racism, namely anti-semitism. The findings of this cross-cultural study in the East End of London was re-examined by the author some years later (Fernando, 1986), taking a different viewpoint from that taken originally.

71

By analysing the findings in the socio-political context of the East End of London during the 1930s, he concluded that:

Jews may have achieved as much as others but they had to struggle a great deal to do so, adopting various manoeuvres to bypass discrimination, for example changing names and such like. 'Straightforward' achievement in open competition was frequently blocked. The consequent sense of failure (as a psychological concomitant) is then understandable as a reflection of anti-semitism. The particular vulnerability to depression of marginal Jews may have reflected their relative lack of protection from blows to self-esteem arising from anti-semitism. The difference in diagnostic subgrouping may reflect the attitudes within an ethnocentric psychiatry toward Jewish individuals and their ways of expressing emotion. The point here is that purely cultural interpretations may miss important issues that determine depression in ethnic minorities. Culture interacts with social pressures in the final analysis of an illness such as depression

This later approach to the findings of the East End study was perhaps more suited to social reality when compared to the earlier approach which ignored anti-semitism. Although the findings of the East End study were not very dramatic in themselves, the study itself points the way for cross-cultural research in the British context.

The second study noted in this section was carried out in Canada and examined subcultural differences in mental hospital admission rates for Canadians of European origin (Murphy, 1974) — differences which were unlikely to be due to variations in hospital policies and services. Canadians of Italian origin had an exceptionally low rate, especially among married males, while those of Irish origin had very high rates until the age of 65 but low thereafter. People of British origin had a moderately low overall rate, but a significant excess of hospitalised patients with senile and arteriosclerotic psychoses, while the French had a high overall rate and a high chronicity except in the white collar stratum and in the over 65s. The author discussed these findings in terms of culturally determined differences in values and attitudes but pointed out that epidemiological studies must be linked to clinical and anthropological ones if they were to be fully analysed. The ethnicity of the researchers and details of the interview techniques used in the study were not reported. Clearly, since all the subcultural groups were composed of white subjects the racial dimension was not relevant in this study. However, the complexity of the findings show up the difficulties encountered in analysing studies of this nature.

The third study considered here is a community survey in Alabama which assessed the prevalence of depressive symptoms in a sample of black people (Dressler and Badger, 1982). By using a symptom check-list used in two other studies, the authors were able to compare the Alabama group with (black) groups in Kansas City and Alameda County. This is really a study within a racially defined population, i.e. black Americans, but still could be seen as one across subcultures. The relationships of socio-economic risk factors to depressive symptoms showed several inter-group differences:

In Alabama rates are significantly higher among females, whereas in Kansas City and Alameda County there is no statistically significant sex difference, and rates are slightly higher for males. In all three studies the prevalence of depression is higher among younger age groups. With respect to marital status, the separated and divorced show elevated rates in all studies, but in Kansas City, single persons have the higher rates. In Alameda County the widowed have elevated rates, while in Alabama the widowed have lower rates of depressive symptoms. In Alabama and Alameda County the persons with the lowest education have the highest rates of depressive symptoms. In Kansas City persons with some high school have the highest rates along with persons with some college. With the exception of Alabama, all persons not working have higher rates; in Alabama it is only those persons who are specifically unemployed who have higher rates. Finally, the effect of low income on rates of depression is attenuated in Alabama, whereas it is marked and significant in both Kansas City and Alameda County.

The intra-cultural diversity within the black population is a striking feature of this analysis. The authors of the paper interpreted it in terms of 'esteem enhancing occupational roles' being less available for black women in the Southern States and the greater availability of extended family support in rural communities in the South, but they accepted that differences in the reporting of distress, differential migration to the North because of the availability of mental health services, and other factors may be relevant. The authors did not, however, examine the differential effects of racism on the black groups and did not define their own racial or cultural position.

The studies quoted above illustrate three points. Subcultural differences within Western culture must be taken into account whenever assumptions are made about large cultural groups such as 'Western' or 'Afro-Caribbean'. The analysis of subcultural differences — even when racial considerations are allowed for — could be extremely complex. Questions of racism, for example in the form of anti-semitism or variations in its type or extent, should be taken into account if socially disadvantaged cultural groups are being studied.

Table 3.1: British research of practical importance

1. *Over-diagnosis of schizophrenia in:*
     West Indian and Asian immigrant in-patients (Cochrane, 1977; Carpenter and Brockington, 1980; Dean, Walsh, Downing and Shelley, 1981)
     Patients of West Indian ethnicity admitted compulsorily in Bristol (Harrison, Ineichen, Smith and Morgan, 1984) and in Birmingham (McGovern and Cope, 1987)

2. *Excess of compulsory admission of:*
     Patients of West Indian ethnicity in Bristol (Ineichen, Harrison and Morgan, 1984) Patients of Asian and of West Indian ethnicity in Birmingham (McGovern and Cope, 1987)

3. *Excessive transfer to locked wards of:*
     West Indian, Indian and African patients (Bolton, 1984)

4. *Excessive admission of 'offender patients' of:*
     People of West Indian ethnicity in Birmingham (McGovern and Cope, 1987)

5. *Over-use of Section 136 of Mental Health Act for:*
     People of West Indian ethnicity (Rogers, 1987)

6. *Over use of ECT for:*
     Asian in-patients in Leicester (Shaikh, 1985)
     Black immigrant patients in East London (Littlewood and Cross, 1980)

British research

Ethnic studies in a British context are a recent phenomenon; some research findings which have important consequences for the practice of psychiatry are summarised in Table 3.1. Epidemiological studies have generally been limited to the analysis of admission rates to hospitals in England and Wales. A survey by Cochrane (1977) revealed that people born in Ireland, Scotland and Poland had very high rates, West Indians and Americans had rates comparable to that of natives, and people from India, Pakistan, Germany and Italy had rates much lower than those of the native born. A later study (Cochrane, 1980), focusing on the Scots, found that there were two groups of Scots who move to England: 'On the one hand there are stable, economically motivated migrants who move south for definite employment related reasons and who show few psychological symptoms. While on the other hand there is a group of migrants who perhaps have psychological problems and who move more in hope than expectation without definite prospects and who account for the high rates of mental hospital admission found in Scottish migrants.' Overall hospital admission rates — especially those that include re-admissions — without taking into account the availability of services and admission policies are of limited value in assessing need for psychiatric treatment or extent of illness within a community. This is particularly so in a transcultural context where the use of services by different cultural groups may be very different, and, the way the services are structured and staffed may tend to exclude some groups and favour others. In a survey using a random sample of migrants from India to the UK, Cochrane and Stopes-Roe (1981) found that they showed less evidence of emotional disturbance when compared to a matched English sample when measured on a scale which had been earlier validated for both English and Indian immigrant groups (Cochrane, Hashmi and Stopes-Roe, 1977). However, a study of general practice in Oxford (Brewin, 1980) showed that an Asian sample had almost identical consultation rates to an English sample for all types of complaint.

A conspicuous finding noted by Cochrane (1977), in his study of hospital admissions in England and Wales in 1971, was the over-representation of patients diagnosed (by hospital doctors) as schizophrenic among most immigrant groups, i.e. people born outside England and Wales, most marked for West Indians and Pakistanis. A study in Manchester (Carpenter and Brockington, 1980) also found that the diagnosis of schizophrenia was given to immigrants much more frequently than it was given to natives — and this was particularly so in the case of West Indians, Africans and Asians. An earlier report (Bagley, 1971), using hospital diagnoses kept on the Camberwell Psychiatric Register, had showed a similar preponderance of schizophrenic diagnoses given to Afro-Caribbean, African, Indian and Pakistani patients; Hemsi (1967) studying patients from the same locality had made a similar observation. A study in South-East England (Dean *et al.*, 1981) found that first admissions given a diagnosis of schizophrenia were five times the expected number for immigrants from the West Indies, four times the expected number for immigrants from Africa (mainly ethnic Asians) and three times the expected number for immigrants from India. Littlewood and Lipsedge (1981a) examined the case notes of 250 consecutive patients admitted to a district general hospital in Hackney, a London borough with a relatively large proportion of ethnic minorities. Migrants were identified as those born outside the UK except that people under the age of 25 were classified as migrants if their parents were born abroad. The researchers found that a diagnosis of schizophrenia was significantly more commonly given to West Indians and West Africans when compared to UK-born patients or other migrant groups; patients from the Indian subcontinent too were more likely to be diagnosed as schizophrenic, but not to the same extent as West Indians and West Africans. A study in Leicestershire (Shaikh, 1985) comparing a group of Asian patients — identified by picking out Asian names from lists of admissions — with a control group of white 'indigenous' patients matched for age and sex, found that schizophrenia was significantly over-diagnosed in the former. A recent report of a survey in Birmingham of patients (legally) detained in hospital (McGovern and Cope, 1987) found that approximately two-thirds of West Indian migrants and British West Indians were diagnosed as schizophrenic, compared with one-third of the Whites and Asians. Also, this study found that 8–16 per cent of the West Indians had been diagnosed as suffering from psychosis induced by cannabis — a diagnosis not given to either Whites or Asians.

Although some researchers, for example, Littlewood and Lipsedge (1982), reckoned that the diagnosis of schizophrenia was likely to be less common among Afro-Caribbeans born in Britain when compared to that among West Indian immigrants, a recent study of first admissions to a hospital in Birmingham (McGovern and Cope, 1987b) did not support this.

After studying patients with 'religious delusions', Littlewood and Lipsedge (1981b) suggested that patients suffering from 'acute psychotic reactions' may be misdiagnosed as schizophrenic and their study indicated that this was more likely in the case of people born in the Caribbean than in the case of those born in the UK or Europe. This study, however, was based largely on unstructured interviews carried out by one author where, as the authors themselves put it, 'good rapport was considered essential to distinguish gently the field of psychopathology, religious experience and cultural values.' The question of how this was established when neither author was black and, according to the authors, West Indian-born patients were more likely than the UK-born to have been compulsorily detained in hospital, is difficult to envisage. However, in discussing the question of diagnostic labelling in Britain, Littlewood and Lipsedge (1982) draw on an observation made in that study to comment that 'twice as many black patients had had their diagnosis *changed* in the course of their psychiatric career, suggesting either that British doctors found it difficult to diagnose them or that the patients did not easily fit into the "classical" categories.'

An extensive study of a sample of admissions to psychiatric hospitals in Bristol reported in two papers (Ineichen *et al.*, 1984; Harrison *et al.*, 1984) identified subjects in terms of four ethnic categories namely, white United Kingdom, West Indian, other (non-white) and other (white). The first paper reported that non-white groups accounted for 32 out of 89 compulsory admissions but only 30 out of 175 voluntary admissions. The authors estimated that, while black people provide an expected proportion of voluntary admissions, they were over-represented among those admitted compulsorily (Ineichen *et al.*, 1984). The reasons for this were not analysed in detail but some findings in the second paper, (quoted below), suggested that public attitudes and police behaviour may play a part; this is in keeping with a recent study by MIND (Rogers, 1987), (also quoted below), which suggested that public attitudes in combination with police power results in an excessive use of police powers to apprehend black people under the Mental Health Act (1983).

The over-representation of both immigrant and British West Indians among male patients compulsorily detained in a hospital in Birmingham was reported at a meeting of the Transcultural Psychiatry Society (McGovern and Cope, 1985) and later published (McGovern and Cope, 1987a). This study compared the compulsory detention rates of white, West Indian and Asian males admitted from a defined catchment area in the Midlands. Both Asians and West Indians were over-represented amongst compulsory detentions. In the age group 16 – 29, the risk of being detained under a section of the Mental Health Act that was applicable to patients who were not 'offender-patients' was 17 times that for Whites in the case of West Indian immigrants — a highly significant difference; in the 30 – 44 age group, the rate for West Indian migrants was seven times and for Asians nearly three times that for Whites. The rates for British West Indians were not significantly different to those for West Indian migrants and there were no British Asians in the study. Although there have been no published accounts of ethnic differences among compulsory admissions in the London area, a one-day census of such admissions to the Maudsley Hospital (carried out as a preliminary to a prospective study), found that 55 per cent were (black) Afro-Caribbeans and 22 per cent (white) Caucasians (Thornicroft and Moodley, 1986).

Harrison et al., (1984) found that West Indians, compared to inner city whites, were more likely to have (allegedly) attracted attention by causing a 'public disturbance'. The authors observed that, 'although West Indian patients differ from their white inner city neighbours in having a greater degree of family contact, when admitted compulsorily, they share a greater incidence of police involvement and assessments at police stations'. In spite of this, the West Indian patients, as a whole, were less violent than the suburban white patients, less often perceived as threatening before admission, and no more likely to be involved in violence on the ward after admission. A common observation of hospital staff is that black patients, compared to white, are more likely to be kept in secure conditions in hospital. Indeed a study carried out in a hospital in South London (Bolton, 1984) found that, of patients recognised as uncooperative but not aggressive, West Indians, Indians and Africans were more likely to be sent to locked wards when compared to (white) English patients — and this was not related to a diagnosis of schizophrenia. This leads on to the question of psychiatric admission for security reasons. Although there is a strong impression that black people are generally over-represented in secure hospitals in Britain, there are no definite statistics on this apart from the observation in a study by Norris (1984), that 12 per cent of male patients who left Broadmoor Hospital — a secure hospital in southern England — between 1974 and 1981 were 'non-white' (defined as black or brown). However, the Birmingham study found that the chances of a West Indian from a catchment area in the Midlands, becoming a (compulsorily detained) 'offender-patient' in a psychiatric institute by being sent there on a court order was 25 times that of a white person in the 16 – 29 age group; the difference in chances was somewhat less in other age groups but still excessive for West Indians compared to Whites.

Section 136 of The Mental Health Act (1983) allows a police constable to remove (under certain conditions) 'a person who appears to him to be suffering from mental disorder and to be in immediate need of care or control', to 'a place of safety' which is usually a hospital. Although there has been a strong impression among both professionals working in the psychiatric services in inner cities and black people living there that this 'section' of the act has been used disproportionately for apprehending West Indian men, there has been no firm evidence published on this question. However, a study based in London and carried out by MIND (The National Association of Mental Health) has recently confirmed this; the number of Afro-Caribbean people placed on Section 136 was about three times that expected (Rogers, 1987). However, the study showed that the reasons for police taking this sort of action were complex; for example, police often acted at the behest of the general public or of relatives, who, presumably, felt unable to get help any other way. Thus, the excessive use of Section 136 for black people may reflect racist hostility of the general public — as well as, perhaps, the police — and/or the difficulties encountered by black people in getting proper psychiatric or social help through 'informal' channels. A disquieting observation in the MIND study was that psychiatrists and police agreed (on the presence of mental disorder and the need for 'care or control') in 100 per cent of the cases in which black men were taken to hospital under Section 136, indicating the extent to which psychiatric staff collude with the public and the police.

In studying the careers of men who were discharged from a special hospital, namely Broadmoor Hospital, between 1974 and 1981 Norris (1984) considered some aspects of ethnicity. In analysing the ex-Broadmoor patients as non-White and White, several significant differences emerged between the two groups. First, 92 per cent of the non-white group compared to 64 per cent of the white were diagnosed as schizophrenic. Although the mean lengths of stay were not significantly different between them, the non-white group had, on the whole, committed less serious offences before admission. Once discharged from Broadmoor, the non-white group, compared to the white, had been contacted by police more frequently but less often charged with serious offences. This suggested that non-whites were harassed by the police, leading the researcher to conclude that: 'For non-white patients the usual perception which divides the "sick" from the "criminal" seemed to be in abeyance so far as the police were concerned.' After examining the interview data on the ex-patients studied, Norris commented: 'Doctors often referred to young non-white (mainly schizophrenic) and to psychopathic patients as not in need of care; and as arrogant, demanding, and generally failing to play the deferential patient role.'

Cochrane (1977) presented figures for estimated suicides in England and Wales by country of birth for the years 1970-2. All immigrants except West Indians had elevated rates, while the Poles had very high rates. He commented as follows:

The very high rate of the Poles can, in part, be explained by the relatively aged nature of the Polish population and the fact that suicide rates are higher in older age groups. Possibly the low rate of West Indians is explicable in terms of their younger average age but structural explanations cannot account for the high rates among other immigrant groups.

Burke (1976a,b) found that the rates of attempted suicide among West Indian and Asian immigrants living in Birmingham were lower than that for British-born people but greater than that found in their countries of origin; Irish-born people, from both Eire and Northern Ireland, were grossly over-represented, with rates that were higher than those in Dublin or Belfast. The reasons behind these differences are not clear. It should be noted that the studies by Cochrane and Burke were based on immigrants, i.e. people born abroad; British-born people of ethnic minorities brought up in this country may well present differently and have very different problems.

The observations noted above on mental health or stress-related problems of migrants should be evaluated in the light of the complex relationship between culture, migration and mental disorder reviewed expertly by Murphy (1977). He designated three groups of variables to be considered: Those related to culture of origin, circumstances of migration and society of re-settlement. The first group is concerned with genetic loading for health or ill-health, attitude to the migration itself, information available to migrants about the country of adoption and cultural influences that may determine personality type. The circumstances concerned with the migration are to do with the forced or voluntary nature of the migration, the difficulties encountered during the process of migration and the perceived permanency of the change of residence. Finally, the last group includes considerations such as the attitude of the host country in welcoming or resisting the migrant, the support available during the settling-in period and the degree of acceptance of the migrant by the host community.

'Maladjustment' among children is usually measured in Britain by a behaviour questionnaire completed by teachers. Using this method for comparing samples of West Indian and English 10-year-old children in London, Rutter, Yule, Berger, Yule, Morton, and Bagley (1974) found that 40 per cent of the former compared to less than 20 per cent of the latter were 'maladjusted' in 1970. The difference between the two groups was accounted for by a difference in 'conduct' deviance (i.e behaviour identified as 'deviant') but not emotional problems (such as worrying, anxiety, etc.). Furthermore, emotional disturbance judged on the basis of interviews with parents showed no difference between West Indian and English children. Six years later in Birmingham (Cochrane, 1979), the 'maladjustment' rates for 9-year-old children, based on teacher assessments, were 25 per cent for both West Indian and English children. The relatively low maladjustment rate — using teacher assessments — for a sample of Asian children compared to one of English children studied in 1973–4 (Kallarackal and Herbert, 1976) was confirmed in another study in 1976 (Cochrane, 1979). Since the measure of 'maladjustment' used in these studies may represent teachers' bias as much as children's behaviour, the observations may be interpreted as conclusions about teachers or about children, or about the interaction between them; racial stereotypes, if not racist myths and images are likely to be involved.

Apart from epidemiological studies, cross-cultural psychiatric research is almost non-existent in Britain although cultural factors are often acknowledged to be important in clinical work. The causes of emotional stress among individuals from ethnic minority groups are often conceptualised as culture-shock, culturally determined goal striving pressures, identity crises and social isolation promoted by cultural factors. Although these concepts may be helpful in understanding individual problems, their use as generalisations tends to obscure the real difficulties that minority groups face in British society. There is a need to shift the emphasis in order to consider the context in which individual problems occur.

Difficulties of communication, racial prejudice, ethnocentricity of health and social services are but a few of the elements within this context. A few British studies throw some light on some of these problems.

A study carried out at a hospital in East London by Littlewood and Cross (1980) examined the case records of (a) 240 patients seen in the out-patient department or on domiciliary visits in a three week period, and (b) 81 patients who had been given electroconvulsive therapy (ECT) during an eighteen month period. The patients were identified as black-immigrant, white-immigrant or British-born. When black patients were compared to white patients, the former were more likely to have been diagnosed as psychotic, to have seen a nurse or junior doctor rather than a senior doctor and to have received major tranquillisers (after allowing for diagnostic differences). These differences were not related to differences in social class, age or sex. Migrant patients were more likely than British patients to receive ECT without a diagnosis of depression and black patients were more likely than white patients to have at least six consecutive ECT treatments. The authors suggested that their findings reflected 'stereotyped attitudes to unrecognised clinical differences' but that 'there appear to be assumptions that (a) ECT is suitable for non-depressive reactions in black patients, (b) black patients require more ECT and (c) intramuscular medication is more efficacious in black patients.' The Leicestershire study (Shaikh, 1985) also reported that 'there was an excess of electroconvulsive therapy use among Asians who received the diagnosis of schizophrenia as compared to indigenous patients with this diagnosis.'

In an important paper, Burke (1984) has analysed the findings of a large community study of West Indian and British people in Birmingham and his experiences in helping the (West Indian) victims of a fire in New Cross, London — an event that aroused little sympathy or concern outside the black community. Burke, a black psychiatrist, noted in his paper how the response rate of black people in the Birmingham study rose to 100 per cent when it became known that the research team was black, although it had been low before that. He found 'equal rates of depression by ethnicity in the suburban zone of the study area but higher black rates in the more densely populated inner city zone.' He concluded that 'although much effort has been spent on identifying stress little attempt has been made to estimate the nature and extent of socially protective factors and how social mobility and social selection may aid this process.' He noted that, when disaster strikes a black community, 'the statutory helping professions and white groups in general will be inactivated if a racial factor is present.' The importance of the interplay between culture, on the one hand, and social pressure arising from racism, on the other, is fairly clear.

Studies in non-Western cultures

Two major community studies will be briefly described — the 'Yoruba study' (Leighton, Lambo, Hughes, Leighton, Murphy and Macklin, 1963a) in Western Nigeria and the 'Kota study' (Carstairs and Kapur, 1976) in South India — and some general observations will then be made.

The Yoruba study was based on a selected number of rural villages and one urban centre in Western Nigeria. Although the essentials of the technique used in the study were the same as those used in the Stirling County Study (Leighton, 1959; Leighton, Harding, Macklin, MacMillan and Leighton, 1963b) in North America, great care was taken to adapt the methods of working to the West African setting. In comparing the Yoruba group with a rural group in North America, the former had 'more symptoms but fewer cases of clearly evident psychiatric disorder.' Also, the male/female ratio for psychiatric disorder, especially psychoneurotic symptoms, was different, being less in the North American sample. However, the researchers were impressed by the similarity of the two samples with regard to symptom patterns (anxiety, depression, etc.) and the prevalence in most of the categories tabulated. As in Stirling County it was found that disintegration, rather than cultural change as such, was associated with the prevalence of psychiatric disorder in Yoruba villages.

The Kota study focused on the population of three South Indian communities defined, on the basis of caste, into Brahmins, Mogers and Bants. Methods of measuring emotional disturbance, social functioning and psychiatric need were devised for the study. The researchers uncovered a high prevalence of psychiatric symptoms in all these rural communities and summarised their findings thus:

1. Women have higher prevalence of somatic symptoms than men. They also have a higher proportion of those with numerous symptoms. 2. Bants have more somatic symptoms than Brahmins or Mogers. Moger women have the highest possession rate. Brahmin males have the highest proportions of those with

psychotic symptoms. 3. Psychoses, epilepsy and mental retardation are commonest in those below twenty. Possession occurs most often in those between twenty and forty years of age. 4. Somatic symptoms appear to be more commonly reported by literates. The nature of somatic symptoms reflects prevailing cultural beliefs.

The Kota study showed the complexity of inter-relationships between symptomatology on the one hand, and gender, age and caste on the other, even within a generally uniform cultural framework. It drew attention to the subcultural differences that exist within non-Western cultures, as in the case of Western cultures. It demonstrated the possibility that subcultural differences may outweigh cultural differences in some respects — that differences *within* cultures may be greater than differences *across* cultures.

Several surveys of psychiatric disorder in non-Western cultures suffer from the major drawback that categories of illness delineated in the West are used to identify emotional disturbance on the assumption that the form, if not the content, of psychiatric illness is universal. The apparently better prognosis of schizophrenia in the Third World, referred to earlier when the question of recognition and delineation of symptoms was discussed, may be related to social organisation and family life (Cooper and Sartorius, 1977), variations in belief systems and ways of labelling across cultures (Waxler, 1979) or a mixture of various influences. Community surveys in India (Dube, 1970; Sethi, Gupta, Mahendru and Kumari, 1974) and Sri Lanka (Wijesinghe, Dassanayake and Dassanayake, 1978) indicate that the prevalence of schizophrenia (as a psychiatric disorder in Western terms) in Asia resembles that in the West, i.e. between 2 and 4 per 1000 (Odegaard, 1970). 'Psychoneurosis' too seems to be common in India and Sri Lanka: a rate of 12.7 per 1000 was reported in the United Provinces (Dube, 1970), 27.1 per 1000 in the Lucknow District (Sethi *et al.*,1974) and 25.0 per 1000 in a rural community near Colombo (Wijesinghe, *et al.*, 1978). Symptom surveys in which initial categorisation was avoided have shown that emotional disturbance is commonly encountered in rural communities in South India (Carstairs and Kapur, 1976) and West Africa (Leighton *et al.*,1963a) with morbidity rates and social incapacitation similar to those in the West: 15–19 per cent of the population were found to be significantly impaired in the West African survey and about 8 per cent in the South Indian one.

Isolated behaviour and 'Culture-bound syndromes'

Cross-cultural studies of isolated cultural behaviour such as toilet training have not yielded any important findings of general applicability. However, the cross-cultural study of guilt (El-Islam, 1969; Kimura, 1965) supports the view of Yap (1965) that a sense of loss and/or failure underlies the overt guilt that is observed in Western culture. Murphy (1973) has quoted studies on alcoholism which show that disinhibited and aggressive behaviour released by alcohol intoxication in Western societies may be culturally determined. He suggests that possession states allow individuals to disclaim responsibility for their utterances and actions in many non-Western cultures in the same way as alcohol intoxication does in the West. Also, Murphy quotes evidence from cross-cultural studies that the relationship between homicide and suicide rates is positive rather than negative and that both variables increase with severity of physical punishment administered to children in the communities studied; he suggests that there may be a common, culturally determined, factor of orientation towards violence underlying all three variables.

The term 'culture-bound syndrome' denotes a pattern of behaviour specific to a particular culture and held (by Western psychiatrists) to be psychogenic. Alternative labels such as 'exotic, unclassifiable, culture-reactive or culture-related specific psychiatric syndromes have been used for these conditions, but the expression culture-bound syndrome (CBS) now seems firmly entrenched.' (Prince and Tcheng Larouche, 1987). Culture-bound syndromes are identified in non-Western cultures reflecting the (racist) ethos within psychiatry that sees the culture of white Europeans as the 'norm'; as Littlewood (1986a) points out, they have been regarded 'on phenomenological grounds not as "real" existing entities but as local erroneous conceptualisations which shaped certain universal reactions.' Littlewood and Lipsedge (1986) believe that 'classic culture-bound reactions follow a triphasic pattern; *dislocation* of the individual is followed by behaviour ("symptoms") which represent an *exaggeration* of this dislocation (frequently suggesting a direct contravention or "inversion" of normative behaviour), followed by *restitution* of the individual back into everyday relationships.' These writers make a valiant attempt to override the essentially racist connotations of the category (of culture-bound disorders) by attempting to identify such disorders within Western — 'industrialised' — cultures as 'Culture-bound Syndromes of the Dominant Culture'; it is preferable, however, to accept the term for what it is.

Socio-anthropological study of culture-bound syndromes tends to render them 'understandable' in psychiatric and psychological terminology, thereby negating the title of 'exotic' syndromes. Thus Koro (or Shook Yang), which is a condition where a male Chinese patient would act out his fear of losing his penis, is understandable in a cultural context where there is a belief in the reverse growth of male genitals and a concept of sexual activity being injurious to life under certain circumstances (Leng, 1971). In terms of Western psychiatry, Koro is a hypochondriacal preoccupation forming a focus for anxiety (Yap, 1965). Windigo Psychosis, described by Parker (1960) and others, is a condition in which an individual of the Ojibwa people of North Ontario broods over, and sometimes acts out, a craving for human flesh. When seen in a context where people believe in the Windigo Spirit — a cannibalistic god representing the souls of people who have died of starvation — this particular condition becomes understandable in Western terms as a depressive state. Various other culture-bound syndromes too have been analysed in this way, e.g. Susto (Logan, 1979) and Latah (Kenny, 1978). The validity of doing so is questionable. The underlying supposition is that an interpretation of the syndrome in terms of (Western) psychiatry is an advance on a purely culture-bound interpretation. One could argue for this on pragmatic grounds if the problem can be dealt with more effectively by redefining the syndrome in this way. But there is no evidence that (Western) psychiatry is effective in dealing with 'culture-bound syndromes' with a base in other cultures. An analogous situation is to argue for the interpretation of (say) anorexia nervosa, which is suspected of being a syndrome that does not appear in non-Western cultures (Prince, 1983), in terms that are alien to Western culture, i.e. non-psychiatric and non-psychological terms.

Possession states, which are rarely seen in Western cultures, are episodic disruptions of behaviour during which it is presumed that the subject's personality is replaced by that of a spirit. They may be seen within the culture as illnesses; the Charaka Samhita, a treatise on Indian Medicine (Ayurveda), is quoted by Haldipur (1984) as dividing mental disorder into two broad categories, humoral (endogenous) insanity and that caused by spirit possessions. However Claus (1979) notes that it is unwanted spirit possession that is seen as an illness while Spirit mediumship (the legitimate spirit possession of a specialist) is not perceived as illness within the culture in which it occurs. A survey in Sri Lanka (Wijesinghe, Dassanayake and Mendis, 1976) found 37 cases of unwanted spirit possession in a population of 7500 — a prevalence of about 5 per 1000.

Psychiatric treatment

The concept of treatment in psychiatry is difficult to define. In a narrow sense, it is limited to ways of intervention aimed at alleviating or eliminating emotional disturbances in individuals. In a wide sense, but still focusing on the individual, treatment includes: (a) ways of coping (by the 'patient', his/her family or community) with emotional distress, and (b) techniques of promoting the coping process of an individual suffering from emotional disturbance. The traditional (narrow) approach to treatment in a medical setting is to consider different forms of treatment subsumed under the headings of physical treatment, psychological treatment and social treatment. A wide definition of treatment must include forms of healing practised all over the world in all cultures, as well as diverse religious experiences and 'ways of liberation' (Watts, 1961), i.e. methods of self-realisation/self-improvement/enlightenment such as yoga. In this sense, healing is about treating the 'illness', which is experienced psycho-socially, as opposed to 'disease', conceptualised as the mal-functioning of biological and/or psychological processes (Kleinman, 1980a).

The commonest physical treatment is drug therapy. Cross-cultural differences in the response to drugs that are used with therapeutic aims have not been substantiated by objective study (Murphy, 1969). If such differences are confirmed, they may be related to biological differences — if these exist to any significant degree between the groups studied — or to culturally determined social attitudes. Social and psychological therapies overlap considerably and have an intimate relationship with culture. Social influences depend on culture for the transference of their effects while psychological changes must depend on the individual's constitution, which is formed by cultural and environmental factors impinging on heredity.

The key to (Western) psychotherapy (of any sort) is communication between therapist(s) and patient(s). Differences between them in cultural background and life experiences may be a barrier to meaningful communication. Even if they share a common

87

language, the type of communication which is appropriate for one culture, — e.g. self-disclosure in a hierarchical doctor-client relationship or interaction in a group setting, may not suit another. A psychotherapeutic method is based on dogma arising from cultural and historical roots, and, to be successful, must be in tune with the basic philosophy of life of the 'patient'. Thus, the extent to which it can be used for people in a setting which is different from the one in which the therapy was located during its development, is very limited. For example, psychoanalysis, which aims at 'the domination of irrational and unconscious passions by reason' (Fromm, 1960), has thrived in the United States — at least among the middle classes — while Morita therapy, a form of psychotherapy which is directed at promoting 'the spontaneous development of the patient's ability to understand his character traits as being acceptable' (Suzuki and Suzuki, 1977), has developed in Japan.

The successful combination of (Western) psychiatric techniques and indigenous healing methods has been reported from Nigeria (Lambo, 1965), Senegal (Collomb, 1967), and Guyana (Singer, Aarons and Aronetta, 1967). Ratnavale (1973) has described a psychiatric hospital in Shanghai which, at least during the time of Mao Tse Tung, used a mixture of herbal remedies, acupuncture, psychotropic drugs and forms of group and individual psychotherapy (referred to as 'heart-to-heart talks'). This sort of cooperation at a practical level may enable each 'camp' to maintain its own autonomy intact. On the other hand a Western psychiatric system may incorporate, or try to incorporate, members of a non-Western healing system as subsidiary workers; else, the healers of one system may adopt the treatment mode of the other system by learning their techniques. For example, Lubchansky, Egri and Stokes (1970) suggest that Puerto Rican healers should become members of a psychiatric team while Carstairs and Kapur (1976) describe Western psychotherapists who become healers within the Indian tradition.

Healing systems which have developed outside a (Western) psychiatric framework may be analysed by using the categories of treatment within psychiatry, i.e. physical, psychological and social components. In doing so, Leff (1975) notes that traditional healing in Africa and Asia often employs psychological and pharmacological methods in combination. However, in analysing non-Western healing systems from a standpoint of Western psychiatry, there is a danger of imposing a structure that is alien to the system and therefore missing its essential qualities and its total impact as a healing system. In other words, the mistake in separating out physical, psychological and social components of a total system is the one made in imposing categories of illness derived within one culture on to a very different cultural setting — a matter discussed earlier. It is therefore proposed to examine, or try to examine, treatment within the socio-cultural context in which it is practised while relating it to the system familiar to the West, the psychiatric approach.

Types of treatment

The perception of health and illness in current Western medicine, including psychiatry, is based on an explanation of reality which is largely determined by experimental science (Pattison, 1977). Modern psychiatry assumes a multifactorial causation for what it identifies as 'illness' — a physiological disturbance of a homoeostatic norm or deviation from an (assumed) norm in terms of functioning and/or behaviour; psychological, biological and socio-cultural factors are recognised as being involved in most, if not all, cases of emotional disturbance or deviance. Treatment is categorised in specific terms under broad headings of physical, psychological and social types of therapy. It is evident, therefore, that the construction of reality on which psychiatry is based is a fragmentary one, without a cohesive picture of human life (Pattison, 1977). Traditional Indian and Chinese medical systems, for example, view malfunctioning of an individual in an integrated somato-psychic framework. The sick individual is seen as disorganised as a whole; physical and mental states are not differentiated. Physical and psycho-social influences in treatment are seen as an integrated whole, and treatment (i.e. herbal remedies, meditation, acupuncture etc.) is perceived as affecting the individual's anatomy, physiology and thinking all at the same time. Thus, in general, explanatory models of illness and concepts of healing that derive from non-Western cultures are linked to constructions of reality that provide a comprehensive explanation of human life.

Various forms of treatment based on psychological theories and/or belief systems alien to the Western psychiatric mode are practised in Western countries. Current examples are meditation and acupuncture. As these 'fringe' therapies become established, they may become absorbed into orthodox psychiatry. The procedure, isolated from its cultural roots and the context in which it has grown, is dealt with as a 'technology', in the way that an indigenous non-Western healer may use antibiotics or tranquillisers in a herbal mixture. The effectiveness, in each case, is likely to be variable and haphazard. Methods for self-improvement which are culturally sanctioned in various societies are subsumed under the heading of 'liberation' techniques (Watts, 1961). These are essentially for 'normal' people but overlap with forms of psychotherapy accepted within psychiatry. Meditation practices appear in many different cultures (West, 1979) and may be considered as a type of 'liberation' technique. The effectiveness of liberation techniques practised in isolation from its cultural context is of doubtful value.

Faith healing exists in some form in all societies and is related to magical practices. Malfunctioning is considered as a consequence of sin, evil intent or violation of religious taboos (Pattison, Lapins and Doerr, 1973). Treatment is based on a strong belief in the healing powers of a person or system and perceived as affecting the whole individual. The type or form of faith healing varies from society to society; the laying on of hands in the context of strong religious conviction is a common structure for faith healing in Western societies. It is akin to magical practices which are used very widely in the treatment of emotional disturbance. These are based on supernatural explanations for certain observed phenomena. 'Treatment' consists of curative ceremonies composed of rituals involving exorcism and/or divinity. Spirit possession is nearly always invoked during these ceremonies but their form is diverse and culture-bound with a strong religious flavour. These practices include mediumship healing and all forms of exorcism (Claus, 1979) such as 'devil dancing' of Sri Lanka (Pertold, 1930). The term 'Shaman' is used to denote 'medicine men' — practitioners of indigenous non-Western medicine — all over the world (Ackerknecht, 1943). There is an obvious overlap between exorcism and certain forms of (Western) psychotherapy, for example abreaction. The beliefs within psychoanalytic theories are recognisable as covertly supernaturalistic (Pattison, 1977) and the process of psychoanalysis could be seen as a form of exorcism. However, since it is sanctioned by Western culture and wrapped up in scientific garb, it is acceptable within psychiatry.

LESSONS

Although fundamental problems concerning recognition and delineation of symptoms and categories of illness have not been resolved for meaningful cross-cultural comparisons to be made about 'mental illness' (however defined), it is evident that there are clear lessons for both clinical practice and research emanating from cross-cultural studies such as those mentioned earlier. These lessons were alluded to in the previous sections but are now described. First and foremost, there is the question of psychiatric nosology — ways of describing illness. Since this question has wide implications, it will be considered in some detail. Then, lessons for the practice of psychiatry among ethnic minorities within Western societies is discussed with special reference to British psychiatry. The conclusions of this section include a discussion of the resistance within psychiatry to the lessons of cross-cultural research and the future of transcultural psychiatry itself.

Psychiatric nosology

In order to evaluate the cross-cultural relevance of current psychiatric nosology, two classes of information are examined: (a) findings on symptomatology in studies outside the West, and (b) information about indigenous healers and systems of medicine in non-Western cultures. In examining the former, it is desirable to avoid studies in which Western categories of illness were used, for reasons described earlier. With respect to the latter, it should be noted that knowledge available in Western literature on the ways of non-Western indigenous healers and systems of medicine is very limited.

Two major studies of mental disorder in non-Western cultures focused on eliciting symptoms rather than diagnoses: a study in Western Nigeria was carried out by a mixed team of Canadian and Nigerian researchers — the 'Yoruba study' (Leighton et al.,1963a); observations in South India were published as a book called *The Great Universe of Kota* (Carstairs and Kapur, 1976). Both these studies were large surveys backed up by careful and extensive information about the communities in which they were based. Symptoms were elicited from respondents in the full knowledge that these may not conform to patterns seen in the West. Physical and laboratory examination was made of some members of the sample in the Yoruba study, so that allowance could be made for symptoms arising from physical illness. A specially constructed interview schedule led to a research instrument devised for the Kota study — the 'Indian Psychiatric Survey Schedule' (IPSS) — to cover the presence or absence of over one hundred psychiatric symptoms, with a special emphasis on those commonly encountered in an Indian setting.

The researchers in the Yoruba study examined symptoms in three ways. First, they evaluated symptom patterns that were recognised by the Yoruba people and not recognised in psychiatry. There were none of any significance, although their informants emphasised some particular patterns: '(1) Sleeplessness, overactivity, and excitement, (2) short episodes of disturbance followed by normal behaviour and by amnesia for the episode, (3) acute confusional states, and (4) acts of violence.' It was not clear whether these patterns occurred at a greater frequency among Yoruba patients as compared to those of Europe and America, or whether the Yoruba had a particular inclination to note them.

Secondly, the researchers considered whether the descriptions of illness among the Yoruba covered all the main categories of symptom patterns recognised in psychiatry. They found that none of the main symptoms found in senile dementia (chronic brain syndrome) were volunteered by their informants, and that many of the 'neurotic' symptoms, such as anxiety, dissociation, neurasthenia, and psychophysiological disturbance were less evident than expected. The (Western) syndromes of phobic, obsessive-compulsive and depressive states were not clearly evident, although their components appeared in various contexts. On further enquiry, they found that: (1) senility was recognised but considered to be a natural event and not treated; (2) night terrors were recognised as symptoms; (3) a syndrome of 'unrest of mind' and sleeplessness was recognised; (4) a condition of crying, worrying and loss of interest, as a reaction to illness of a valued person, was recognised; (5) people who are excessively aggressive, socially anxious, 'always wanting things in a hurry', or generally inconsiderate of others, were not seen as ill although recognised as abnormal; (6) a condition when someone acts as if drunk without insight was seen as one that 'can go on to insanity' but can be stopped if treated in time; and (7) sociopathy and addiction were recognised but not treated.

Finally, on examining ideas about cause of illness, the researchers found that the views of the Yoruba people differed widely from those of psychiatrists. They identified two major points of difference: 'The belief in magical and supernatural agencies and the belief that an illness is a being with a volitional force of its own.' However, they made the point that, 'to the Yoruba, a magical or supernatural explanation does not mean that a psychiatric disturbance is any less a disease.' In summarising their observations, the researchers concluded that:

> When it comes to classifying and explaining any particular case, there is room for considerable difference of opinion about the combination of causes, about which is primary, and about what the treatment should be...It is now apparent why there is so little correspondence between Yoruba and psychiatric diagnostic categories. In each the main outlook on the nature of cause, despite certain similarities in mode of thought is radically different. The Yoruba group together symptoms and causal ideas in ways that have no counterpart in psychiatry.

The researchers of the Kota study categorised symptoms in a variety of ways for different purposes. In one method they were able to delineate groups (of patients) with predominantly somatic symptoms, possession states, psychoses, and depressive symptoms. They found that no respondents described obsessive-compulsive symptoms and very few expressed worries about loss of semen or masturbation — contradicting clinical experience elsewhere in India, according to the authors. The overall impression, from the report of the study, is that Western nosology had some relevance to, although is far from identical with, symptom patterns recognised indigenously.

The evaluation of categories of illness recognised by indigenous healers in Jamaica (Kiev, 1963; Wedenoja, 1983) and Senegal (Beiser, Winthrob, Ravel, and Collomb, 1973) suggest that they have similarities to Western nosology. Jamaican healers recognise six kinds of mental disorder namely 'silent-mad, Kumu kumu, rush-a blind, pregnancy-mad, fatuation-mad and nervous breakdown' (Long, 1973), resembling (respectively) endogenous depression, personality disorder, acute transitory psychosis, disorders around childbirth, mania and neurotic disorder. In Senegal there are three major types of 'illnesses of the spirit' — a concept that corresponds to Western notions of mental illness — O'Bodah, O'Dof, and M'Befedin (Beiser et al.,1973). The last is clearly a description of epilepsy but the two former categories resemble psychotic states described in psychiatry since they are identified by bizarre systems of thought, speech and behaviour.

There are two well-established systems of Medicine in Asia — the Indian and the Chinese. Ayurveda, a system of medicine practised widely in India and Sri Lanka, has a somato-psychic model of insanity (Obeyesekere, 1977) but takes into account the aetiological role played by psychological factors (Haldipur, 1984). Traditional Chinese medicine regards mental disorder as a mixture of organic illness and mystical possession (Leng, 1971). Forms of madness are recognised as illnesses in both these systems. In *Commentary on the Hindu System of Medicine* Wise (1845) describes different kinds of madness recognised as illnesses and notes that the possession state, or 'devil-madness', is also denoted as an illness. The syndromes described by Wise clearly do not correspond to Western categories of mental disorder although some features of (Western) functional disorders could be recognised in them. His descriptions are in line with the observation by Haldipur (1984) that Indian texts on mental disease do not mention subjective symptoms of hallucinations or depression, nor the typical history of the categories of illness recognised by psychiatry. Leng (1971) quotes a standard textbook of Chinese medicine written in 610 AD describing eight types of mental disorder. These categories too do not correspond to those of Western psychiatry except for syndromes resembling puerperal psychosis and mental subnormality.

Conclusions

A consideration of symptom patterns observed in non-Western societies (e.g. in Nigeria, and India) and of indigenous practice (e.g. in Jamaica and Senegal) indicate that categories of illness developed in the West are probably usable for describing the emotional disorders encountered in non-Western societies, except that the possession state needs to be considered as a separate entity which may or may not be an illness. The practicability of using Western nosology for diagnosing schizophrenia is supported by the success of the IPSS (World Health Organisation, 1973, 1979), at least as far as acute schizophrenia is concerned, in diagnosing the condition (as defined in the West) reliably in nine centres in Asia, Africa, Europe, North America and South America. However, practicability and reliability is one thing, suitability (in terms of relevance) and validity is another. Western categories may be usable but may not be superior, or even equal, to indigenous categories in terms of indicating treatment or prognosis within the culture. They would, of course, have the advantage of opening up the possibility of Western treatment being applied (since treatment is geared to diagnosis), but this raises the issue of the efficacy and relevance of treatment across cultures. After all, the IPSS, which used Western diagnosis of schizophrenia, found that prognosis was better in areas where Western treatment was less available.

The drawbacks of using Western nosology become really apparent when non-Western systems of medicine (e.g Indian and Chinese) are examined. Since these systems represent the modes of thinking within their cultures, the imposition of a structure (for evaluating illness) that is inconsistent with their basic tenets may, at best, be useless and, at worst, be undermining to the society itself — unless, of course, the alien structure is considered superior in some way. Although Western nosology may be usable, it may not be the best way of describing emotional disorder in non-Western settings if nosology is to lead to an understanding of the 'illness' and an approach to treatment. Western nosology may indeed miss important aspects of illness and certainly miss the meaning of the illness in its cultural totality. But it must be accepted that illness within non-Western communities can be pushed into a (Western) psychiatric framework if this is necessary. If the ultimate aim of studying emotional disorder in non-Western cultures is to benefit the people who are studied, the question is whether the use of Western nosology is useful or justifiable or even the most economical way of proceeding. If, however, the aim is to ensure that Western ways of conceptualising illness are spread around the globe there is no argument.

It is evident, therefore, that, if psychiatry is to develop a theory and practice that is of universal relevance cross-culturally, the very first move should be to re-assess its diagnostic system. The current thinking in psychiatry is reflected in the diagnostic systems called DSM-III (American Psychiatric Association, 1980) and ICD-9 (World Health Organisation, 1978); Good (1987) in an editorial to an issue of *Culture, Medicine and Psychiatry* which includes a special set of papers on 'culture-bound syndromes' and psychiatric diagnosis, refers to 'current efforts to revise DSM-III and ICD-9 to make them more inclusive of clinical phenomena seen by Third World psychiatrists.' But developing a system with universal relevance needs much more than that. Murphy (1986), in supporting criticisms of the existing classifications 'as being too orientated towards European and North American practice while paying only superficial attention to numerically much more important syndromes afflicting the rest of the world', suggests that 'the time is now overdue for the world's psychiatric authorities, who are mainly of European origin, to confront the question of how far their writings and teachings are being distorted, unknowingly, by cultural factors.' Obviously, this would be a start but should not obscure the need for European psychiatry to confront the issue of race as well.

Ethnic minorities

Since ethnic minorities are, by definition, subcultural groups, conclusions about the extent of subcultural differences apply to them. However, differences, other than specifically cultural ones, between them and the majority community in the way psychiatry deals with them must not be overshadowed by cultural differences. In other words matters such as racism should not be obscured by cultural considerations.

The question of psychiatric nosology in the case of ethnic minorities in Western societies is a complex one. In general, the diagnosis of schizophrenia is double edged. On the one hand, its use may be helpful to someone who may benefit from treatment and/or need protection from punishment for a misdemeanour that he/she is not legally responsible for carrying out; on the other hand, social problems may be concealed by the psychiatrisation (via this diagnosis) of the intolerance of personality 'deviance' or social protest (however disguised) in the way (for example) that political dissent is psychiatrised in the Soviet Union. The over-representation of ethnic minorities among those people diagnosed as 'schizophrenic' raises questions, not just of diagnostic methodology, but also of the *social function* of this diagnosis within society. The diagnosis of depression among ethnic minorities may also obscure social problems unless applied sensitively and carefully. The use of the concept of depression among ethnic minorities has been described elsewhere (Fernando, 1986):

> Depression is an individual experience in a social context...In the case of black and ethnic minorities, the social context is concerned with the criteria that differentiates them from the majority community, namely culture, minority status (in terms of power) and racism.

The survey of British studies points to lessons for practical psychiatry. The need to explore interrelationships between culture and race — in particular racism — and their effects on the practice and theory of psychiatry is of paramount importance. In so doing it is inevitable that racism within the institutions of psychiatry has to be recognised and dealt with. The well-established observation that black people are over-represented among compulsorily detained patients and patients in secure hospitals has to be investigated, not just as a cultural phenomenon but as a social injustice. The differential use of treatment needs to be investigated and corrected if it represents practices that are unjustified. The need for psychiatric institutes and professionals to be sensitive to both culture and race — including their own racism — has to be accepted. The main lesson from British research is that culture and race are so intertwined that the profession and institution of psychiatry will eventually have to recognise the need for a policy on race if it wishes to promote a culture-sensitive psychiatry. A matter of particular concern is the connection between psychiatry and social control. Cross-cultural research in Britain suggests that race is being drawn into psychiatric evaluations of dangerousness. When this is seen in the context of the over-representation of ethnic minorities in non-psychiatric penal institutes, i.e. prisons (Home Office Statistical Bulletin, 1986) considerable doubt is cast on the independence of psychiatry as a discipline.

Conclusions

Although some of the lessons of cross-cultural research are reasonably clear, there is very little indication that they are being incorporated into clinical psychiatry or into methods of research being developed by organisations such as the WHO. DiNicola (1985a) argues that the failure of research generated by transcultural psychiatry to have any clinical impact is 'because no therapeutic approach has been able to incorporate its cultural observations'. In other words, he argues that the therapeutic models of mainstream psychiatry do not have room for cultural considerations. But the context in which this is happening — or rather not happening — is important, at least as far as Britain is concerned.

Britain has just emerged from being a colonial power that dominated (militarily) a large part of the world. As Rushdie (1982) states: 'One of the key concepts of imperialism was that military superiority implied cultural superiority.' British institutions continue to maintain the fantasy of cultural superiority linked to racist thinking that characterised the Empire. Therefore, it would seem that one reason for the resistance within psychiatry to the lessons of cross-cultural research is psycho-political — a psychological resistance arising from political considerations. From this arises questions of prestige: British institutions cannot accept that observations on people whose culture is seen as an anomaly (i.e. a deviation from the established order) and inferior (being native to black or brown people) carry equal validity to those made on Western people of white, European stock. This attitude of mind comes through very clearly in the paper from the Social Psychiatry Research Unit at the Institute of Psychiatry in London which was quoted in Chapter 2 (Bebbington, 1978). The author refers to non-Western cultures as 'primitive' and to illnesses of depression in non-Western people as 'cross-cultural anomalies'. Although it is unusual to see these attitudes expressed quite so obviously, many discussions of culture and mental illness, for example Rack (1982), are concerned with re-defining belief-systems, illness models and patterns of symptoms of non-Western people in Western terms. By using the term 'culture' instead of 'race', or 'priority' instead of 'superiority', and by avoiding terms such as 'primitive', the racist nature of the discussion is camouflaged. But yet, the underlying theme, the view that black experience is an inferior version of the experience of white people, is discernible to a careful reader. This is sometimes revealed by a flash-back reference to overt racism of earlier years. For example, in discussing linguistic factors in the perception and interpretation of subjective experience, Rack (1982) writes:

> This brings us back to the issue of somatization. In order to make a distinction between distress in the mind and distress in the body, and describe each one separately, it is necessary to recognise a clear dichotomy between the concepts of 'mind' and 'body'. Such a dichotomy though tacitly accepted in European thought, has no inherent validity nor can it claim universal acceptance. An earlier statement about this was: 'the primitive not only does not separate the diseases of the body and mind in his medical concepts, but does not recognise such separate units' (Ackerknecht, 1943). This statement appears to be the same: but it is in fact slightly different...Our explanation is in terms of cultural priorities.

Another reason for the resistance of psychiatry to take on the lessons of cross-cultural research is the economic advantage for the West in maintaining the *status quo* . This concerns the need for Western institutions to ensure that they remain the centres to which trainees come, the source from which international advisers go, and the base for the generation of new methods of psychiatric practice and research. In the background (or perhaps the foreground) there is the power of vested interests, namely (Western) drug companies, which are dependent on a bio-medical model of psychiatric disorder which disregards culture. Finally, and perhaps most importantly, a reason for the resistance of psychiatry to transcultural lessons is the complacent ethnocentricity of psychiatric institutes and the assumptions within European culture about non-European peoples and their cultures. All this within the overall context of the international power structure tends to protect present diagnostic models and to spread them around the globe. Unfortunately the present power structure is unlikely to change very soon. Western ideas and concepts about people in the shape of psychiatric nosology are likely to continue spreading across the globe like the Western version of Christianity did in the nineteenth century and coca cola in the twentieth.

The future of transcultural psychiatry

Transcultural psychiatry is being pulled in several directions at present. Psychiatry seems to see it as a means of imposing traditional nosology and methodology around the world in the cause of 'epidemiology', and, in dealing with black and ethnic minorities in the West, of sweeping under a cultural carpet potentially explosive problems concerned with race. In practice this means that, if it remains bound to psychiatry, transcultural psychiatry would, at best, become an instrument for communication between the powerful and the powerless. Social anthropology pulls transcultural psychiatry towards becoming a *cultural* psychiatry. If it succumbs, and this is a real possibility since powerful forces are at work, transcultural psychiatry will become a mere umbrella for many different types of cultural psychiatry, or, an intermediary between psychiatry and social anthropology. Transcultural research in Britain has veered, during the past few years, away from the traditional approach of examining rates of 'illness' as well as from the approach named by Kleinman (1977) as 'the new transcultural psychiatry' — essentially an anthropological approach. British workers seem to be reaching out for studies of a useful nature attuned to clinical needs in a social setting. This pragmatic approach points the way for transcultural psychiatry to develop and play a special role, distinct from both social anthropology and traditional psychiatry. It may then be able to feed into social anthropology the need to view human experience in terms of social realities, the real problems of real people, and to alert mainstream psychiatry to the disturbing issues of culture and race that psychiatry must contend with if it is to survive as a credible discipline in a multicultural and multiracial society.

4

Socio-cultural Psychiatry

INTRODUCTION

The background and present standing of psychiatry as a part of Western European culture with its ideology of racism formed the backdrop to a consideration of the cultural dimension in psychiatric research in Chapter 3. This chapter deals with some practical issues of applying psychiatry, as it stands at present, in a multiracial and multicultural community. In a recent paper on psychiatric services for ethnic minorities in Britain, two British psychiatrists, John Bavington and Abdul Majid (1986), point out that, in order to achieve 'cultural sensitivity' to minority cultures, 'health professionals need to become aware of their own culture and how this may influence their attitude towards patients as well as their clinical judgement.' It is a matter of self-awareness as much as an awareness of other people. It would be clear, from the first two chapters of this book, that it is also essential for these professionals to become aware of the culture of the discipline that they practise, the institutions that they work in and the social climate of the society that they belong to. And, it would be evident from Chapter 3, that they must take up some, at least, of the lessons of cross-cultural research.

The cultural viewpoint in psychiatry is generally seen within the aegis of social psychiatry (Wittkower, 1965). But a social psychiatry, geared to a strict medical model of illness, cannot allow a cultural viewpoint which has much meaning in practice. In this model, social stressors are held to precipitate psychiatric illness and social milieu is used to treat the person suffering the condition. Thus 'life events' are studied in order to understand 'social factors' in the aetiology of illnesses; strategies for treatment, for example the 'therapeutic community' approach, are designed to promote the recovery from diseases which are seen primarily as biological disturbances. When viewed within this type of social psychiatry, cultural factors are special types of social factors and culture merely one of several aspects of a person's milieu. In following this way of thinking, the practice of psychiatry would attempt to allow for the culture of the individual patient, or at least those aspects of his or her culture that deviate from the accepted 'norm', in order to formulate the 'real' (biological) illness or to understand what is 'wrong' with the patient. In doing so the 'symptoms' of a patient from one of the non-Western cultures may be dismissed as 'cultural', or, 'atypical' of the particular illness which is being sought. In either instance, the patient is very likely to be seen as deviant — deviant in terms of normality or deviant in illness presentation. Thus, the patient is seen as harbouring 'strange ideas' rather than delusions, or a 'peculiar manner' rather than behaviour disturbance; alternatively, if diagnosed as suffering from an illness, 'atypical depression' or a 'culture-bound syndrome', usually seen as a 'primitive' form of real illness, is recognised. Thus, just being 'culturally sensitive' is not enough; the way of thinking about illness, and about people, is crucial.

A cultural viewpoint emanating from a social anthropological approach has been advocated by Littlewood (1986a):

> Ethnopsychiatry offers an alternative to traditional social psychiatry by regarding psychopathology not as a particular individual's state of mind at a given time or as nature thinly disguised, but as a cultural datum with complex linguistic, political and historical determinants. It approaches the mind through the examination of shared cultural categories of thought and action rather than through the statistical study of individuals.

This approach in clinical method corresponds to the 'new cross-cultural psychiatry' identified by Kleinman (1977) as an emerging framework for the study of psychiatric epidemiology. A cultural psychiatry based on anthropology may yield a formula, or rather formulae (since each culture or group of similar cultures may have to be considered separately), for a theoretical understanding of 'the unique experience of being a member of a particular society' (Littlewood, 1986a), but it must depend on psychological theory to give it meaning in the context of practical psychiatry. It is psychoanalytic theory that social anthropology has drawn upon for this purpose. Thus, in practice, an anthropological approach is a sort of culturalised psychoanalytic method which, like psychoanalysis itself, disregards the social universe that people live in. Psychiatry, however, cannot ignore social realities of people with problems of 'coping' with the 'here-and-now' as well as with their 'inner selves'. Hence, although ethnopsychiatry may be a useful approach for academic psychology, and possibly for some aspects of research in a multicultural society, it is of little use as a means of bringing cultural sensitivity to practical psychiatry. For example, a cultural analysis which renders the personal distress of a Bengali woman in East London understandable in terms of her culture is hardly much use to a social worker or psychiatrist trying to help her if, and a likely 'if' in the present day, she is fearful of racist attacks and the local hospital services regard her as a nuisance. In such a case, professionals must be sensitive to her 'culture', which to a social anthropologist means the analysis of her (seemingly) exotic beliefs and customs. But to a psychiatrist, an understanding of culture (of the anthropological type) must be integrated with an understanding of the social conditions that disable her in the society that she lives in with a sensitivity to the realities of life and ways of coping from her angle, in order to appreciate something of what it feels like to be that person.

It has been argued by DiNicola (1985a) that family therapy and transcultural psychiatry cover 'similar maps of the same territory'. After reviewing the 'portability' of family therapy cross-culturally, DiNicola (1985b) concludes:

> Transcultural psychiatry has lacked a clinical model while family therapy has been enlarging its scope. For transcultural psychiatry, family therapy can be a clinical tool for cultural research, since the family is a window on cultural process. For family therapy, transcultural psychiatry offers a comparative tool to pose questions about family functioning in different cultures, testing the limits of its models and suggesting necessary adaptations of its techniques.

Clearly, family therapy and transcultural psychiatry may enrich each other reciprocally (Palazzoli, 1986) in the future. But family therapy has already built up theories based on assumptions about families observed in Western Europe. These are reflected in culturally loaded perceptions of family functioning denoted by terms such as 'the parental coalition' (Haley, 1963), and 'enmeshment'

(Minuchin, 1974). Concepts of family pathology, for example, the 'dysfunctional family system' (Glick and Kessler, 1974) characterised by 'defects' in families such as 'non-cohesiveness' or the 'lack of differentiation between its members' (Wynne, Ryckoff, Day and Hersch, 1958) are clearly inapplicable cross-culturally. Thus, although one may accept, with some reservations, DiNicola's view that some methods of analysis used by Western family therapy, such as structural family therapy (Minuchin, 1974), are portable across cultures and that the central tenets of family therapy with large systems may be used for cultural analysis, family therapy, as practised today in Western Europe, cannot be a model for an effective practical psychiatry that is sensitive to culture in a social context.

What is needed, therefore, is not the cultural psychiatry of anthropologists nor that of family therapists. It is a '*socio*-cultural psychiatry' that is sensitive to culture in a broad sense while maintaining a practical, perhaps pragmatic, stance in insisting on being relevant and useful to people that psychiatry is supposed to deal with. Socio-cultural psychiatry is a means whereby psychiatrists, and other health workers who use psychiatry in a multicultural setting, can examine themselves, their institutional practices and their disciplines for social influences that produce and perpetuate bias. However it is not the recognition of bias that is so important as its abolition. One must always be followed by the other in practical terms. Socio-cultural psychiatry is not seen in this chapter as just sensitivity to 'cultural factors' or just an 'emic' knowledge of the individual's culture — although it may include both these. It is not a matter of extending the scope of psychiatry from the individual, through family, to cultural group — although this too may be included. It is a viewpoint, as well as a way of working, that is relevant to the needs of a multicultural society, taking in social realities that affect cultural groups. It is, in effect, a compromise, a coming to terms with a psychiatry that is basically hostile to non-Western cultural groups which are designated as racial groups. It is an attempt to make the best of the present arrangements within psychiatry. Therefore, it is not an answer to the serious faults in the theory and practice of psychiatry; ways of rectifying these will be considered in Chapter 7. It is, however, a way of applying psychiatry that may be useful for health professionals right now.

In its clinical application, socio-cultural psychiatry is first and foremost a way of working for health workers to relate to their clients. This involves establishing a rapport, with one or more persons, that enables the professional to think and feel through the cultural viewpoints of the individuals concerned (including the professional himself or herself); it is concerned with incorporating culture in the evaluation process while taking note of the limitations of diagnostic nosology and methodology of psychiatry; finally, it means a sensitivity to the conceptual frameworks of the patients/clients in determining the type and degree of professional involvement. In all this, it is important that the professional views the individual and his/her culture within a type of social psychiatry that is not tied to a medical model of illness. Psychiatric disorder, as well as psychiatry itself, should be seen in the context of social forces in society reinforced by ideologies (Banton *et al.*, 1985). Stereotypes about individuals must be avoided and generalisations about culture viewed with caution. Above all, there must be a constant awareness of the context within which the interaction between the professional and the client or patient takes place. The practice of socio-cultural psychiatry is not just a clinical matter. It must pervade the institutional structures of psychiatry to ensure that services are equitably available to all cultural groups within the population served. This involves specific recruitment policies, training methods and evaluation of the opinions of consumers, in particular those from ethnic minorities.

RAPPORT

People go to psychiatrists because they want to, because they have to, or because they are persuaded or pressurised to do so. In other words, they are 'informal', 'compulsory' or in-between. The expectations of a person who goes willingly is likely to be patterned by his/her cultural expectations of a healer or someone like that; a person who is forced to see a psychiatrist is likely to perceive the latter in terms of social control in the society at large and may well see the professional as a part of the 'system' that is against him/her. Thus, the starting point for rapport is influenced by the context in which the initial interaction takes place. But, in general, the rapport between a professional and a client or patient is determined to a large extent by their mutual perceptions of each other on two dimensions, first, in terms of role as a doctor, social worker, etc., ·and, secondly as a person with a social designation — black, white, female, male, etc.

Communication through language is an important part of establishing rapport but not necessarily the key to it. Sympathy, humility and a willingness to learn are qualities of a professional that may well outweigh the importance of a common language between professional and client. However, if there is an obvious language barrier, interpreting becomes essential. It is always preferable to have an interpreter who, being a member of the professional team, can speak on behalf of the team rather than interpret for the team (Bavington and Majid, 1986). In an ideal service, the cultural mix of the population being served by a psychiatric team must be reflected in a similar mix among professional disciplines within the team. If an interpreter is used, he/she must have the ability to translate concepts, feelings and ideas rather than mere literal meanings of words. Such a 'cultural interpreter' must, not only, have the requisite linguistic and cultural knowledge to perform his/her task, but also, be able to speak up boldly when the two sides are misunderstanding each other (Rack, 1982). An interpreter may, therefore, border on being an advocate, a two-way advocate, representing the client to the professional and *vice versa*. However, once an interpreter is brought into the picture, rapport becomes a three-way matter.

The perceptions of professional roles may be culturally determined and lead to misunderstandings on both sides. Professional health workers usually see their role as broadly benevolent and independent of the 'state' as represented by, for example, the police. But for black people, all white institutions may form one indivisible whole just as they, black and ethnic minorities, are seen by white society as one mass of black people. Hence, an individual working for a 'white' institution may need to demonstrate his/her independence from that institution before rapport with cultural sensitivity can even begin to develop. In these circumstances black professionals cannot expect automatic acceptance from black clients any more than whites can, although blacks are at an initial advantage by being black, or being perceived as such by the client. The first line for a professional to take, in establishing rapport with a black person, may be to loosen the professional role dimension and strengthen the personal relationship, showing clearly where he/she stands on issues of race. The following incident was experienced by the author:

I was called to see an Afro-Caribbean man in the Accident and Emergency Department of a general hospital as he had been brought there by the police for assessment by a doctor and a social worker. He was reported to have been abusive and threatening violence and apparently aggressive towards nursing and medical staff. On meeting me — away from the others — he gave a clue to establishing rapport by asking me where I was 'from'. My answer did not identify me with the institution but: 'I am from Sri Lanka and where are you from?' This set the basis for a very reasonable conversation. Everyone else had been doctors or nurses or police all identified as such, but I had separated myself from them and approached him as a Sri Lankan — and fortunately his previous experience of Sri Lankans had been good.

In establishing independence from an institution that is seen as racist and hostile to ethnic minorities, there may be an advantage in professional contacts being made away from the institution. Thus, home visits are likely to yield much greater gain in the case of ethnic minorities than in the case of the 'majority' community. The assessment in a casualty department of a hospital, or, worse still, a police station, makes the task of establishing rapport very difficult because the context itself intimidates black and ethnic minorities.

Manoeuvres that are adopted by a client in order to establish rapport may have a cultural basis and meaning. Rack (1982) has observed that 'Indian and Pakistani families have an endearing habit of adopting outsiders into the family, ascribing names like "auntie" or "sister"'. If viewed in the context of establishing rapport, such a move by a patient is a way of side-stepping the professional's problem of being saddled by his (professional) role. A professional who is culture-sensitive would take this on and incorporate it into his/her role, but, one who finds it 'disconcerting' (as Rack claims it is) or sees it in paternalistic terms (as 'endearing') is indicating an unwillingness to establish rapport in the client's mode or an inability to accept the client on equal terms. In order to be culture-sensitive one has to deal with one's own racism first.

A patient who goes to a psychiatrist for some form of healing may be from a culture in which the division between healing of the mind and that of the body is not so distinct as it is in Western culture, and hence in psychiatry. A serious dissonance in understanding and rapport between the psychiatrist and the patient may then ensue. If the psychiatrist tries to maintain a psyche-soma split, the 'holistic' patient is pushed into a forced choice, and the choice is invariably a somatic one since, in the final analysis, medicine is about something *physical*. The result is a form of communication based on 'somatic symptoms', a reflection largely of the failure of proper rapport.

Although the healing function of a medical person is evident in all cultures, the perceptions held by a patient about psychiatry and its ways of working may be very different to those held by the psychiatrist. In practising socio-cultural psychiatry, a professional may have to alter his/her role-perception to fit into the particular expectations of the patient from an ethnic minority, or at least go some way towards that, if proper rapport is to be established. All health workers practising in a multicultural setting must feel their way into a compromise between, on the one hand, the particular role that the culture of the patient ascribes to him/her and, on the other hand, that which society denotes. Triseliotis (1986) quotes a study in West Yorkshire which shows that Asians feel unable to trust health workers without having personal knowledge about them and that West Indians distrust formality in professional – client interactions. Therefore, being culture-sensitive in a multicultural setting may mean revising ethnocentric role models taught on traditional training courses and expected by traditional institutions. Although the concept of 'healing' is present in all cultures, that of social work is not clear to many people without, or even with, a Western background. The role of a social worker in intervening within families is a difficult concept for people whose cultures place a high premium on family integrity. In working with such a culture, a social worker must see his or her role as more akin to a participant observer rather than an interventionist, as an intermediary between the family and the state rather than a family therapist.

In order to avoid using the familiar stereotypes of ethnic minority families referred to in Chapter 2, the culturally sensitive social worker must take an individual approach to each family. General information about the culture must not obscure the personal information derived from members of the family themselves. These are the experts — not transcultural psychiatrists or self-styled cultural specialists. The latter may be able to help in elucidating ways of approach and obtaining rapport if this is failing, but cannot make judgements — *in absentia* — as it were.

It is evident that rapport is dependent on many variables some of which have been referred to above. The failure to establish rapport is largely to do with attitudes of professionals both as individuals and as representatives of the institutions they work for — which in turn represent society. But a professional working for an institution that is racist may find it very difficult to step outside that label.

On the other hand, a professional who is culturally insensitive and/or racially biased is unlikely to establish rapport whatever the context of work.

ASSESSMENT

Psychiatrists are called upon to make assessments of other people for various reasons. While adhering to a basic medical model of illness in the framework of Cartesian mind – body dualism, psychiatrists vary in their approaches to diagnosis and assessment. If orientated towards organic explanations, the psychiatrist thinks in terms of physical causes for both psychological and physical symptoms; the psychologically orientated psychiatrist leans towards psychological explanations for symptoms, while the social psychiatrist brings in a multifactorial explanatory model of illness. Sensitivity to 'cultural factors' (as the psychiatric jargon puts it) is always important but becomes crucial when there is a 'culture-clash'. This may be said to exist on two counts in a multicultural society. First, it occurs when the cultural base of a professional in terms of personal background and/or professional training is at variance with the cultural background of the client. Secondly, a clash occurs when the cultural base of psychiatry invests the discipline with a bias against the culture of the client. Socio-cultural sensitivity in assessment entails the acumen to look beyond the 'presentation' of symptoms by the individual patient and to view diagnosis as, primarily, a social concept rather than a biological 'thing'; it requires the psychiatrist to interpret communication in terms of the cultures of those involved and the different social realities of their lives; it means that the conclusions of an assessment are about each person as a member of a family, within a culture, in relation to the culture of psychiatry itself. A socio-cultural psychiatrist must be aware of the context in which psychiatric assessments are being made: the confusion between race and culture, racial prejudices of individual professionals and racism within institutional settings, and, most importantly, the racist traditions and present ethos of psychiatric theory and practice.

All psychiatrists, and consequently their 'multidisciplinary teams', strive, first and foremost, to distinguish between physical disease and psychological disease. A patient, perhaps with a family, from one of the non-Western cultures, holding a holistic frame of reference regarding health and ill-health, is unlikely to share very much of the conceptual model held by the psychiatrist. The consequent lack of rapport may lead to both people, or groups of people, taking a fall-back position; negotiation takes place over tangible symptoms, each testing the other. Inevitably, racial stereotypes come into play. People deemed inferior are seen as employing inferior ways of communication. This is the origin in many instances of the 'somatisation myth' — the view that black and ethnic minorities cannot feel their emotions (in the way white people do) in terms of real emotions but do so *physically*. Socio-cultural psychiatrists do not get 'hung up' on the somatisation issue but perceive symptoms as a part of the communication process between patients, on the one hand, and doctors or other health workers, on the other. Psychiatrists in any community who concentrate on counting presenting symptoms and add them up to identify illness may indeed miss the patient in the process, but this is particularly likely to occur in a multiracial and multicultural society.

The diagnostic process is an important part of psychiatric assessment. The most important diagnoses in terms of social consequences (for people given the diagnoses) are depression and schizophrenia. In summarising an account of depression in ethnic minorities, Fernando (1986) writes as follows:

Depression is an individual experience in a social context. Symptoms are the interface between the individual having the experience and others — both people and society in general. In the case of black and ethnic minorities, the social context is concerned with the criteria that differentiate them from the majority community, namely culture, minority status (in terms of power) and racism. The culture (of an individual) affects the nature of presenting symptoms and the significance of life experience. Marginality may promote vulnerability to depression, and a strong ethnic identity provides protection from blows to self-esteem in a society that devalues the status of minorities. Racism causes depression by promoting blows to self-esteem, inducing experience of loss, and placing individuals in a position of helplessness.

The use of the term 'depression' to describe a state of subjective dysfunction that does not include the traditional presenting symptoms of the 'condition' described in the West is theoretically dubious. But denying the sort of help (to the individual 'patient') that the application of this concept might lead to, may be unfair, given that society ties up sources of help with institutions such as psychiatry. Therefore, a balance has to be struck: diagnostic concepts have to be used, with care and sensitivity, but their use must be geared to a particular aim of helping the 'patient'. If the aim cannot be realised by employing a particular diagnosis, or, socio-cultural sensitivity cannot be exercised in making it, there is no justification for using the diagnosis. In other words, if the diagnosis helps, use it, but giving a diagnosis cross-culturally for the sake of doing so is not acceptable.

The account of depression in ethnic minorities, referred to earlier (Fernando, 1986), describes how the concept of depression may be used 'helpfully and realistically' in a multicultural community. An example of so doing is the case of a woman of Indian origin first seen by the author in 1982:

> Mrs C was referred by her general practitioner as complaining of various physical symptoms. It was evident, on talking with her and her husband, that they both fully recognised the psychological nature of the disturbance which caused her to suffer what doctors call 'physical' symptoms. In other words neither the patient nor her husband saw a mind–body dichotomy in illness or symptomatology. She felt devalued in the only job she was able to get and felt a sense of loss in her separation from close contact with Asian people. She had no difficulty in identifying these features of herself as causing her to feel pain all over her body. Since then, she has been using anti-depressant medication on and off balancing it with other types of 'treatment' such as a visit to India and a job in an Asian community project. She seems to see the psychiatrist as a person with knowledge about medication but welcomed his interest in family matters once she detected his non-judgemental understanding of it.

This patient made a full recovery. A very different outcome may have emerged if the traditional approach had been used. The fact that she had an arranged marriage may well have been identified as a significant 'factor' in her illness and her presentation with physical symptoms an indication of her lack of 'insight'. In these circumstances she is likely to have resisted joint interviews with her husband and been reluctant to discuss family matters. Explanations that there is 'nothing physically wrong' would have been resisted and a prescription for antidepressants, a physical remedy, confusing.

The use of the diagnosis 'schizophrenia' in cross-cultural assessments has serious inherent problems concerned with social stigma, questions of personal responsibility and expectations of behaviour disturbance. However, a total exclusion of the term may be counter-productive in Western society; however a sensitivity to socio-cultural issues is an essential part of any assessment where this diagnosis is considered. The following experience of the author exemplifies the ways in which the cultural dimensions and its social concomitants have to be carefully weighed up before a diagnosis of schizophrenia is made.

I was asked to see a 29 year old Afro-Caribbean man who was on remand (in prison) for a court report. A (white) psychiatrist who saw him had reported that he 'suffers from a chronic schizophrenic illness, with mainly negative symptoms (withdrawal, social deterioration, emotional blunting). He lacks insight and is not willing to have treatment informally. He does, however, require re-admission...' I was told that he was near-mute hardly saying a word to anyone, had said nothing when asked to plead in court to a (minor) charge and showed little emotional response. I had met him about six months earlier on a home visit soon after he had then moved into a flat to live on his own for the first time; he was one of the few black people housed in the area and was considered to be a 'nuisance' by the local white population — a matter that he had discussed with me at the time.

On visiting him in prison, he welcomed me with a smile and chatted quite freely. He claimed to have been picked up by the police when he was looking at a new car in a car-park. He wandered around because he had given up trying to get a job or get his flat into order. He had not spoken to anyone because 'if you say something they pin something on you'. He did not speak in court because 'the courts are for criminals'.

I disagreed with the diagnosis and declined to collude with a compulsory order for hospital care but offered to have him in hospital (without a diagnosis). I volunteered the observation that his attitude to his offence was 'consistent with attitudes generally in the community to this type of situation'. Later, I had a telephone call from the prison medical officer. He reckoned that the person concerned had 'relapsed' in that he was again withdrawn etc. and also seemed to be 'pre-occupied', possibly with hallucinations. He tried to persuade me to change my mind and help the 'patient' by giving a diagnosis that would get him into hospital from where he could be released, since, otherwise, he would 'continue to get picked up by the police on minor charges', and 'the courts did not know what to do with him'; compulsory admission to hospital may 'save' him from a prison sentence.

Thus, a socio-cultural psychiatrist has to recognise the nature of social pressures on black people and ways of dealing with them. A judgement has to be made on the overall helpfulness (to the 'patient') of intervening socially by making a diagnosis. This has to be done with a recognition of the prospective patient's right to deal with society in a manner of his own choice, and in the light of the reality of unjustified police action against black people and of courts which are unable to cope with protests against racism. The option of walking away from this type of situation, designating it as a social problem rather than a psychiatric one, is not open to a socio-cultural psychiatrist. Psychiatry in a multiracial and multicultural society must be seen as a social institution and the making of a diagnosis as a social action. To stay with the person assigned to the psychiatrist for an assessment and to use psychiatry sensitively and helpfully in a socially appropriate way, to the patient's overall benefit, is the challenge.

Psychiatric assessments that embody diagnoses of neuroses and personality disorder are really semantic issues when undertaken in the cross-cultural arena. However, here too, the designation of a diagnosis may carry a practical meaning in terms of help-giving. The failure to recognise subjective distress cross-culturally coupled with a lack of empathy because of cultural dissonance between psychiatrist and patient may lead to patients being denied psychological or social 'treatment'. The degree to which a form of behaviour is 'neurotic' or indicative of 'personality disorder' is dependent on cultural norms. Culture-sensitivity, therefore, involves a degree of knowledge about the person's culture as well as a rapport within which the person's own views can be assessed. An earlier discussion indicated how 'somatisation' can complicate the issue because of the psychiatrist's failure to establish the rapport that is needed. If this is overcome, a socio-cultural psychiatrist should compensate for any cultural dissonance by bringing in the patient's family at an early stage thereby widening the scope of the assessment procedure.

The traditional practice for involving the family in the course of a psychiatric assessment is for a social worker to see the family and

113

report back to the psychiatrist. An exploratory type of approach, rather than a traditional investigative interview, should be used in socio-cultural psychiatry since the assessments are being made cross-culturally. But it requires a professional of considerable skill to work with a family in this way. Lau (1986) states:

> The family therapist must first know the family's cultural and religious background in sufficient detail in order to assess the content of the clinical materials. If necessary, the services of a cultural interpreter should be obtained. The therapist must be aware of the stresses, both present and historical, of the particular ethnic group to which his client family belongs.

A psychiatrist, or some other health worker, who is an outsider to the family and alien to its cultural roots must be aware of his/her position *vis-a-vis* the family, and, more importantly, aware of what the alien professional person brings into the situation, both from his/her personal culture and the culture of psychiatry. These include personal prejudices and misconceptions of family life of the client and myths about families that have been incorporated into psychiatric traditions. Rapport in a family setting is even more complicated than it is in relation to one individual client. Psychiatrists are tuned to differentiate normality from illness and to look for 'pathology' — a notion which is conceptualised in terms of 'problems' and 'dysfunction'. In a cross-cultural context, the professional must desist from using this dichotomous approach in trying to understand the family life of clients.

Psychiatric assessments should not be seen as objective facts but rather as statements within a social context. This may of course apply to all psychiatric assessments but there is an important difference. A 'social statement' of this kind made within a relatively uniform cultural system, where culture-clash and racist judgements are not involved, may approximate to an 'objective' fact, at least for practical purposes. But this cannot be said to occur in the case of psychiatric assessments which entail cultural differences between the participants of the assessments and where an inbuilt bias exists within psychiatry against the cultures of its clients. The approach to assessment that is proposed in this section does not amount to a deviation from traditional psychiatry but is an attempt to modify it sufficiently to enable psychiatry to function in a multiracial and multicultural society. Assessment plays a large part in the 'gatekeeper' role of psychiatry in determining the use of resources which are tied up with psychiatry as a social institution. Also, a psychiatric assessment may have legal implications, determining questions of personal responsibility and freedom. Therefore, the need to introduce a socio-cultural approach into psychiatry is a matter of considerable importance for natural justice in society and social stability in the community.

ORGANISATION OF SERVICES

The quality and extent of a psychiatric service is dependent, first and foremost, on its staff. If the managers of a psychiatric service wish to provide a service that is sensitive to social and cultural needs and issues, they must insist on an honest approach that focuses on policies within three broad areas — training, recruitment and race-relations. These will be discussed in terms of broad policy rather than detailed content. In many ways the three stand together: a failure to implement any one is to undermine, or even reverse the effects of, the other two.

The training of professionals to practise socio-cultural psychiatry, which is sensitive to both the cultural and social needs of ethnic minority groups, must be related to the setting in which it is practised. It must emerge from an appraisal of the cultural differences as well as the social needs and disadvantages of the groups that the service caters for. A training 'package' applicable to all areas and to all professional groups is not feasible. But certain common themes that should be covered are evident. First, there is the question of racism in the way it affects (a) cultural or ethnic groups among the consumers of the service, (b) recruitment and promotion of professional staff within the service, considered in the context of the particular functions of each profession, and (c) service provision through its effect on rapport, assessment and treatment. Racism awareness training may be helpful in some areas as an aid to the promotion of socio-cultural psychiatry. But it must be carried out in a way that is applicable to practical service delivery, rather than via a 'package' supposed to be of universal relevance, and, more importantly, it must be carried out within an overall framework of anti-racist action by the institution. Secondly, training should focus on socially and culturally determined expectations (from the service) of ethnic minorities living within the 'catchment area' covered by the service: their linguistic and cultural needs, and ways of providing for them, should be included. Specialist input

115

may be required into training professionals in ways of understanding particular groups and developing special services. Thirdly, each professional group within psychiatry should concentrate on understanding its own particular professional background and current practice with respect to race and culture. Since this book is concerned primarily with the psychiatric profession (in addition to the institution of psychiatry), its subject matter, especially in Chapters 1–3, is largely applicable to training of psychiatrists and allied professional groups, such as clinical psychologists and social workers.

Recruitment into the higher grades of any of the professions working in psychiatry, and possibly any other institution, is linked to concepts of 'qualification' and 'acceptability'. For example, a person who is recruited as a charge nurse must have certain qualifications in terms of degrees and experience, and be judged as acceptable for the job. In a socio-cultural psychiatric service, these criteria need to be defined carefully. The term 'qualification' must be interpreted in the light of the cultural and racial composition of the consumers of the service, as well as degrees and previous experience of the individual concerned. On the whole, ethnic minority patients/clients need professional staff at all levels with whom they could identify at a personal level, while people of the majority community do not need this sort of response from the service since the service clearly belongs to them.

Cultural sensitivity and an understanding of social pressures on ethnic minorities must be seen as important qualifications for working in the service, especially in positions of responsibility. The term 'acceptability' should be defined in relation to the consumers of the service as well as to professional colleagues. Hence, a service which caters for several cultural and racial groups must contain within it professional staff easily identifiable and self-acknowledged as being from those groups, at least in a broad sense. Moreover, the hierarchy within each profession must be balanced so that the service projects an image of being fair and just — counteracting the situation in society. Linguistic problems in a psychiatric service arise from the failure of professional staff to speak the languages that their clients are used to. Clearly this should be dealt with by having members of staff who speak the languages that are needed — a matter that should be reflected in recruitment policies. In exceptional circumstances, however, adequately trained interpreters may be employed on the staff. In order to establish a recruitment policy that would promote a socio-cultural psychiatry, people involved in staff-selection must be trained and tested in their ability to implement the policy. Specially designed racism awareness training may be necessary and/or firm vetting of procedures may have to be introduced. Specific problems in implementing the policy have to be picked up early and dealt with.

A race and culture policy for a socio-cultural psychiatric service should cover recruitment and training but also deal with various other issues such as culture-sensitivity in the provision of food and the easy availability of interpreters when they are needed. A main feature of the policy should be one of continuous evaluation and change. Consumer research into the cultural sensitivity of services and ethnic monitoring of staff appointments should feed back sufficient information to implement changes in services and influence planning. For example, the observation (if verified) that the psychiatric services in the inner city areas of London, which have a relatively high proportion of black and ethnic minorities, are largely staffed at a senior level by white people working in prestigious institutes must be acted upon by changes in recruitment. Therefore, the appointment of a race relations officer and a development officer advising the general manager of each health district is a necessary part of an effective race and culture policy that can back up a socio-cultural psychiatry.

TREATMENT

A broad definition of treatment includes specific techniques directed at the individual as well as changes within his/her family or community (Chapter 3). If viewed in this wide context, a socio-cultural psychiatry must place the eradication of racism as the most important (public health) remedy for the treatment of social stress impinging on ethnic minorities. The aim of this section, however, is to consider the practice of socio-cultural psychiatry in providing treatment defined in the narrow sense of 'something done in order to relieve or cure an illness or abnormality' (Oxford Paperback Dictionary, 1979) and divided, for convenience, into physical, psychological and social therapies.

Physical treatment with psychotropic drugs is generally geared to diagnosis — in theory. Since the validity of making clear-cut diagnoses in a multicultural population is doubtful, physical treatment should be under-used in treating people from minority cultural groups. But in reality, drugs are used empirically and are not precise in their actions; the 'mystique' surrounding their use

117

derives from biochemical theories about their actions in conditions of 'illness'. In practice, most psychiatrists prescribe psychotropic drugs on a 'trial' basis, to 'see whether it will work', rather than as a specific 'cure' for an illness. In the case of black and ethnic minorities, this approach should be extended; the broad action of a drug that may be useful should be explained to the patient and/or the person's relatives, leaving them to try out the drugs. The use of electroplexy should be limited to extreme instances when biological changes supervene and threaten life in conditions analogous to 'depression'. In the course of under-using physical treatment, the use of psychological and social treatment procedures become more important in the case of ethnic minorities, compared to the majority community.

Psychotherapy, or 'talking treatment', depends for its practice on rapport and communication between therapist(s) and client(s); it is ethnocentric in its conceptual basis being imbued with traditional beliefs and ideologies of the West. Three models of psychotherapy are recognised: individual, group and family psychotherapy (Brown and Pedder, 1979). The applicability of individual psychotherapy, as it is currently organised and practised in Britain, as a treatment method for people of non-Western cultures is dubious. Bavington and Majid (1986) suggest that a 'culturally consonant' therapeutic approach that is applicable to the Asian population in Britain is feasible but think that 'considerable research and work are needed' to develop this. However, if the concept of psychotherapy is demystified and examined for what it is, its cross-cultural applicability becomes evident. Psychotherapy is about three interrelated matters within a relationship between a therapist and a client: communication, interest (of the therapist in the client's personal affairs, feelings etc.) and analysis (of the client's feelings, personal life, 'symptoms' etc., and/or the relationship between the client and the therapist). It is the philosophy of life (as a psychological model or set of beliefs instilled during training) held by the therapist that gives the process of psychotherapy its status as a technique of treatment and its mystique and/or 'scientific' aura. But it is this very system of thinking that may block proper communication across cultural and racial barriers. In using psychotherapy as a vehicle of cross-cultural therapy the therapist must focus on questions of rapport (discussed earlier) and then take on board the client's cultural perceptions and realities of his/her social life as an ethnic minority in a racist society. In analysing 'illness', the client's 'explanatory model' (Kleinman, 1980b) must be given precedence over that of the therapist. In assessing problems, the client's viewpoint must be uppermost; in determining goals, the client's aims must be paramount.

An approach to psychotherapy for ethnic minorities (as indicated above) does not require special training but does require the therapist to be culturally sensitive, aware of the social pressures on black and ethnic minorities and mindful of their ways of coping with these pressures. The relationship between therapist and client, and any consequent concepts of 'transference', must be seen in the context of the power structure in a racist society and majority – minority interactions in the experience of the client — which may be very different to that of the therapist. Thomas and Comer (1973) give this advice to therapists in the United States:

> The only successful way of dealing with a black person in a psychotherapeutic mode is to fail to accept and even to raise the challenge to the basic societal assumption and not to offer solace to an individual at the potential price of leaving the group behind. The therapist clearly does not have to engage in the reorganisation of his society. Indeed, it is important at some point in the treatment of all patients to help them realistically assess themselves and their responsibilities. But first the interactional set must reflect the acceptance of the reality that the society can be wrong and can be responsible; that makes the difference in the degree of communicative intimacy and trust that can be attained.

In seeking to promote self-knowledge and self-awareness in a client, the therapist must, first and foremost, be mindful of the danger of invalidating social realities of the client's life situation. For example, explaining away the client's sense of victimisation in terms of 'projection' or 'denial' may have damaging effects; in describing ways of coping with the black experience in Britain, the writer Remi Kapo (1981) states: 'The identity of anyone *aware* of being victimised is always clear-cut'.

Although there are doubts about using group therapy cross-culturally, it is not too difficult to apply this approach in a multicultural setting. Bavington and Majid (1986) describe an Urdu/Hindi/Punjabi mixed weekly group which has been highly successful, and the author is conversant with multiracial groups where racial and cultural differences are an asset to exploration of personal problems. In fact, the group situation is probably an ideal vehicle for providing psychological therapy across cultures in that it is potentially flexible in many ways. But this form of therapy too must be demystified and separated from complex theories of 'group dynamics' which are invariably ethnocentric in their derivation and application. The therapist(s) must see the group as an open system to be guided into a group matrix by its members rather than the therapist(s). The comments (made earlier) about cultural sensitivity and the need to recognise and understand the social realities of the clients' world still apply, but, if group therapists are open minded and sufficiently self-aware of their personal prejudices about race and culture, they could develop these attributes in the course of participating in multicultural groups.

Family therapy may appear to be well suited as a form of treatment for ethnic minorities 'because of the frequency with which stresses and illness appear to arise from family conflict, and because of the importance of the extended family in the culture of some of the minorities in Britain', (Bavington and Majid, 1986). However, this is a dangerous generalisation. First, in a situation where the therapist's knowledge of the culture of the client-family is limited, he/she is likely to 'detect' family conflict because of the tendency to view family patterns that are alien to one's own experience as pathological, especially if they are derived from what society considers to be 'primitive' parts of the world. Thus a 'diagnosis' of 'family conflict' may be no more than a racist assumption about family life. Secondly, even if the therapist is knowledgeable about the culture of the client-family, he/she would be bringing into the 'therapy' assumptions about family life based on concepts derived by (Western) family therapy. In this light, it is evident that a family approach in treatment is much more difficult cross-culturally in a racist society, when compared to that where therapist(s) and family share a common culture or where the client(s) are from an identifiable Western culture. Therefore, socio-cultural psychiatry must discourage family therapy in any formal sense; but the involvement of psychiatrists and social workers in discussions with families may help if the professional sees his/her role as a participant learner rather than a therapist or interpreter of dynamics.

Clearly, many of the problems of using psychotherapy for the treatment of black and ethnic minorities can be overcome by employing black and ethnic minority therapists. But psychotherapy being a prestigious (and remunerative) occupation, various devices are used by psychiatry and institutions allied to psychiatry to keep psychotherapy 'white'. The situation requires administrative action of the type suggested in the section on 'Services'.

The therapeutic community approach was the first formalised 'social therapy' to be introduced in psychiatry. The essence of this approach being open communication and the shared examination of problems (Brown and Pedder, 1979), its applicability to a multicultural clientele and its use in a situation where there is a cultural dissonance between staff and clients are fraught. If black and ethnic minorities are in a minority in the community in terms of numbers and/or power, it merely reinforces the destructive social situation in society at large — hardly 'therapy'. However, if the community concerned is different from society in its power arrangements, it may have the potential of providing a 'therapeutic milieu' for ethnic minorities. Nevertheless, the detailed structure of meetings etc. may have to be revised to suit cultural differences in notions of hierarchy and interpersonal relationships. As in psychotherapy, staff must be culturally sensitive and socially aware, preferably by personal experience.

Crisis intervention is a social 'technique' that is allied to family therapy. If stripped of its mystique in the form of 'crisis theory' (Brandon, 1970), it is seen as a means of defusing highly charged situations by 'intervention' at a time when clients are most vulnerable to accept the views of professionals. Clearly, the professionals participating in 'crisis intervention' must have a deep and detailed knowledge of the culture of the family and a sensitivity to the social pressures around it if intervention is to be justified during a crisis. If this does not apply, the danger is that action would be taken on intuitive judgements which naturally emerge from 'common sense' — and 'common sense' carries within it all the prejudices and racist assumptions current in society. Therefore 'crisis intervention', as a form of treatment, is open to serious abuse unless it is used in a very limited way, for example, in social crises where the professional acts to protect the individual and/or family from a situation identified by the client(s) as intolerable. However, a socio-psychiatric service, which is staffed by black and ethnic minorities within a system where the overall policies are sympathetic to these groups, may find it possible to evolve a type of 'crisis intervention' that can be used constructively and effectively as a form of 'treatment' in a broad sense.

CONCLUSIONS

The foregoing paragraphs indicate that the practice of psychiatry in a multiracial and multicultural society must be mindful of rapport between the people involved, the extent to which professionals are sensitive to cultural and racial issues and the need to organise services that take note of the realities of life for black and ethnic minorities. This chapter is by no means a complete guide to the use of psychiatry cross-culturally. The remarks and suggestions in it are designed to provide an ethos for the health worker who wishes to make something of psychiatry in the present context, while waiting for, or trying to make, those fundamental changes in psychiatry — and indeed in society at large — that must come if psychiatry is to be a component of British society that is relevant to all its people.

British psychiatry today is hardly credible with many of Britain's ethnic minorities. The complaints about its practice and its practitioners are legion. The demands for an equitable service are mounting. The over-representation of black and ethnic minorities among compulsorily detained patients are seen as directly related to both cultural insensitivity of psychiatrists and racist practices in the profession. The psychiatric services are seen as biased and unjust. Yet, there is a recognition that psychiatry may be of potential help to ethnic minorities as shown by the protest against so-called 'mis-diagnosis'; the implication here is that if only diagnosis is accurate, there would be no problem. In fact tightening up the diagnostic criteria will not alter the injustice, irrelevance and racism within psychiatry when it is applied to black and ethnic minorities. The perversity of some diagnostic practices are merely indicators of the ethnocentricism of psychiatric methodology. It is the use to which diagnosis is put that is at fault. It is harmful to black people because psychiatry has got drawn into the social oppression of black people.

The application of psychiatry, with its racist heritage and its ethnocentric bias, to cultural minority groups who are identified in racial terms raises a basic ethical question. The revisions to a traditional psychiatric approach that have been considered in this chapter may modify, but certainly do not negate, the question. The question emerges very clearly if one accepts the sort of argument put forward by Sashidharan (1986) in identifying the subject matter of transcultural psychiatry as 'something to do with white psychiatrists or mental health professionals and black patients or clients' culture, 'defined in a simplistic and manageable way' is then seen as providing an 'explanatory variable in understanding black deviance (or psychopathology)'. The result is a marginalisation of the 'structural and political dimensions of inequalities in a racist society'. Cultural psychiatry may be seen in this context as 'isolated from the day to day struggles of black people' and therefore undermining the progress of the very people it hopes to help. The attempt in this chapter to bring into practical psychiatry some of the lessons of transcultural research and (seemingly) to compromise with an essentially racist society may then be seen as an unethical position to take.

The answers to ethical questions in psychiatry are seldom clear-cut. Ethics cannot be separated from real life which is often a series of compromises. It is important, however to keep a clear distinction between a compromise and a solution to a problem. A psychiatry that is both culture-sensitive and racially aware — presented in this chapter as 'socio-cultural psychiatry' — is not a solution to the problems within British society that result in the oppression of black and ethnic minorities. It may, however, alleviate that oppression and enable psychiatric services to provide more benefit and/or do less harm to them. Progress towards a more equitable and just society cannot come from psychiatry alone.

5

Racist Psychiatry

INTRODUCTION

The public face of psychiatry is that of an objective, applied science based on a body of knowledge built up over the years. It would be evident, from the previous chapters, that such a view of psychiatry is so limited as to be fallacious. But the significance and meaning of psychiatry as a social process depends on its impact on the people at the receiving end of its practice and the part it plays in society generally. At a personal level, psychiatry may be felt as aggressive, liberating, educative, condescending, etc., depending on various factors, in particular the attitudes and aims of the participants in the process. At a more general, social level, in its effect on groups of people or society in general, psychiatry may be felt as repressive, ineffectual, interfering (for example, with individual or group rights), reformist, feminist, ageist, or racist. The particular adjective that is used would vary from place to place, time to time, and circumstance to circumstance. Further, the general approach often determines the effect it has on the individual: for example, a generally sexist psychiatry will be destructive (in most cases) towards women because the judgements made by professionals and/or the organisation of services will reflect sexist attitudes and practices. In fact, the level of underlying sexism may be indicated by observations of gender-linked diagnostic preferences (of depression, for instance) and service priorities (in providing creche facilities for instance). The purpose of this chapter is to trace racism, both implicit and explicit, in the practice of psychiatry in Britain. It should be considered as an extension of Chapter 2 and overlapping with it to some extent. While in Chapter 2 general features of psychiatric practice and services were examined, this chapter looks at the specifics of psychiatry—its methods of evaluation and details of service provision.

Racism is not a unitary concept that can be clearly defined and scientifically investigated. A psychological view tends to see it as a kind of prejudice—ethnic or racial prejudice. In his classic psychological analysis of prejudice, Allport (1954) identifies two essential (psychological) components in prejudice namely, an attitude of hostility and a belief that is overgeneralised and erroneous:

Ethnic prejudice is an antipathy based upon a faulty and inflexible generalisation. It may be felt or expressed. It may be directed toward a group as a whole, or toward an individual because he is a member of that group

Allport designates the acting out of prejudice as discrimination 'which has more immediate and serious social consequences than has prejudice.' Benedict (1942), a social anthropologist, marks the lack of rationality in racist beliefs in likening racism to a religion and she too emphasises the importance of its social consequences: 'Like any belief which goes beyond scientific knowledge, it can be judged only by its fruits and by its votaries and its ulterior purposes.' Racism is much more than just prejudice with social consequences. Wellman (1977), a sociologist argues: 'Without an understanding of the structural context within which attitudes occur, we cannot grasp their meaning. Their importance is also exaggerated; it seems as though the attitudes cause the structures.' In fact, once racism is embedded within the structures of society, the prejudice of individuals is no longer the main problem. According to Wellman, racism is not just about attitudes but about 'institutionally generated inequality'. A culture of racism in the fabric of society does not need prejudice for its survival. And it affects the behaviour of individuals; 'Prejudiced people are not the only racists.' Racism then arises from thinking that is rational and correct within the culture.

In analysing the function of racism in present-day British society, Lawrence (1982a) rejects the view of racism as prejudice and racist ideas as a relic of a distant imperialist past: 'Racist ideologies ... are an organic component of attempts to make sense of the present crisis. The fear that society is falling apart at the seams has prompted the elaboration of theories about race which turn on particular notions of culture.' In this context, racist ways of dealing with people have developed in order to keep British society together. Psychiatry being a part of the society that is felt to be 'falling apart', goes along with this in line with the rest of society. Therefore, to point out the racism in psychiatry is to shake the position and status of psychiatry as a pillar of present British society; psychiatrists and others concerned with its status and power are bound to feel threatened.

The terminology concerned with racism is confusing and muddled. Richardson and Lambert (1985) identify three uses of the term among sociologists—racism as ideology, racism as social structure and racism as practice. The first, which they call 'cultural racism', has some aspects of the psychological view of the concept: 'A whole cluster of cultural ideas, beliefs and arguments which transmit mistaken notions about the attributes and capabilities of "racial" groups.' These attitudes and ideas may come from belief systems in the culture, theological or pseudo-scientific doctrines, or ordinary folk-wisdom or 'common-sense'; they may have historical origins and/or be related to structural factors in society. Institutional racism denotes the extent to which racism is embedded in the 'dominant organisations and power structure of society, resulting in distinctive patterns of social disadvantage.' Racism in practice is referred to as 'racialism' or racial discrimination; it is the acting out of racial prejudice by individuals towards other individuals, or more generally, racially prejudiced behaviour. This may be determined by cultural racism or institutional racism. Cultural racism, institutional racism and racialism (as described by Richardson and Lambert) cannot be seen as distinct entities since they are closely related to each other at various levels. One can refer to the cultural racism of an institution such as psychiatry; racialism—the practice of racism—is a direct consequence of cultural racism when a racist individual exhibits racist behaviour, but is a part of institutional racism when racist behaviour is a result of institutional processes which are racially discriminatory.

Hall (1978) looks at institutional racism both historically and politically:

It does not always assume the same shape. There have been many significantly different *racisms*—each historically specific and articulated in a different way with the societies in which they appear. Racism is always historically specific in this way, whatever common features it may appear to share with other social phenomena. Though it may draw on the cultural and ideological traces which are deposited in a society by previous historical phases, it always assumes specific forms which arise out of the present—not the past—conditions and organisation of society.

In defining racism for practical purposes the most appropriate approach is to relate the definition to the context. It is different in different places, at different times and with different people. In general, the term racism covers many facets of a basic concept that is recognised in terms of attitudes, beliefs, institutional structures, ways of working, life-styles etc. A definition of racism must be geared to the particular purpose for which it is needed. For example, a definition that is appropriate for examining a psychotherapeutic relationship must be very different to that used in assessing the functioning of a day centre. Furthermore, since psychiatric practice is not uniform throughout the country, racist psychiatry in one place may be unlike that in another. The sort of racism at a psychiatric centre that takes a predominantly organic stance (as opposed to a 'social' approach) may be very different to that at a centre where 'cultural psychiatry' is practised. However, certain generalisations are applicable to most of British psychiatry.

The historical and theoretical background to racism in psychiatry was presented in Chapters 1 and 2. In assessing the manifestation of racism in psychiatry, it must be analysed from various angles. There are questions of power—power with respect to racial categorisation and power within the psychiatric system. Cultural and racial bias in techniques and methods used in psychiatric practice must be considered. Finally, it is necessary to examine the experience of black and ethnic minorities as patients, or as staff within the psychiatric system and the professional disciplines that come together in (psychiatric) multidisciplinary teams.

QUESTIONS OF POWER

Power is a major factor in many aspects of human relationships. It may be considered in terms of the power of individuals—individual power—and the power of groups—collective power (Goldman, 1972). However, a person's power in British society, as in many others, is derived in most instances from his/her membership in groups that have collective power. Dahl (1968) analyses power relations in society in terms of 'controlling' (social) units (Cs) and 'responsive', or 'dependent', (social) units (Rs). Matters to consider then are 'the *magnitude* of the power of the Cs with respect to the Rs, how this power is *distributed* in the system, and the scope, and *domain* of control that different individuals or actors have, exercise, or are subject to.' The magnitude of C's power over R is measured in 'amounts' (of power); the distribution of power among individuals or groups is determined by historical, economic and other factors; the power of C may apply to some class of R's activities—the range or scope of C's power; and the Rs over whom C has or exercises control constitutes the 'domain' (of C's power).

The power structure of the psychiatric system in a clinical setting places the doctor, or psychiatrist, at the top and the patient at the bottom, with other professionals distributed somewhere in between. Thus, psychiatrists always belong to 'controlling' units, (Cs), and patients to 'responsive' units, (Rs), while others would vary in their designation to Cs or Rs within the psychiatric system depending on various complex factors. For example, social workers or clinical psychologists as a group may be a 'C' with respect to nurses as a group in one district or one hospital because (for example) they are strongly led, while the situation may be very different in another district or hospital. Further, subgroups within each category including patients may be 'C' with respect to other subgroups because of their status or wealth or economic power—or race. It should be noted that having power is different from exercising power. The amount of power actually exercised by psychiatrists and others belonging to controlling (social) units over patients and others belonging to responsive (social) units may vary considerably. The range and domain of power of a 'C' over 'R' is subject to many factors. It is modified by the limitations imposed by the system within which psychiatric practice is carried out, for example the National Health Service, or the legal framework of society, especially the laws concerned with mental health. Official bodies, such as the Mental Health Act Commission, may challenge the scope and domain of medical power. According to the chairman of the commission, Lord Colville (1986): 'The essence of the Mental Health Act is that medical dominance should be diluted...'; voluntary bodies, like MIND, and civil rights organisations, such as the National Council of Civil Liberties, may do likewise.

Racism is to do with power both historically and in the present. It formed the backbone of the power of slave owners over 'Negroes' and colonial civil servants over 'Natives'; the amalgam of racism and military power enabled white Europeans to establish myths of their superiority over people in Africa, Asia and parts of America. Today, in Britain, attacks on racism are perceived by the establishment as threats to the power of the state; appeals to racism through discriminatory immigration policies are used by political parties as means of obtaining power; the response of the state to black protest is to strengthen the power of the police. Looked at from an individual's angle, prejudice in people's minds is of little concern to others unless acted out, and action is only effective if backed by power; institutional racism is innocuous to the individual if divorced from power. To a large extent, racism in contemporary British society *is* the manifestation of power of white people over black.

When racism and psychiatry come together, a highly dangerous mixture results. Race-power works its way into the exercise of psychiatric, mainly medical, power; and medical power is expressed through race. At an individual level, black professionals sometimes become confused as to their power-position since the power of the individual working in psychiatry is derived from (at least) two sources—the social unit designated as 'whites' and the professional category that he/she belongs to. As black individuals become institutionalised into the white institution of psychiatry, many assume the 'honorary white' position although few are accepted as such by their colleagues or the institution itself. But the individual's dilemma has little consequence as psychiatry functions as a discipline and social system with a tradition and way of working. As groups of professionals (i.e. psychiatrists, social workers, nurses and others) in positions of power over patients take on racially determined power-positions of society, behaving as if they are white people (even if they are not white) whenever they confront black people as patients. In other words, the black–white divide of the racist society is translated into the professional–patient divide of the psychiatric system. The exercise of professional power becomes one with the exercise of race-power. Racially biased judgements, of dangerousness, for example, passing as psychiatric or social-work judgments gain in significance and credibility because of the power of the professional status behind them. Professionals slip into seeing patients as black or white in the way that the racist society sees people in these terms.

Power in social situations may be analysed in terms of 'those conditions which create the potential for its exercise' (Ben-Tovim, Gabriel, Law and Stredder, 1986). The power of racism is seldom manifested directly in British psychiatry but certain conditions within psychiatry are conducive to it. The colour-blind approach which fails to acknowledge racism as a specific dimension independent of (say) classism and urban deprivation (Ben-Tovim *et al.*, 1986), is freely used in psychiatry: neglect of patients based on racism is identified as 'general' neglect. For example, the racist dimension of the events leading to the death of Michael Martin at Broadmoor Hospital was evident at the coroner's inquest but the verdict referred to (general) 'lack of care' only (Francis, 1985). Racist judgements of black and ethnic minority patients and punitive actions against them are frequently seen as *general* 'mis-diagnoses' or mistakes—at worst based on cultural misunderstanding—thereby avoiding the specific racist dimension in the exercise of power within psychiatry. A colour-blindness ideology linked to a liberal philosophy of 'treating everyone alike' is used as an argument for rejecting special consideration for black people when the real reason is a racist one. Racist practices at appointment committees are dismissed as idiosyncrasies of individuals and positive action is rejected as a form of preferential treatment within a colour-blind ethos.

The way of working in psychiatry, in particular the diagnostic process, is conducive to the application of racism in a scientific guise. The resulting 'psychiatrisation' of black and ethnic minorities with excessive numbers being compulsorily detained, diagnosed as 'schizophrenic' and admitted to secure hospitals has been dealt with elsewhere in this book. The status of psychiatry as a medical discipline and the power of people working in it as an institution provides a 'cover' for racism to operate unchallenged. However, the most effective manoeuvre by which psychiatry conceals, defends and maintains racism is that of 'culturising' it: Injustices and disadvantages suffered by black and ethnic minorities are attributed to their culture which causes *them* to distort illness patterns (for example by somatising psychological symptoms), make unreasonable demands (for instance by exaggerating symptoms or not expressing them) or not benefit from treatment (by not speaking a European language, by communicating in ways that psychiatry sees as 'primitive', etc.). By culturising the problem of racism, both the power structure within psychiatry and the power of white over black is maintained because the remedy is looked for in the 'alien cultures'—with all the connotations of this term used by Margaret Thatcher (cited in Barker, 1981)—and the blame for the problem is attached to *them* — the 'cultural aliens'.

RACIAL BIAS

Psychiatric practice aims at objectivity in assessment, diagnosis and treatment by standardising its techniques and methods using scientific procedures to do so. Traditionally, scientific method is associated with measurement and quantification of observed phenomena. A less restricted view of scientific method is that it is an 'approach to knowledge that satisfies two conditions: All knowledge must be based on systematic observation, and it must be expressed in terms of self-consistent but limited and approximate models.' (Capra, 1982). Techniques used within psychiatry are related to knowledge in this sense—or at least should be. However, the 'systematic observation' on which psychiatric knowledge is based is itself influenced by various models often related to schools of thought. Thus, the psychoanalyst makes observations within a particular model and the behaviourist does so within a very different one. The 'organic psychiatrist' sees illness in a strict medical model while the 'social psychiatrist' has a much wider framework for conceptualising illness. Thus, the fund of knowledge on which the practising psychiatrist draws is held in many pools rather than a sea, each pool being linked, more or less, to a way of thinking if not a definite school of thought. The technology of psychiatry consists of various tests (clinical tests and psychological tests) and ways of observing (for example the 'mental state examination') which have been standardised, to a greater or lesser extent, to render them 'objective' and to give some sort of 'measurement'. The term bias in this context refers to the meaning given to the word in *The Concise Oxford Dictionary* (Sykes, 1982) namely, prejudice, influence and distortion of results (of measurements) by 'neglected factors'—in this case those related to race. The interplay between cultural influences and those arising from racism have been referred to in previous chapters. The difficulty of separating one from the other applies to racially determined bias.

Bias in testing and observing may arise from three sources. There is bias resulting from the tester/observer, his/her attitudes, beliefs etc., but also from what the tester/observer represents in terms of (for example) role, class and race. Secondly, there is the bias inherent in the tests and observations themselves, or the way that inferences are drawn from them. Finally, the circumstances in which the tests are given or the observations made, may introduce bias. A generalisation that applies to all three sources is one of context: the training and (usually) the background of the

131

tester/observer, the standardisation and development of tests and ways of observation, and the assumptions regarding the factors that determine the results of tests or influence observations are all constructed within a Western cultural mode and racist ways of thinking about people. Thus in general terms, the extent to which psychiatric technology is 'objective' in a multicultural and multi-racial society is arguable.

Psychological Tests

In the past, clinical psychologists were 'ancillary' to psychiatry in that they provided test results for psychiatrists to use for the understanding of patients. The modern clinical psychologist is a co-worker alongside the psychiatrist. The clinical psychologist brings to the psychiatric scene special skills and ways of assessing people. A discussion of bias in psychological testing is meant to show how bias may affect the working of clinical psychology within psychiatry. Classically, psychological tests are concerned with intelligence and personality. A general criticism of using standard tests in a multiethnic society is stated in a paper on educational evaluation by Jenkins, Kemmis, MacDonald and Verma, (1979):

> Testing in the area of race raises perplexing and difficult questions about the possibility of objectivity and neutrality. Some of the explicit concepts underlying the measurement of ability and achievement, like 'intelligence' itself, involve constructs that have sprung from the demands of an industrial society (even the notion of 'adaptability', as it is used in the context of I.Q. testing, is rooted in an economic market where the ability to cope with rapid change is at a premium). If cultural and ideological perspectives are built into the tests themselves, the notion of using such tests fairly is a mystification which conceals exploitation...and there is a growing concern that non-Western cultural and ethnic groups are heavily handicapped by their in-built biases.

The authors point out that the American Association of Black Psychologists has expressed its alarm about bias by calling for a moratorium on all testing of black people 'until more equitable tests are available'.

In a recent British book Shelley and Cohen (1986) highlight some of the less-obvious errors inherent in many of the standard tests and the procedures for testing. While making a plea for 'improving well-validated tests so that norms do not discriminate against ethnic minorities or women' and arguing that the issues of 'fairness of testing' should be raised by the Commission for Racial Equality, they ignore in their book a serious defect of present day testing—namely the 'colour-blind' way in which it is carried out in clinical (and possibly educational) settings. Although the cultural bias of intelligence testing is well recognised (Anastasi, 1976), the influence of racism in testing is a subject that clinical psychologists, like most psychiatrists, seem to ignore. In that sense, clinical psychology has not moved from the position of one of the fathers of testing in Britain, Francis Galton, whose contribution to a racist ideology in Western psychology was discussed in Chapter 1.

The process of testing cognitive function is not a simple matter of measurement but invariably involves a transaction between two or more people. Characteristics of the examiner, such as gender, social class, behaviour and expectations have been shown to affect the results. Watson (1973a) quotes several reports from the mid-1930s onwards that testify to a significant negative effect on black people tested by Whites. In reviewing American research on the performance of black people in inter-racial situations, Katz (1973) identifies three models for negative effects on Blacks being tested by Whites: first, emotional reactions that are detrimental to intellectual functioning arise from the 'social threat' arising from the power and prestige of white people in society. Secondly, motivation is affected by a relatively 'low expectancy of success' induced by a 'demeaning role' in American society. Finally, the fear of failure—which he calls 'failure threat'—carrying a particular social meaning elicits emotional responses that are detrimental to performance. All these models of ways in which institutional racism affects testing are based on experimental work in the United States and may not apply in the same form in Britain. However, it is reasonable to assume that if there is a perceived racial difference involved and there is a subjective element to the testing procedure or the deduction of inferences from it, one should assume that racist value judgements are likely to affect the outcome of testing — unless of course there is an inbuilt mechanism to prevent it. Neither the subject nor the psychologist is ever 'neutral' in being uncritical (Shelley and Cohen, 1986), but when the racial dimension comes into the picture, cultural assumptions derived from racial ideologies

133

form the content of the bias. These assumptions are woven into so many aspects of social life, language and professional training that the only way of minimising such a personal bias is to curtail the extent of subjectivity in the testing procedure. However, depersonalising procedures for testing introduces its own bias. In a racist society, where black and ethnic minorities are perceived as being inferior, the lack of human contact may be perceived by them as discrimination, thereby introducing a racially determined differential—a racial bias.

Since tests of cognitive function are usually presented in terms of scores which are combined into an intelligence quotient (IQ), the question of norms is an important consideration. Clearly, if a test has been standardised in a particular cultural setting, the norms apply to that setting alone. Applying irrelevant norms is a common mistake made on the assumption that everyone should be measured on the 'ideal' of what happens in white (Western) society. Moreover, IQ tests are standardised to correlate highly with school performance and economic success, thereby building into them additional biases: 'In as much as IQ tests measure anything, they measure the likelihood of educational and social success in a particular society.' (Ryan, 1972). Apart from questions of norms and standardisation, there are more fundamental issues that cast doubt on assumptions about cognitive testing in a multiracial and multicultural society: first, the 'test event' (Erickson, 1968) must be seen in its historical and social context. The test situation, which is an artificial one for all subjects, may be more so for those who are disadvantaged—and feel so—in society. As Pettigrew (1964) states about the American scene: 'After all, an intelligence test is a middle-class white man's instrument; it is a device whites use to prove their capacities and get ahead in the white world.' When administered in a racist setting, the IQ test may be felt as a threat to someone from a non-white group, and scoring low may be a 'rational response to perceived danger.' Secondly, a particular test or group of tests may measure different qualities of 'intelligence', assuming that such a concept is useful, in different cultural settings. Irvine (1973) describes experimental studies which show that children from two different cultures perceive the same test items differently, so that 'the probability of the same score, particularly around the average, being made up from the same set of items in *both* cultures' is remote. In discussing this question of test equivalence across cultures he writes:

Intelligence tests and reading tests usually sample a number of psychological processes. Mechanical information and dexterity tests are likewise complex. The more heterogeneous a test is in its demands on processes, the more liable it is to change its meaning in other cultures. By this we mean that the mental processes that the logic of constructs compels us to assume to be necessary for problem-solving in any one culture may indeed be identical for any other. On the other hand, they may be different ...

The content of standard intelligence tests themselves have been criticised as being culturally biased, favouring the cultures in which they were devised. Irvine (1973) has distinguished a test's explicit and overt content from its implicit or covert content. The former includes 'the language the test is printed in; its modality (that is, whether it uses figures, symbols or words); its declared sampling of the abilities or skills measured by the test; its format (whether it is multiple-choice or open-ended). In short, any aspect of a test that is observable and subject to experimental control.' Both verbal and non-verbal intelligence tests are subject to implicit restraints determined by culture. The culture-bias in verbal tests is obvious, but 'the giving of a test where no words are used is no guarantee of the fairness of that test. The test merely becomes more difficult to label because the meaning of the test score for an individual from another culture cannot be easily made *explicit*.

Thus, it is not merely a matter of standardising established cognitive tests; the content of the tests needs to be derived from within the culture in which they are to be used. However, IQ tests derived in the West, and often standardised on Western groups alone, continue to be used in a culture-blind manner. Rex (1972), a sociologist, argues that 'the misrepresentations of the psychometricians' in continuing to regard IQ as an objective measure applicable to everyone 'is not simply a matter of a random "mistake" but is directly related to the beliefs of the society in which they operate.' A society that believes in the superiority of Western cultures identified with the 'white race' is apt to regard a test that is standardised to predict success for white people as the ideal. Tests continue to be used because they confirm the 'common sense' within society—the racial inferiority of black people. For example, Vernon (1969) defends the use of psychological tests in a multicultural setting on the basis that they confirm the 'everyday observations' about certain groups of people:

Although the psychologist's tests are highly inadequate instruments for bringing out the full strengths and weaknesses of different groups or individuals, particularly when applied outside the cultural group for which they were constructed, they nevertheless tend to confirm our everyday observations. Each group certainly shows variations in patterns of abilities: members of an underdeveloped country may reach, or surpass, western standards on some tests, and fall below what we would regard as the borderline for mental deficiency on others. But the average performance on quite a wide range of tests only too strikingly fits in with the observed inequalities of mankind. Similarly, within any one western country, there are obvious differences in the status, vocational and educational achievements of subgroups such as the social classes, the coloured immigrants in Britain, the Negroes and the Indians of North America; and, however open to criticism our tests of intelligence and other abilities may be, they tend to reflect these differences.

The experiences, aspirations and values of non-whites are not seen within this racist ideology as important.

There is a considerable American literature on the likelihood of racial bias intrinsic to the Minnesota Multiphasic Personality Inventory (MMPI)—a comprehensive test of personality that is particularly popular in the United States. The results obtained by many researchers 'suggest that, compared with whites, more black normals are likely to be falsely identified as deviant, and fewer black patients are likely to be incorrectly classified as normal.' (Gynther and Green, 1980). Pritchard and Rosenblatt (1980) point out that this suggestion is largely based on comparing differences between mean scores of racial groups which are assumed to have similar levels of psychopathology; they challenge this assumption and argue that the MMPI is valid in terms of its ability to predict 'maladjustment', 'schizophrenia' etc. Of course this merely means that the test is in line with other methods of assessment which too may be equally biased in the same direction, and there are no 'culture-free' external criteria for verification of this point. But, as with IQ tests, it is not merely a matter of devising norms for different groups; the totality of the test is in question. For example, although groups of black and white alcoholics produce similar mean scores on a particular alcoholism scale (MacAndrew, 1965) derived from the MMPI, this scale does not discriminate between black alcoholics and non-alcoholics while doing so in the case of

Whites (Walters, Greene, Jeffrey, Kruzich and Haskin, 1983). Much of what has already been stated about bias arising from standardisation, content, and test procedure with respect to IQ tests are applicable to personality tests—perhaps more so. Unfortunately, personality tests are generally used with little or no consideration of cultural or racial bias because, by their very nature, they substantiate stereotypes current in society and (as Vernon stated in defence of IQ tests) they confirm 'everyday observations'.

This discussion of bias in psychological testing is far from comprehensive. It may be summarised in three statements: clinical psychology, like psychiatry, is very much a part of the society that has invented it; as such, clinical psychology reflects the ideologies within that society; racial bias is inherent in its practice.

Psychiatric assessment

A psychiatric evaluation is primarily based on a patient's history, basic personality and examination of the current 'mental state'. The history is often regarded as being composed of objective facts but in reality, it is a highly selected account of whatever information has been given by the patient and others—the crucial sorting out being done by the psychiatrist. The psychiatrist influences the content of what is obtained as 'history' in two interrelated ways within the overall (variable) limitations of communication: First, the type and extent of information given by the patient and others are fashioned by the perception that the psychiatrist has of the people providing the information and *vice versa*; for example, a black patient, aware of the negative value attached to non-European marriage customs, is unlikely to tell a white doctor or social worker much about his/her marriage. Secondly, the picking and choosing—the emphasis given to one item of information as opposed to another or the meaning attached to an incident—is dependent on the beliefs, value-judgements, understanding and knowledge of the psychiatrist; for example, a psychiatrist who is a part of an establishment that does not appreciate the extent of racial discrimination in employment is likely to take down a history of persistent unemployment of a black person without qualification, i.e. as having the same significance for both black and white patients. It is in this context that Asian patients are said not to discuss their family affairs with doctors; it is the author's experience that there are no such inhibitions when the doctors are perceived by the patients as accepting and appreciating Asian family life. The author recently visited a black patient, who is well known to him, who was temporarily in a hospital in the Midlands. After discussing with her the difficulties she was having in obtaining employment, the author attended her case review. The history given by the nurse referred to the patient's failure to get a job as being caused by a 'chip on her shoulder about being black'. This is another example of how racist psychiatry distorts history-taking.

The personality of the patient prior to the onset of 'illness' is an important matter in the medical model of illness because the general aim of treatment is to get the patient back to his/her 'old self' again. The bias inherent in personality assessment by psychologists (noted above) applies to the psychiatric interview too. The psychiatrist asks questions about social relations, hobbies, mood changes, character, etc. (Slater and Roth, 1960) and makes judgements as to what might be 'normal' in terms of the patient's culture and background. Clearly, the extent to which these judgements are realistic depends on the knowledge of the psychiatrist about the patient's culture and background. More importantly, however, in the case of black and ethnic minorities, the judgements are likely to be influenced by the stereotypes in society. Since Asian women are assumed to be passive, an Asian woman patient who says very little will be judged as being 'passive'. A man of West Indian origin may well be seen as aggressive for similar reasons. In both cases, culture and race are confounded, the judgement being based on physical appearance. The particular constellation of stereotypes that influences the psychiatric judgement may vary, but in the case of black and ethnic minorities they are invariably racist; the judgements are related to 'racial' coding and carry derogatory connotations.

The 'mental state examination' is a description of the patient in terms of (the patient's) behaviour, thinking and emotional state in a form which is designed to isolate particular pathological characteristics designated as retardation, overactivity, agitation, anxiety, depression, delusions, hallucinations, thought disorder, confusion, etc. These characteristics are essentially a framework of concepts related to the definition of 'illness', derived from a mixture of direct observations and inferences about the patient's thought processes and feelings from his/her behaviour (including speech). There have been various attempts to standardise the procedure to increase reliability—the Present State Examination (Wing et al., 1974) is the best known of these. Questioning the validity of the mental state examination in terms of external criteria is a non-starter because the 'findings' of the mental state examination are not objective facts, and validity in terms of its predictive value is difficult to evaluate because of the nature of what is called 'illness' in psychiatry. However, it is the mental state examination that forms the main reason for the diagnosis of illness—'diagnosis' too being a conceptual configuration rather than an objective fact. The problems inherent in applying the concepts within the 'mental state examination' and 'diagnosis' in a multiracial and multicultural society are immense.

Depression

This is a very common diagnosis in Britain today. Like others, it is based on an assessment of history (of a person's complaints) and observations made of the patient by the psychiatrist and (sometimes) other people. At the same time, some judgement is made as to whether the person concerned is reacting in an appropriate way to personal circumstances. In observing the (prospective) patient, various aspects of behaviour and speech are noted and evaluated in order to make a judgement of his/her subjective feelings and thinking; facial expression and eye-contact are considered to be of particular significance. If the person looks 'depressed'—not just 'miserable'—seems withdrawn or appears pre-occupied, the diagnosis of depression is strengthened. The observations made by the psychiatrist are clearly judgements of someone else, based on empathy and rapport with the patient as a vehicle for communication. It is easy to see that, when the (prospective) patient and the diagnosing psychiatrist do not have very much rapport and are used to different ways of expressing feelings and behaving (especially in the context of an interview), 'findings' of the psychiatrist cannot be described as objective. Add to this racist value judgements that the psychiatrist may have absorbed from society, and a seriously misleading situation could emerge. For example, the white English doctor, who fails to appreciate the feelings that he or she has about the cultural background of a black Bengali patient, and furthermore, who has no real appreciation of the racist pressures under which the latter lives, is very likely to misinterpret the patient's behaviour, attitude and thinking quite apart from missing the causes of stress that the patient may be suffering from. Judgements are then made on surmise or guess-work, or, worse still, beliefs that arise from 'commonsense'. The patient's reluctance to expose deeper feelings or apparent suspicion of other people may be seen as symptoms of illness. In a more direct way, a person who fails to establish eye-contact is often seen as being evasive or unassertive although in some cultures averting one's eyes when speaking with someone in authority is a mark of respect.

It is well known that the concept of guilt, which is used as a hallmark of depression diagnosed in the West, is not universally valid, particularly in African and Asian cultures. But how often do psychiatrists allow for this? And indeed are psychiatrists *able* to allow for such differences when, for example, guilt is so much a part of the illness called depression? What happens in the case of guilt is that a failure to detect it is attributed to a (cultural) primitiveness or lack of sophistication in people who are perceived in racial terms as African or Asian; at best, a (so-called) depressive equivalent is diagnosed. When somatic (physical) symptoms are presented by a person who is emotionally disturbed, this is seen as 'somatisation' of psychological feelings—reflecting the ethnocentric basis of psychiatry as a discipline; concomitantly, 'somatisation' by a black person is conceptualised as an inferior way of expressing feelings—reflecting the racist bias of psychiatry. To appreciate feelings psychologically is considered to be the norm because that is the fashion in Western societies; somatic experience of feelings is seen as deviancy. Thus, although the concept of depression is widely used, its validity in a multiracial society is limited by racism disguised in cultural terms.

Schizophrenia

This is the diagnosis in psychiatry that is most likely to get involved in political and social pressures. For example, this is the diagnosis given to Soviet dissidents sent to secure hospitals. The tendency in Britain is to tighten the criteria for diagnosing schizophrenia but the over-diagnosis of black people as 'schizophrenic' suggests that the concept may be used unfairly. The judgements that have to be made by the psychiatrist in differentiating schizophrenia from other illnesses, and from normality, concern another person's thinking, beliefs and emotional reactions. The psychiatrist has to decide whether the (prospective) patient's beliefs are true or imaginary, whether the patient is thinking in an organised way, and whether emotions are blunted or in keeping with what is expected. All this is largely dependent on judging interactions between persons, usually the doctor and the patient, but influenced by society's norms which are institutionalised in education, training and so-called commonsense. It is in this context — the overall social expectation, professional training, and rapport between doctor and prospective patient—that certain symptoms of schizophrenia such as delusions, thought disorder and incongruity of affect are recognised. If the psychiatrist cannot understand why someone is suspicious, the latter is likely to be seen as paranoid. Further, rapport depends on background and affinity. In a racist society where skin colour determines the nature of one's experiences, at least as far as black and ethnic minorities are concerned, and the way people treat each other, a white person would find it difficult to feel the same way about many aspects of society and other people as a black person would. Training is supposed to make up for this type of drawback. But training does not and cannot do this when psychiatric and social institutions themselves are implicitly racist. Even when training has an anti-racist slant or incorporates an anti-racist package, everyday experience counteracts the benefits this may bring.

Psychosis

Schizophrenia is one of the psychoses; the other main one is manic-depression. The hallmark of a psychosis is the (supposed) lack of contact with reality—of the patient. In manic-depression the patient exhibits 'overactivity', undue elation, etc. at times, while at other times, he/she is profoundly depressed. A person deemed to be suffering from mania—or a lesser form of it, hypomania—is someone who is excited, and under pressure to an abnormal extent. As in many other instances the psychiatrist has to judge what is normal and abnormal for the individual in his/her particular circumstances—a matter that could be very difficult if, for instance, the individual is a black person who has been apprehended by the police. The judgement of 'contact with reality' is often based on the patient's ability to give explanations for his/her behaviour and beliefs that sound reasonable to the psychiatrist. If the latter is unable to appreciate the patient's life circumstances, such a judgement is likely to be made on the basis of assumptions which, in the case of black and ethnic minorities, may be biased in line with racist stereotypes. For example, the author has seen black patients whose religious explanations for behaviour are discounted and then their anger interpreted as 'excitement'. Thus the diagnosis of psychosis may be inappropriate because of cultural misunderstanding complicated by racist bias.

Other Diagnoses

It could be argued that, within a particular cultural and political context, the diagnosis of depression or schizophrenia or a more general designation of 'psychosis' could be a very useful label to describe a particular constellation of problems (which may or may not identify an illness in the bio-medical sense of the term). Also one could argue—and there is some evidence for this—that these diagnoses could be made in a reasonably reliable way if strict criteria are used consistently. In other words the diagnosis of depression or schizophrenia may be valid and reliable within a particular context. The same could not be said for the diagnosis of personality disorder and neurosis.

The term personality disorder is applied to a person who is found to behave, think and feel in certain ways which are judged as being abnormal without any explanation in terms of another disorder such as schizophrenia. The abnormality is recognised as being composed of deviations from hypothetical norms which are based on a body of information or general commonsense—a basis that must be ethnocentric. Psychopathic disorder is an extreme form of personality disorder where antisocial tendencies are identified. Few people see personality disorder as a disease in the way that schizophrenia and depression are viewed as diseases; and virtually nobody thinks of an organic disturbance as being the cause of it. Thus personality disorder is, essentially, a judgement on the way someone functions in society and therefore as much a reflection of society as it is of the person. Diagnosing personality disorder cross-culturally is likely to be unreliable at best but when racist attitudes complicate the process of diagnosis, highly suspect.

Neurosis is a concept allied to personality disorder in that it is diagnosed by identifying deviations from supposed norms. People who suffer persistently from symptoms of anxiety, whether somatic ones (such as headaches, palpitations or paralyses) or psychological ones (such as worries, obsessions or depressions), may be classified as suffering from neuroses of various types, for example, obsessional neurosis, hysterical neurosis, anxiety states, phobias etc. Although it may be reasonable to identify individual symptoms as neurotic ones the designation of any particular person as being 'neurotic' is probably misleading and certainly extremely unreliable. Neuroses like personality disorder should not be seen as diseases but as theoretical concepts which may be useful for discussion. Their application without a consideration of differences in norms and social attitudes in a multiracial society is extremely hazardous for black and ethnic minorities.

Dementia is a psychiatric disorder with an organic basis which could therefore be a reliable, valid and relevant diagnosis across racial and cultural barriers. But psychological tests for identifying levels of intellectual functioning and memory are not culture free and may be misleading in borderline cases. Here, as in other situations, clinical observations may be distorted by prejudiced attitudes about black people. Another point is that expensive investigations are done selectively often on the basis of cost-effectiveness; for example, if a firm clinical diagnosis is made, a brain scan may not be done unless of course the patient or the relatives make a fuss. Thus a combination of passive families, racist attitudes of staff, a biased system of health-care and cultural misinterpretation may render the diagnosis of dementia too an uncertain one for black and ethnic minorities.

Conclusion

The observations of psychiatrists based on interviews where there are cultural and racial differences between the participants of an interaction are of doubtful relevance in many cases, especially if the interaction takes place in a society where value judgements about culture and race are institutionalised. Over and above fundamental cultural differences (complicated by value judgements), there are problems of communication concerned with language and other practical difficulties in psychiatric practice. These are obvious but they are unnecessarily difficult to circumvent or resolve because of racist attitudes. Western languages and cultures are usually assumed to be superior to those which are seen as alien to Western civilisation and hence 'uncivilised' or 'primitive'. Western views of illness are held to be correct and other views are generally thought of as 'primitive' unless given a special status, for example in hyped-up guru worship or by a white person who goes 'native'. An important bias stems from the formalised, and therefore highly ethnocentric, mental state examination that is a fundamental part of the psychiatric assessment procedure. This cannot be dismantled without unscrambling the diagnostic system itself. But psychiatry today has a large investment in both and is hence unlikely to let go very easily. A way of doing so will be considered in the final chapter of this book.

SERVICES AND PATIENTS

The sensitivity of a psychiatric service to social and cultural issues is inseparable from that of its service providers, i.e. health professionals in psychiatric and social services. They are the gate-keepers who control the use of resources available to people designated as 'patients' or 'clients' through the National Health Service and the social services. Black and ethnic minorities are deprived of their rightful share of these resources because the structure and content of the services are often irrelevant to their needs or exclude them selectively through racism and cultural insensitivity at various levels. However, there are other wider issues within a service that foster racism. By projecting an image, often an accurate one, of being a racist organisation, a particular service may exclude (indirectly) black and ethnic minorities from applying for staff positions and attending as patients—since most people avoid institutions that do not want them. For example, obviously discriminatory recruitment practices or failure to appoint ethnic minorities to higher professional and administrative posts indicates a particular stance by an organisation. These are the institutions that usually claim to be 'colour-blind' in recruitment and patient care. Further, authorities may marginalise the needs of black and ethnic minorities in various ways: promoting voluntary groups—which are often under-funded—to cater for ethnic minorities and using this as a reason for not providing for their needs within the statutory services; a development officer may be appointed but not given much power, so that recommendations for the improvement of services for black and ethnic minorities get entangled in a morass of committees and rarely see the light of day; a request for change may be countered by a demand for further research and/or 'hard facts'—a demand that can be pursued endlessly; an unending dialogue may be established with the local Community Relations Council (CRC) or voluntary groups. These manoeuvres have been used in various parts of the country in response to expressed concern of black people, and they may have been highly successful in defusing overt protest. But they should be recognised as essentially racist courses of action unless they are geared to the mediation of change. Thus, if a health authority extends a helping hand to a voluntary group, the latter should offer to match and support services rather than take on their provision; a development officer concerned with services for black and ethnic minorities must have direct access to the general manager of the health district; research on needs of ethnic minorities must be 'operational research' i.e. research into the operation of services as they are being instituted.

In the introduction to a book on transcultural psychiatry, John Cox (1986) draws attention to the danger of training and educational programmes in which characteristics of ethnic minority groups, as they impinge on the provision of health care, are 'given as facts without attempting to understand the systems of cultural meaning'. The danger is that discriminatory practices are worsened. The same comment applies to education about culture without a racial dimension. Training can exacerbate cultural stereotypes and confirm racial prejudices unless it is done within a context that takes an anti-racist stance and is even-handed in considering cultural difference. Thus racism awareness training done in a racist institution is likely to worsen racism in the practices of the institution for two reasons: First, it marginalises racism as something to be dealt with as a 'course' and/or personal 'therapy', thereby strengthening the general policies of the institution; secondly, it encourages a complacent attitude among professionals who, once they have 'taken' the course, feel that their work is now free of racism, enabling them to ignore the institutional and personal racism that they continue to operate. Educational courses that deal with culture and race as theoretical concepts without applying them to real situations is a common racist practice in psychiatric training of medical staff and nursing staff. The ideally racist educational course that claims to tackle issues of race and culture is one that is held well away from the scene of psychiatric practice with no reference to real 'cases' and an emphasis on academic lectures about race and culture—preferably of an anthropological variety.

Psychiatric services in Britain are in the process of changing from the original hospital-based provisions to community-based care. Since there is a great variation from place to place in the pace of change and methods employed in changing, a particular service may have a variety of facets to it. Additionally, there is the 'social control' element in psychiatry, which means that some patients are held (as in-patients) compulsorily and others are treated informally. The over-representation of black people among compulsorily detained patients and the possible under-use by them of informal care, particularly out-patient care, is explicable in terms of psychopathology (of Blacks) or racism (of Whites and psychiatric institutions). In discussing the alternative explanations, Littlewood (1986b) seems to give equal importance to both types of

145

explanation. Although the former suits the establishment in psychiatry and society in general, most black people have little difficulty in seeing that the latter explanation must be more important in terms of practical value and natural justice.

The experience of black nursing staff in the National Health Service is analysed by Agbolegbe (1984), who reports a survey carried out within six District Health Authorities serving a population of 240,000 to 280,000 of which 18–24 per cent was made up of ethnic minorities. Although it is a pilot study for determining areas of concern, there are clear indications for both further research and immediate action: selection procedures adopted by schools of nursing seem to be racially biased with some schools being particularly racist; working relationships between white managers and black nurses are often 'oppressive', while black managers are deterred from confronting racial prejudice within the nursing profession by intimidation; there is marked discrepancy between the promotion prospects of black nurses when compared to that of their white colleagues; and there is a disproportionately large number of black nurses appearing before the professional disciplinary committee while there is no black member on this committee. Two consultants at St George's Hospital report that a computer program used for the selection of students for a medical course at St George's Hospital Medical School downgrades applicants if they are female and non-white (Veitch, 1986). A study by the Commission for Racial Equality (Anwar and Ali, 1987) into the position of ethnic minority doctors in Britain shows that nearly half the white doctors and over half those from ethnic minorities believe that racial discrimination is practised against black doctors; at least 14 per cent of white consultants consider that it is 'natural to discriminate' in this way. In discussing the findings of a survey of overseas medical graduates practising psychiatry in Britain, Bhate et al., (1986) comment on the racial discrimination that occurs in appointments to senior psychiatric posts in the National Health Service. The extent of racism within the disciplines of social work and occupational therapy is unlikely to be very different from that in the medical and nursing professions, except perhaps that some local authorities have begun to tackle the problem of racism within social service departments, and there is a marked paucity of black occupational therapists perhaps because of selection policies of the schools of occupational therapy.

The experience of black patients within the psychiatric service has some similarities to the experience of black staff within it. Just as black staff may be seen as lacking those qualities needed for leadership, patients who are racially identified as 'alien' (by colour of skin) are perceived as having inferior family patterns and personalities. Just as the positive qualities in the background and training of black staff are ignored, patients who are perceived as being from non-Western cultural backgrounds (because of the colour of their skins) are seen as culturally deficient and unable to benefit from 'sophisticated' methods of treatment such as psychotherapy. Just as black staff who show signs of protesting against racist practices are seen as 'difficult' or lacking in self-discipline, black patients are often stereotyped as hostile and dangerous. This brief resume implies that racist practices are determined by misperceptions and unconscious discrimination. But this is not usually the case and racism has to be examined in a socio-political perspective of institutionalised practices and the reality of their social advantage for white people. Discriminatory practices result from ways in which the services are organised—selection procedures, points of comparison for promotion, etc. (in the case of staff) and diagnostic processes, selective criteria for types of treatment, indicators of 'dangerousness' etc. (in the case of patients). Racism may have direct advantage for the dominant (white) population in that, for example, the exclusion of black staff from management, and the easing out of black patients from time-consuming types of 'sophisticated' treatment modalities or their labelling as (psychiatrically) dangerous, allows white society to continue its dominance.

The racist stereotypes of the Asian and Afro-Caribbean patient that pervade British psychiatry were referred to in Chapters 1 and 2. In general, British stereotypes of the patient who is perceived as non-Western (usually on the basis of colour) are similar to the American ones for black patients described by Sabshin, Diesenhaus and Wilkerson (1970): 'Hostile and not motivated for treatment, having primitive character structure, not psychologically minded, and impulse-ridden.' These, and other, stereotypes that result in racist practices within the psychiatric service are not just in the minds of psychiatrists and other staff; they are woven into the fabric of the institution of psychiatry and ways of working of the discipline through its history and ideology (Chapter 1) and the 'psychiatric machinery' underlying diagnosis and treatment (Chapter 2).

The effect on the individual patient of racist psychiatric practice has not been documented in a systematic manner. An attempt to do so by the Black Health Workers and Patients Group (1984) loses impact by its presentation within, or rather as a part of, a political philosophy that sees racism and psychiatry as aspects of state oppression of the 'working class'. Furthermore, it may be argued that the cases presented by this group represent generally 'bad practice' rather than racist psychiatry. It is when apparently good practices, or practices that are not particularly 'bad', are at the same time racist that society is duty-bound to pay attention. The author has selected three cases, known to him personally, as examples to illustrate such instances. The histories are given in abbreviated form with some deliberate distortion in substance and changes in names and dates designed to obscure the true identities of the people concerned.

The first case is that of a man of Turkish origin from North London.

Hassan was aged twenty at the time of admission to hospital after being brought there by his uncle. He had a history of one previous episode of illness within the previous one year; this had been diagnosed as 'hypomania' and he had been treated as an in-patient for three months with drug therapy followed by family interviews. The same diagnosis was made on this second admission with the additional observation that he had an 'imma-ture personality and family conflicts'. He was treated with medi-cation but disappeared from hospital on the day after admission. Later, he was apprehended by the police in an alleged stolen vehicle and remanded in a remand centre. He was transferred to hospital under an order of the Mental Health Act a week later. His symptoms of overactivity, 'flights of ideas and pressure of speech' improved over the following three weeks during which time he was treated with medication, but he remained very angry at being detained compulsorily in hospital. He was re-graded to informal status and his anger abated. He talked of the abuse and physical violence that he had experienced at the remand centre. He began to abuse members of staff and made a general nuisance of himself by interrupting group sessions and other activities. At this point, the question of his dangerousness was raised by staff who were not closely acquainted with him. His reputation spread around the unit and there were several episodes when he fright-ened members of staff by seeming to threaten violence without actually hurting anyone physically. He was then known to be associating with a female nurse living in the nurses home within the hospital grounds. In the face of demands by senior members of staff that doctors should 'do something' to quieten Hassan since he was a patient, the consultant in charge of his case discharged him from hospital and arranged out-patient attendance, thereby establishing clearly that Hassan was not in need of in-patient care and not in need of compulsory treatment. Further complaints by members of staff that Hassan had frightened them were reported to a meeting of senior staff. Since the consultant did not consider that his behaviour amounted to dangerousness caused by illness, the hospital administration took out an injunction restraining Hassan from entering the hospital grounds. Meanwhile, the hospital consultant arranged for Hassan to be treated at home by a community nurse and social worker with a combination of medication and counselling. He gradually let up on his antagonism towards the hospital staff. His medication was tailed off and discontinued about nine months after his admission and he declined further visits from the community nurse.

The racism that affected the patient in this case centred on his alleged dangerousness. He was frequently referred to as 'that Turk'. And 'turk' is defined in the *Concise Oxford Dictionary* (Sykes, 1982) as 'ferocious, wild, or unmanageable person' as well as 'native of Turkey'. The problem was conceptualised by the majority of senior staff of all disciplines as being located entirely in the patient, and consisting of *his* behaviour and *his* antagonism to staff. When the author, as consultant in charge of the case, attempted to widen discussion, his explanations were discounted once the patient's Turkish origin was evident. It was mainly white staff who were seen as being in danger and statements by black staff—such as the community psychiatric nurse, the charge nurse of the ward and the doctor—that the patient was not dangerous were seen as biased. The patient's behaviour in scribbling anti-white graffiti on walls were seen as hostile acts towards the institution and his dating of a white nurse perceived as a threat to it. In this instance, institutionalised racism interacted with the fears that are typical of institutions—the fear of established authority being challenged and of traditional ways of working being undermined. Thus the institutional reactions were essentially 'normal' and normal in being racist.

The second case is that of a woman from a Punjabi family settled in England for many years.

Reka was aged twenty six when referred to a psychiatric hospital, known to the author, and admitted at her request. She had arrived in England with her family of origin about ten years earlier. She then worked in a factory but disliked her place of work because of colour prejudice. Her parents arranged a marriage for her when she was twenty-one and she accepted it. About two years after her marriage she became hostile towards her husband. She was diagnosed as being depressed and paranoid and treated in a psychiatric hospital for three weeks. The marital relationship remained unstable but the couple stayed together and their first child was born when she was twenty-six.

At the time of admission Reka was miserable and complained about racial discrimination and about her husband's (alleged) infidelity. She was treated with marital counselling and later given a small dose of a tranquilliser. She left, dissatisfied, and later left her husband to stay with her parents. She was referred back soon after she returned to her husband and the couple were seen jointly in conjoint therapy. It was then noted that she had strange experiences that may be delusional and she was given medication too. She was referred one year later and noted to have symptoms that were 'frankly schizophrenic'. She was prescribed medication but was admitted compulsorily after she had gone to the police station in despair. She was treated with regular medication and improved considerably. She remained well on medication but stopped it when she became pregnant two years later at the age of thirty-two.

Reka was referred back for psychiatric assessment when her younger child was nearly two years old and the patient thirty-four. Compulsory treatment was recommended but not pursued after a social worker managed to persuade her to accept medication. However, this did not last and she was admitted compulsorily under the Mental Health Act nine months later. A diagnosis of paranoid schizophrenia was made. She refused medication and appealed (against her detention in hospital) to a Mental Health Review Tribunal. The Tribunal discharged her from hospital. She went to stay with her parents and (unmarried) brother. About five months later she died as a result of a violent altercation with a member of her family.

In this case, the staff had difficulty in deciding whether Reka was suffering from an illness, i.e. paranoid schizophrenia, or reacting to marital disharmony. Many of the white staff tended to see the marriage as inherently 'bad' because it was an arranged match. Therefore they tended to identify with the patient's apparent wish not to be married and dwell on the issues she raised about the marriage, thereby failing to understand her wider difficulties and concerns, in particular the alienation that she felt in society. However, the sort of intervention that was attempted over nine years made little or no impression on her sense of dissatisfaction with the marriage. When, ultimately, an 'illness' model was applied and compulsory powers enforced to detain her in hospital for treatment, a new group of people came on the scene: the (entirely white) members of the Mental Health Review Tribunal perceived her presentation to them in a colour-blind way. They sympathised with her apparent wish to be free of the husband arranged for her by her parents and her expressed intention to be 'independent'. Their arrogance is evident in the failure by the tribunal to interview any of the family members before coming to a decision; in fact her husband was specifically told that he need not attend the hearing. While their emphasis was on the autonomy of the patient, there was an implicit assumption that her (Asian) family of origin was there for her to go to—and that *that* was where she belonged. Reka was treated 'like anybody else' with all the assumptions about black and brown people held in white society.

The third case is that of an Afro-Caribbean man from London.

Lester was born in England about ten years after his parents had migrated there from the West Indies. His adolescence was marked by considerable conflict with his parents. He had a struggle at school where he felt that teachers did not give him adequate credit or encouragement and his parents never took his side when he reported this to them. Soon after failing the first year of a course at a polytechnic, he was charged with assaulting a bus conductor who, Lester claimed, insulted him first. He was sent to Borstal for two years but was noted to be behaving oddly and then admitted to hospital with a diagnosis of schizophrenia. During the next 2–3 years he was in and out of hospital care, either as an in-patient or day-patient, for 2–6 months at a time with breaks of similar periods. He was then sent to a hostel located at a considerable distance from his home until he moved to one near his home.

Lester was 23 when he moved to live in the second hostel. He was soon found to be exhibiting himself sexually to females. His tendency to do this was known but had not been a problem previously. However, the extent of this behaviour increased as the members of staff at the hostel became increasingly concerned about it. A consultant psychiatrist who discussed the problem with the staff noted that they had various unfounded fantasies of what Lester might do to (white) female members of staff. Since Lester was reasonably intelligent and his 'schizophrenia' was under 'control' with medication, he was referred to a psychotherapy centre for treatment. He was turned down as being 'not suitable for psychotherapy'. After various attempts to deal with his 'exhibitionism' had failed, Lester was expelled from the hostel. It was noted at the time that Lester was the only black resident of the hostel and that the one black employee, a cook, had left because of alleged racist abuse. Later, Lester was admitted to hospital after an apparent 'relapse' of schizophrenia. Once again this was treated successfully with medication. Since no hostel would consider him, Lester applied to the Housing Department of the Local Authority for a flat. After considerable pressure from professional staff insisting on his rights, the Housing Department yielded. He now lives in the community and shows little or no signs of schizophrenia although the exhibitionism seems to be continuing.

All statutory authorities in this case professed, both implicitly and explicitly, to have dealt with Lester in a colour-blind fashion. No one service can be faulted specifically over any particular decision made. The result was a highly racist service being provided for a black person. While the staff at the hostel sincerely liked him and gave him an 'honorary white' status, they continued to see his 'blackness' in terms of sexual fears (of rape and violence) although, when challenged, everyone agreed that Lester was not dangerous. The decision to expel him was rationalised as being in *his* interests. The psychotherapist clearly saw him in terms of a stereotype, as did the Housing Department. His alienness as a Black played into the perception of Lester as an alien to society. Ironically, and tragically, his parents too were drawn into the overall ethos of the service-providers and wanted him locked up.

Racist practices in the context of 'bad practice' are easier to detect than those within seemingly 'good' practice. However, the three cases described above exemplify the importance of examining ordinary, and seemingly good, practice. Ordinary services carried out by ordinary, honest and decent people can be racist for several reasons: racism is embedded and institutionalised in the methods and training of professionals; little, if any, thought is given to the counteracting of racism in psychiatric practice; and it is assumed that 'good practice' is automatically non-racist. Racism in psychiatry occurs in different ways in different settings. This chapter points to a few of these.

6

The Race– Culture Argument

INTRODUCTION

Earlier chapters of this book have referred to various aspects of culture and race. The aim of this chapter is to examine the confusion between the terms 'culture' and 'race' in everyday psychiatry in Britain today. The concept of culture is generally used very loosely in practical psychiatry. A person's upbringing, childhood environment, or family life may be designated as his or her 'culture'. Thus, psychiatrists may refer to a person's culture being different to another person's culture; or they may identify one family culture as being different from another. Following on this, various aspects of family life or upbringing, or even the entire life-styles or life-experiences of certain individuals or families, may be identified as 'cultural factors' which are involved in the genesis of specific illnesses or conditions perceived as 'pathological'. Thus, a standard British textbook of psychiatry, *Clinical Psychiatry* (Slater and Roth, 1960) makes the following generalisation in one of the few references to culture: 'The prevalence of alcoholism appears to be markedly affected by social and cultural factors. In under-developed countries and among individuals living within a simple culture, drunkenness is generally agreed to be rare...' Culture as a part of someone's background is generally seen as influencing the 'content' of illness (as perceived within the medical model) by reflecting beliefs and practices of the individual; but the extent to which culture is seen as determining 'form' of illness—the 'symptoms'— is variable. In whatever way that culture is seen as affecting illness, it is seen essentially as distorting the illness; 'true illness' is conceptualised as being 'free' of culture.

Psychiatrists also use the term culture in a different way. When a psychiatrist is confronted with an apparent deviance of behaviour or feeling (in an individual), the question may be raised as to whether it is 'pathological' or 'cultural'; the former denotes the possibility of an illness while the latter suggests that the person's background or family context is causing the deviance. This is a particularly ethnocentric use of the term 'culture'; it implies a culture that is alien to that of psychiatry—other people's culture, non-Western culture. It is easy for 'culture' seen in this way to slip into being seen as pathological in itself: cultures that are 'different' become cultures that are problematic (to people outside the culture); when 'problem' cultures are associated with people who are perceived as racially inferior, the concept of pathology arises within the context of the medical model.

The use of the term 'culture' in ordinary psychiatry is further complicated by the fact that Freud used the term as synonymous with 'civilisation' (Freud, 1927); and Freud believed firmly in the supremacy of Western civilisation (Hodge and Struckmann, 1975). This connotation to the term culture is reflected in the use of the term in reference to, for example, 'a cultured person', and is the opposite of the connotation when psychiatrists use it to denote pathology.

The term 'race' is usually used in psychiatry with a biological meaning carrying the implicit assumption that people are different genetically on the basis of their colour. Thus, Slater and Roth (1960) discuss differences in suicide rates between black and white Americans as 'race differences'. But, psychiatrists in Britain are generally reluctant to talk about 'racial' issues since, to do so, would seem (to them) to acknowledge colour prejudice if not racist behaviour on their part. The social construction of race (Brittan and Maynard, 1984) is seldom, if ever, appreciated in psychiatric circles.

In a multicultural society where racism is prevalent, cultural issues are not easily differentiated from racial ones. Consider, for instance, a psychiatric interview where there are cultural and racial differences between the participants. This is an interaction taking place within a certain power relationship and where value judgements about culture and race, that are institutionalised and generally accepted, affect the outcome. For example, the white English doctor may be ignorant about the cultural background of a black patient but still carry definite views about it—views derived from the doctor's culture and linked to racial images; add to this the likelihood that the doctor lacks any real appreciation of the patient's life circumstances, in particular the racist pressures impinging on the latter, and the outcome is a serious misinterpretation of the patient's behaviour, attitude and thinking quite apart from a failure to detect the causes of stress that the patient may be suffering from. Furthermore, the patient's reluctance to expose deeper feelings or apparent suspicion of other people may be seen as symptoms of illness and the patient's unwillingness to accept the doctor's judgement as a sign of unsophistication. The breakdown in such an interaction is to the disadvantage of the patient because of the power relationships inherent in the situation. Such a set of circumstances is common in practical psychiatry and may appear to be a cultural problem. But what is the real difficulty here? Is it the (white) doctor's lack of knowledge of the patient's culture or the doctor's view of that culture—based on Western tradition, the 'commonsense' of society, cultural assumptions or whatever. Or is it the way in which both individuals are 'set up' by society—by the racism in society that gives different values to different cultures, thereby enabling white people to feel superior to blacks etc.? Perhaps both ignorance and value judgements play their part at an individual level, but the larger social scene is really to blame for giving rise to the mistakes that the doctor might make. In any case, it is difficult to designate the problem as one of culture or race exclusively.

Straightforward, and seemingly obvious, misperceptions which arise when specific behaviour patterns are misinterpreted by psychiatrists have been designated as 'cultural pitfalls' in the recognition of 'illness' (Rack, 1982). For example, a person who fails to establish eye-contact may be seen as being evasive or unassertive although, in some cultures, averting one's eyes when speaking with someone in authority is a mark of respect. Is this type of misperception culturally determined? Is it a cultural problem? If so, whose problem is it? In such instances, the problem is perceived as the black person's problem determined by his or her culture. It does not make any difference which side of the fence the black person is on—whether as patient or doctor—the problem remains with the (black) colour. Is it purely ignorance that leads to misperception or is it the fact that the behaviour of an Asian or African or West Indian is seen as inferior, and therefore abnormal or not sufficiently evolved, that is the problem? It is difficult sometimes to identify the real problem. Many books on transcultural psychiatry tend to dwell on the cultural aspect of this sort of problem. But if it is purely cultural, why is it that the problem is mainly to do with people with black or brown skins? It seems easy enough to allow for this sort of 'cultural problem' when it concerns white Americans, white Australians, or even white South Africans whose ideas are supposed to be so different from those of the white British. Are these problems then cultural with racist undertones or racist with a cultural presentation?

The presence or absence of certain symptoms, such as guilt or somatic complaints, are often interpreted in a context that confounds cultural and racial matters. Biased diagnostic processes in psychiatry (described in Chapter 5) result in ethnocentric concepts feeding into racist thinking, so that culture and race become intertwined. Research papers reporting that people from underdeveloped countries are 'found' to be unable to discriminate between different types of emotion (Leff, 1973) and that Blacks (so-called 'West Indians') are 'found' to deal with distress by 'cheery denial' rather than depression (Bebbington et al., 1981), were described earlier (in Chapters 1 and 2). These myths are getting into psychiatric literature as 'facts' because of the way in which 'facts' are made in psychiatry—the process described in Chapter 5. For example, the chapter by Lloyd and Bebbington (1986) in a recent British textbook (Hill, Murray and Thorley, 1986), which according to its foreword represents the 'Maudsley approach' i.e. the 'knowledge' imparted to trainees at the Institute of Psychiatry, quotes Leff (1981) uncritically in arguing that 'there has been an evolution of the ability to express and differentiate emotions', so that 'people from traditional cultures tend to express distress in somatic terms and fail to distinguish between the emotions of anxiety, irritability and depression' while 'we in the industrial West have learned to make these distinctions and have developed a language to accommodate a subtle diversity of emotional experience expressed in psychological rather than somatic terms.' Are these cultural 'facts', expressed so patronisingly, really about culture or are they racist statements where the word 'traditional' is used as a euphemism for 'non-European' (identified racially by skin-colour)?

What happens in practice (how the 'facts' emanating from biased research 'findings' are actually used) depends on the context in which psychiatry functions. A psychiatry that fails to recognise the racism within it or takes no action to counteract that aspect of its own culture, must inevitably succumb to the common practice of using the term 'culture' as a cover for racist conduct. Thus, cultural difference is 'pathologised': in everyday discussion, 'cultural' behaviour is the name for the behaviour of people who are perceived as (racially) inferior; differences in emotional expression or differentiation are seen on an evolutionary scale with 'industrialised' Whites being higher than 'traditional' Blacks; illness presentation in Whites is assumed to be the standard against which deviant forms (of illness) seen in black and ethnic minorities are analysed as being pathoplastically distorted by their ('deviant') cultures. Overall, racist statements about cultures and people are wrapped up as observations about culture or 'transcultural psychiatry'. Since psychiatry does this, is there any point in attempting to separate culture from race in psychiatric theory and practice? In discussing a similar dilemma in the realm of public policy Ben-Tovim *et al.* (1986), state:

> The tendency to focus on 'ethnic' culture *per se* does serve to shift the emphasis of discussion onto minority groups themselves; the quaint and the exotic as well as the alien and the pathological characteristics of their culture. Predictably and correctly many have come to regard this form of analysis as a diversion from, and by implication an abdication of, institutional responsibilities for inequality. Although we accept the thrust of these criticisms we do believe that it is both possible and necessary to develop a knowledge of culture which neither pathologises the group in question nor eschews the reality of racism.

Thus in psychiatry too, while recognising the situation for what it is, some attempt has to be made to disentangle race and culture, at least at an individual level, in order to seek a way forward. It is proposed to do this by considering one against the other as a text within a context.

CULTURE IN THE CONTEXT OF RACISM

The reality and importance to practical psychiatry of cultural differences between groups of people are easily apparent. The aim of this section is to examine, in broad perspective rather than in detail, the extent to which cultural knowledge can influence the practice of psychiatry in a multicultural society while allowing for the racist context in which psychiatry functions.

The practice of psychiatry in Britain can be considered at two levels: the personal (professional) practice of psychiatry by psychiatrists at the individual level and the (social) practice of psychiatry through an arrangement of services to provide help, care and treatment. Individual practice is mainly within a 'medical model' where assessments lead to diagnoses and treatment; the cultural dimension affects each stage of this process. But many psychiatrists working in the National Health Service indulge in a less formal approach, seeing their function as one member of a multidisciplinary team bringing help to people, families and communities that are in need. The current organisation of psychiatric services is characterised by three basic ideals: first, there are the concepts of 'sectorisation' and 'multidisciplinary teams'; a catchment area served by a psychiatric service is divided into 'sectors', each containing about 60,000 people and served by a team of mental health professionals liaising with social workers and others working in the community. Secondly, there is the concept of 'community care'; the aim is to deploy professional staff in such a way as to deliver services (i.e. provide treatment) to patients without admission to hospital. Finally, the concept of 'the least restrictive environment' for an individual being treated for mental illness; the intention is that restrictions on personal liberty are avoided and only resorted to under clearly defined conditions that are subject to strict legal checks.

Individual psychiatry

The problem that arises in an individual psychiatrist's encounter with a patient of a different culture to himself/herself may be evaluated as follows: an honest psychiatrist in this situation must recognise the need to view the patient in terms of the latter's culture. In doing so, the psychiatrist has to recognise and understand the barriers to communication that may arise from the cultural difference. First, there are the (psychiatrist's) personal prejudices about the patient's culture usually reflecting images and ideas present in society at large; secondly, there may be a linguistic problem; and finally, the psychiatrist may be deficient in knowledge and information about the patient's culture with resulting misconceptions and misinterpretations of emotional responses, ways of thinking and behaviour. The first of these barriers is largely to do with racism, while the other two may also have racist connotations.

Therefore, the psychiatrist's primary duty is to confront racism by understanding its nature in society at large and the extent to which the discipline of psychiatry itself is involved in it. It is then, and only then, that the psychiatrist is ready to grapple with the cultural aspects of the encounter. In fact the problems presented by cultural difference are then not likely to be very great.

Once barriers to communication determined by racism are broken down, the information about (the patient's) culture can be obtained from the patient without too much difficulty—although of course knowledge derived from extraneous sources can help. It would then seem natural to evaluate the culture of the patient in the way that other aspects of the patient's life are considered. Cultural information is then no different from any other information that the psychiatrist obtains, from the patient, his/her family or society at large. However, using this knowledge in a constructive and imaginative fashion may be difficult.

In the normal course of psychiatric practice the psychiatrist would naturally use concepts of morality, behaviour and ways of relating that he/she is used to, as a standpoint from which to judge the extent to which a person's feelings, behaviour etc. are acceptable as being within 'normal' limits. A knowledge and understanding of the patient's culture may give a very different perspective; but, however much the psychiatrist tries to objectify observation, some degree of intuitive assessment enters into the formulation that is made. In a cross-cultural encounter, the intuitive element has to be diminished to a minimum. The patient's own interpretations have to be taken in conjunction with those of his/her relatives and others familiar with the culture when an assessment is being made. The psychiatrist has, as it were, to stand apart to start with, and then feel his/her way into the patient's culture to make the judgements that are necessary. Exactitude in diagnosis is less important than the need to establish rapport and evaluations in terms of 'problems'. When rapport is being established, an understanding has to be reached with the patient and (possibly) members of his/her family in an ambience of cultural equality and sensitivity. Since the psychiatrist uses ethnocentric concepts of 'illness', both for his/her own convenience and as a vehicle for communication, some trouble has to be taken to allow for different concepts that may be held by the patient and his/her family. Ideally, some compromise has to be found between explanatory models of illness (Kleinman, 1980b) relevant to the culture that psychiatry springs from, and those relevant to the patient's culture. Clearly, cultural difference *per se* need not be a hindrance in establishing communication; in fact a qualitatively better, more beneficial, rapport may well be established in an encounter where there is a cultural difference compared to one where everyone concerned is very similar in cultural background. The main pre-requisite is the overcoming of cultural arrogance and establishing, and conveying, genuine concern.

In evaluating the forms of treatment to be used, the psychiatrist needs to start by seeing their meanings through the culture of the patient. Once this is done, the value of the treatment should be evaluated in terms of the patient's explanatory model (of illness). The final result, in the framework of the 'medical model' used by psychiatry, should be that the psychiatrist and the patient, with a variable involvement of the family, comes to a joint (compromise) arrangement for treatment. The assessment of progress during treatment must be sensitive to the viewpoint of the patient and people who are in tune with the (patient's) culture.

Multidisciplinary teams

A team of people from different disciplines brings to the client variety in terms of professional training and experience. Clearly, this team must be equipped to establish proper communication with clients and to understand their cultural setting and background. This presents relatively little difficulty in the case of populations that are culturally homogeneous, European and English-speaking. But when ethnic minorities are present, especially including people who do not speak English very well, the team needs to be multicultural and, perhaps multilingual, as well as being multidisciplinary. This is difficult to establish because of racism—often in the very places that it is most needed. For example, it is a commonly observed fact that senior staff of all disciplines in the psychiatric services in inner boroughs of London, served by highly prestigious teaching hospitals, are white Europeans although populations in these areas contain relatively high proportions of black people. Meanwhile, black professionals are relatively commoner in outer suburbs of London, although less so in senior positions, where health service posts are considered less prestigious, although the populations there contain lower proportions of ethnic minorities. The need to think in terms of cultural needs of the population served by a multidisciplinary team requires employing authorities to confront racism in the first place. If and when this is done effectively, the cultural considerations should become obvious and manageable. Then, cultural matching of the multidisciplinary team will not seem such an emotive subject and becomes a natural part of service planning.

The aim of cultural matching is to facilitate communication, provide information about cultural background and enable helpful relationships to develop. A good verbal understanding between the professional staff and the people served by the team, in a background of clear and accurate information about them, is essential for proper assessments to be made so that the correct help may be offered. The team should aim at providing, within it, proficiency in most of the languages spoken by the population it serves. However, communicating is not just a matter of language and making a relationship does not depend simply upon clarity of information available. The most important blocks to establishing good rapport arise from the inability of professionals to cut through racial stereotyping by accepting people as individuals and from the misinformation that arises from biased images of non-European people and their cultures that pervade society.

Community care

Many psychiatrists and other professionals working in the National Health Service see the aim of community care as delivering services where the community lives, rather than in institutions 'cut off' from it geographically. This approach to community care, which may be called the traditional approach, is the usual basis for current planning as described (for example) by Leff (1986b). It presupposes that the present (largely institution-based) services are basically sound and beneficial to the communities they serve, and that they are 'transportable' for re-location in 'the community'. On the other hand, some people take a radical view to see the concepts of 'community care' as being very different from the concepts underlying the present psychiatric service; they see professionals working in a community service responding to needs of communities without analysing individuals in terms of 'illness', promoting mental health instead of dealing with mental illness, and using technologies such as drug therapy, behaviour therapy and psychotherapy very sparingly, and then only to bolster up natural support systems in community life. Unfortunately, neither model has integrated into itself the social realities of community life of minority groups, especially those of ethnic minorities living in inner cities of Britain. If the traditional psychiatrists are serious in wanting to make psychiatry more accessible to those who need it, psychiatry itself must become relevant to the needs of all races and all cultures; if the radical approach is looked at from a racial and cultural viewpoint, the first impediment (to health) that must be removed is racism. The reality that is developing, in practice, is a hotchpotch of services which vary from place to place in their theoretical bases and practical detail; the final result in any one location is likely to be influenced by financial expediency more than by the needs of the community, and by the politics of inter-professional rivalries as much as by the co-ordination of effort by professionals in the mental health field. Inevitably, the exercise of power plays an important role in decision-making; therefore, the influence of ethnic minorities is very limited. Although the need to consider the cultural differences in the communities for which services are being planned is often accepted, the importance of tackling racism is seldom confronted. It is the view of the author that whatever 'community care' may mean in practice, racism has to be confronted before its cultural dimension can be properly dealt with.

A service that is close to a community must inevitably be influenced by the way that community functions. Therefore, if psychiatry is involved in community care, it must be 'cultural'. In a multicultural society it must be multicultural. People have to be seen as individuals in their diverse cultural settings and subject to different social pressures. Community services need to be organised in different ways for different cultural groups. As clients/patients tend to stay in their homes (rather than being admitted to institutions) while relating to the psychiatric service, the types of intervention practised by professionals have to be adapted to suit the cultural norms of clients/patients. The changing pattern of psychiatric services provides a chance for psychiatry to change; the need for it to absorb the cultural dimension and relate it to service provision cannot succeed without a recognition of the racist context in which the changes are taking place.

Restrictions on liberty

Any patient who is compulsorily detained under the Mental Health Act (1983) is subject to restrictions on liberty. In attempting to devise ways of avoiding such restrictions, two questions arise. First the reasons for a differential application of compulsory powers under the Act resulting in a relative over-representation of black people among those detained; and secondly the question of assessing dangerousness of patients diagnosed as suffering from mental disorder. The evaluation of cultural aspects of these questions must first take account of the part played by racism in both matters. Littlewood (1986b) has discussed the first question in an academic paper analysing alternative 'patterns of explanation'. But an analysis of this sort fails to incorporate real-life experiences of black people who can easily recognise, in their everyday lives, the racist attitudes in society that are reflected in the workings of the Act. A similar situation exists with regard to perceptions that underlie the assessment of dangerousness. Although psychiatric assessments of dangerousness are unreliable (Steadman, 1983), psychiatrists continue to make predictive judgements on this matter. The racist images prevalent in society about black people must feed into the bases of these judgements since they must inevitably be a reflection of prejudices of individuals and the 'commonsense' of society. If racism is removed from the line of action that determines compulsory detention and the prediction of dangerousness, it is doubtful whether any cultural considerations would be necessary in examining the ideal of treating patients in the least restrictive environment.

RACIST PRACTICE IN THE CONTEXT OF CULTURAL DIFFERENCE

The extent of racism in British society is the measure of its extent in psychiatric practice. The way racism works in the practice of psychiatry must be seen within the overall social context of society, in particular, the multicultural nature of British society. The aim of this section is to consider the ways in which racist practices are legitimised as cultural practices. A book written for practitioners (Rack, 1982) contains a series of chapters each of which has a title starting with 'Cultural Pifalls' and continuing by referring to the recognition of depression and anxiety, mania, schizophrenia, paranoia, and hysteria; these chapters are preceded by the chapter 'Culture and Concepts of Mental Illness' and followed by the chapter 'Culture-Bound Syndromes'. This approach to culture represents the way in which the cultural dimension is usually adopted by practical psychiatry. Cultural difference (from the culture that psychiatry has developed in) is seen more as an impediment to the recognition of diagnoses rather than a matter that has to be incorporated into the diagnostic system. The psychiatric practitioner is supposed to learn how to avoid the 'pitfalls' in getting to the diagnoses that psychiatry has defined. But diagnoses are really concepts devised by psychiatry for particular purposes to suit particular cultures; they are not natural conditions that have been 'discovered' but rather devices that have been 'invented'. Further, non-Western cultures are seen as exotic—and *so* exotic in some instances that they are supposed to generate 'culture-bound' syndromes that are beyond understanding in some way. It is not surprising that the 'pitfall' approach to the place of culture in psychiatry coupled with the exoticism attached to African, Asian and indigenous American cultures leads to a psychiatric practice that is often racist in the guise of being 'cultural'.

Most racist practices in British psychiatry do not claim to be cultural, but they are justified (if challenged) as (allegedly) traditional, sensible, scientific, or fair by being 'colour-blind' or by a mixture of two or more of these reasons. For example, the application of diagnostic criteria devised in a particular cultural setting arising from ideologies, philosophies and life-experiences of white Europeans such as the Present State Examination (PSE) (Wing *et al.*, 1974) may be seen as 'scientific' as well as 'sensible'; but, apart from being anti-cultural it is distinctly racist. When the relatively excessive compulsory detention of black people as patients is interpreted on the basis of 'commonsense' or 'scientific' reasoning in terms of 'explanations orientated to the black patient' (Littlewood, 1986b), the racist connotations of this fact are ignored. The underrepresentation of black people in senior positions in the mental health services is often ignored on the grounds of being fair, or explained as being a consequence of tradition—again ignoring the racism in the appointment procedures.

Racist practices carried out under a cultural label are particularly pernicious because they appear to be based on 'understanding' and culture-sensitivity. Diagnostic difficulty arising from cultural difference may be used as a reason for negating the need for treatment in the case of black people. For example the author is aware of a black woman who presented to her doctor complaining of hearing voices which she attributed to spirit possession. Although this excited the doctor's curiosity into the 'exotic' presentation, the underlying distress of the patient was ignored for a considerable time. The doctor, in this case, saw himself as unable to understand or help. The author is aware of many equally 'unusual' presentations by, for example, Italian people without evoking that sort of response from a doctor. Similarly, when (for example) a black client says to a (white) social worker 'you don't understand me', the latter is likely to respond by confirming the client's contention; in the case of a white client the response may be to examine the client's statement on the assumption that the social worker *should* understand. In both these instances, the stereotypes and assumptions are based on racial images. Since they are interactions in a power structure of white over black, reflecting that in society at large, the 'problem' is one of racism masquerading as one of culture.

Cultural arguments are used to justify racism in the provision of services. Since black people are viewed as somatising their emotional problems and preferring physical treatment to psychological treatment, the relative overuse of electroplexy and underuse of psychotherapy as treatment modalities are justified on 'cultural' grounds. Quite apart from the lack of reliable evidence to warrant this widespread notion held in psychiatry, the perception of black people is that white professionals, as well as many black professionals trained in 'white institutions'; are disinterested in listening to 'problems' of black patients and only take note of precise physical complaints. The underlying difficulty of white professionals to relate to Blacks at an emotional level is often a result of the influence of racism in distorting their perceptions of Blacks— although, again, cultural explanations are usually given for this too. The (alleged) tendency of Asian families to be closely knit is often used as a 'cultural' reason for not providing services to them in time of need. The (alleged) hostility of Afro-Caribbeans to the psychiatric and social services is used as a reason for professionals from these services not getting too involved with them. In each instance, 'culture' is a cover for the racist service that results. Cheetham (1982) has described how racism at institutional and personal levels results in unnecessary reception into care of black children. A less obvious matter is the failure by social and psychiatric services to provide black families with help on the grounds that the (white) professional staff cannot understand their cultural ways and that intervention is culturally inappropriate. Thus, sometimes, child neglect by black parents is overlooked and excused and families are allowed to suffer on the basis that they are being allowed to live according to their 'culture'. The result is a racist service based on expediency with 'culture' as an excuse.

The culturally sensitive psychiatrist or social worker needs to be sensitive to racial issues, in particular the racism that is enmeshed within the normal practices of the two professions. In analysing her experiences of working with black women, Ahmed (1985) states:

> In social work there tends to be an uncritical reliance on cultural theories and culture-based explanations of behaviour, which frequently stop short of a more fundamental analysis which might be crucial in explaining the actions of minorities. It is significant that family disruption and breakdown are seen simply in terms of the innate deficiency of a culture, and the next critical step towards structural explanation is not taken.

An emphasis on culture, however well-intentioned, may lead to a racist approach in practice. Ahmed concludes the paper quoted above by emphasising the danger of 'cultural studies which lack a political analysis' and the need for a system that 'incorporates the centrality of racism in the assessment and treatment process.'

CONCLUSIONS

The attempts in this chapter to differentiate (from each other) culture and race indicates that there is a serious confusion in the way these words are conceptualised and used. In practical terms of service provision, the need is for the understanding of the issues involved: 'cultural factors' are inevitably and inextricably bound up with racism since the society is racist, views about culture transmitted in training are racist and psychiatry has a racist heritage with a power structure that is racist. Therefore, the identification of racist practice, and its elimination, is the primary need. Understanding the 'cultural dimension' of psychiatry is important too, but it is unrealistic to try to do so without incorporating the fact of racism. Furthermore, the promotion of cultural sensitivity without challenging racism may result in the reinforcement of racism by masking it and thereby inducing complacency. For example, the denial of racism in appointing white staff with training in culture-sensitivity to senior posts with responsibility to organise services for black people, when black staff are available at lower levels, provides a 'cover' of culture-sensitivity and good intention which postpones equal opportunity for staff *and* patients.

Disentangling culture and racism at the level of personal interaction is less difficult than doing so at a more general level. The first problem here is an individual one: the professional has to understand the nature of his/her race attitudes and prejudices, then to fathom the depths of racism in the social processes of society, and finally to grasp the ways in which racism is entangled within the theory and practice of psychiatry, in particular its central position in diagnosis and assessment. Once this problem is overcome, the professional is in a position to draw on knowledge of cultural differences and benefit from training in methods of incorporating this knowledge into psychiatric practice. Then, 'cultural factors' may be analysed; a culture-sensitive approach may be used for making psychiatric assessments; and cultural judgements made about the patient.

7

A Blue-print for Change

INTRODUCTION

The cultural heritage of psychiatry, the fallibility (in a cross-cultural context) of the diagnostic and assessment process within the discipline, the ethnocentricity of treatment processes used by psychiatry, and the racism that is active within it, have together created a situation that excludes black and ethnic minorities in most parts of Britain from the full benefits of a psychiatric service that should be accessible to, and appropriate for, the whole population. A change in this situation requires changes in professional practices and in the nature of psychiatric institutions. If the change is to last, society itself has to change. The purpose of this chapter is to examine changes in psychiatry that are both feasible and practicable without necessarily postulating significant changes in society. But changes in established institutions and professions do not occur spontaneously. They have to be initiated and worked at; aims have to be formulated and strategies devised. Psychiatry is both a discipline and a (social) institution. Changes in the way that the discipline fulfils its functions must come from psychiatrists primarily, but pressures to reform may come from other sources. Changes in psychiatry as a (social) institution may be effected through various means although psychiatrists and other professionals working in the field need to be involved in implementing them.

Since the argument for change arises from disadvantage, changes that are required may be seen as means to combat disadvantage. This (usual) approach leads on to examine the groups (of people) identified as being disadvantaged and to evaluate the nature of their handicaps. But there is a serious drawback in doing so: the study of ethnic minorities in this way is likely to reinforce the racist perception that the problem is in *them*. Another common approach is to increase the awareness of professionals to racism, through race-awareness courses (for example), and to cultural issues, through specific training courses. But this approach too may accentuate the real problems of ethnic minorities by (for example) diverting attention away from the central issue of racism in professional institutions and training. The rule then, in considering change, is to keep alive—at the top of the agenda for change—the central issues concerned with racism while, at the same time, analysing, evaluating and effecting changes at various levels.

At present, psychiatry is closely bound up with the society in which it functions. In considering ways of changing psychiatry so that it operates in a fair and just manner in a society that is not fair and just, the first strategy is to separate psychiatry from the direct influence of society, particularly the forces of control. With such a 'de-politicisation' of psychiatry, it would be in a position to evolve strategies to combat racism within it. While this is being done, the discipline needs to incorporate the lessons (however meagre) of cross-cultural research, primarily by redefining the concepts underlying diagnosis and reforming the practical use of the diagnostic procedure. This would enable psychiatry to incorporate cultural and racial dimensions into its practices and to develop ways of ensuring that the experiences of black and ethnic minorities are reflected in its theory and practice. Although the changes that are recommended in this chapter derive from a consideration of racial and cultural issues, their impact is not particularly of sectarian advantage. They are likely to improve the practice of psychiatry as a whole, to benefit all consumers of the service, and improve the standing and self-respect of all professionals involved in it.

DE-POLITICISATION

The strategies suggested in this section should be seen as an exercise in preparing the ground for change. They are directed at psychiatry as a professional discipline and as a social institution; they are given as suggestions, against a discussion of the background within which psychiatry functions in Britain.

Profession of psychiatry

The profession of psychiatry is under the influence of social pressures that restrict it to traditional ways of working, tie it to supporting the *status quo* in society and involve it in colluding with
racism. The Royal College of Psychiatrists (RCPsych.) is concerned with the standards and status of the profession and controls
the training of psychiatrists. The members and fellows of the college belong to 'divisions' and/or 'sections'; each division covers a
geographical area and each section a 'special interest' or subspe-
cialty such as child psychiatry, forensic psychiatry, and community
and social psychiatry. The RCPsych. is the organisation that is normally consulted when the views of the profession of psychiatry are
sought at an official level about psychiatric services or professional
matters concerning psychiatry. Strategies to free psychiatry sufficiently so that real changes can take place, must seek to enlist the
support of the RCPsych., or rather, to break through the 'dynamic
conservatism' (as described in Chapter 2) of the college representing that of the profession itself. The main aim, however, is to
mobilise the forces in society that may support change and to lead
psychiatry into becoming a force for reform. The following is a
possible plan of action:

> Those psychiatrists who are members or fellows of the RCPsych.
> and are dissatisfied with its present role combine to form a 're-
> form group' within the college with specific aims, including the
> confrontation of racial and cultural issues. This group to seek
> recognition within the established structure of the college, out-
> side its 'sections' and 'divisions'.
> The College be called upon to appoint a committee with a wide
> brief to consider the practice of psychiatry in a multicultural and
> multiracial society. This committee to include representatives
> from statutory bodies, such as the Mental Health Act
> Commission and the Commission for Racial Equality, semi-pro-
> fessional organisations such as the Transcultural Psychiatry
> Society, and some voluntary groups representing interests of
> patients.

If these suggestions, or similar ones, are implemented, the way
should be open for the profession of psychiatry, led by the
RCPsych., to face up to the challenges of the present time by
confronting current issues, particularly racism, both within the

profession and in its dealings with patients. If the RCPsych. does not prove able to give this lead, progressive psychiatrists may have to combine with other groups of professionals to devise strategies to by-pass the College.

Institution of psychiatry

The question of devising strategies for detaching the practice of psychiatry within the National Health Service (NHS) from conditions that prevent or restrict changes in its functioning is one of pragmatic politics. The psychiatric services in Britain, which are a part of the NHS, is funded by central government through the Department of Health and Social Services (DHSS). Each District Health Authority (DHA) organises its own (district) service with a variable degree of liaison with departments of social services which are funded and controlled by local authorities. The health care policies for a district are determined by both central advice, or instruction, and local decisions made by a (political) body of appointed people—the members of the DHA. In addition, a managerial system was introduced in 1985 to establish (with slight variations) a line of management, and authority, stemming from the General Manager of the NHS, through Regional General Managers, District General Managers and Unit General Managers to Service Managers for Psychiatric Services. Meanwhile, there are two national bodies directly responsible to the DHSS, which inspect individual (district) psychiatric services: The Health Advisory Service (HAS) and The Mental Health Act Commission (MHAC). The former examines each district service as a whole; the latter was established in 1983 as a special health authority to carry out certain specified functions on behalf of the Secretary of State. The functions of the MHAC are limited, at present, to helping (legally) detained patients and reporting on their care (Jones, 1985). The members of the MHAC are appointed by the Secretary of State from the three main groups of professionals concerned with psychiatry, namely (medical) psychiatrists, (psychiatric) nurses and social workers, supplemented by solicitors and some lay members.

There are two features of the institution of psychiatry within the NHS that must be noted: it is wedded to a system of medical, as opposed to social, care by being a part of a service organised to deal with 'illness'; as a result, its power base is largely in the hands of psychiatrists taking a medical role, and its practical organisation is strongly influenced by models of care analogous to those of general medicine and surgery. Secondly, the consumers of the service have very little power, either in terms of public pressure or influence on those who control services, when compared to consumers of other segments of the NHS. The author proposes, therefore, that administrative changes should have two aims: A separation of the psychiatric service from the totality of the NHS and the provision of a voice in its control for potential consumers. Since it is unrealistic to consider major alterations in the organisation or funding of health and social services, the following approach is one possible way of effecting these changes:

A Mental Health Agency (MHA) be established in parallel with the NHS, with a similar management structure to it and relating to it at all levels. The funding of the MHA at a district level be supplied by both central government and designated local authorities, being paid into a common pool. Thus, each district, or group of districts, in conjunction with one or more (appropriate) local authorities to have an independent local MHA managed by a (local) Manager (equivalent to the present Service Manager for Psychiatric Services), responsible to the General Manager at the DHSS. The Health Advisory Service (HAS)—with a permanent membership representative of the professions involved in psychiatry as well as consumers—become a Mental Health Advisory Service (MHAS) to advise the General Manager of the MHA, and appoint local Advisory Services to advise local Managers. Special provision be made for the representation of ethnic minorities on all advisory bodies. The Mental Health Act Commission (MHAC) continue its present functions but be re-organised to enable it to voice clearly the concerns of people liable to be detained under mental health legislation. In order to implement this, individual members of the MHAC be overtly designated to represent particular issues concerning detention— including the over-representation of black people among those detained—and/or particular organisations or groups of patients.

The changes envisaged above should enable psychiatry, as an institution within the NHS, to become amenable to the influence of its consumers either directly or through people nominated to speak on their behalf. Further, it should be able to widen its base into becoming less 'medical' and more 'social' gaining a direct input from social services without losing the benefits of a medical input.

These, or similar, changes would free psychiatry from some of the constraints that prevent it from responding to current needs arising from racial and cultural issues.

ANTI-RACIST STRATEGIES

Professional psychiatry

Since racism has extensive ramifications within the profession of psychiatry at various levels, diverse strategies are required to combat it. However, action in particular carefully selected areas may result in changes that spread through the system (of psychiatry): these 'sensitive' points are identified (by the author) as the organisation and methodology of psychiatric research, the editorial policies of learned journals, staff appointments to senior posts, the diagnosis of schizophrenia, compulsory detention, the estimation of dangerousness, and a policy about psychiatry in South Africa.

Research

At present, research in Britain is often carried out and reported in a 'colour-blind' mode, ignoring the reality of racism (based on colour) that (a) influences research findings by its effect on researchers and their methods of study, and (b) forms a source of stress to black and ethnic minorities. Furthermore, researches on black and ethnic minorities are structured and reported in such a way as to reinforce racist concepts about black people. Therefore:

> Grant-giving organisations and ethical committees that consider psychiatric research projects to have a policy on race and culture. Such a policy, drawn up in consultation with professional people with a knowledge of racism and cultural issues in British society to include guidance on methods of allowing for racist misconceptions and cultural differences, the usefulness or otherwise of particular lines of research, and the qualities necessary in researchers who are deemed suitable to carry out the research. They should ensure that all research projects that involve black and ethnic minorities take on the racial dimension in terms of its effect on researchers' attitudes and misconceptions determined by the racist context of society, and, the fact of racism as a major cause of social stress to black people.

174

There is at present a dearth of psychiatric research that addresses the serious concerns of black people in Britain. It is known to the author that ethical committees tend to prevent such research being carried out. Furthermore, professionals who carry out such research are frequently misrepresented as being politically motivated. Cultural research fostered by anthropologists obscures the problems of ethnic minorities by avoiding the racial dimension of their experiences in Britain. Therefore:

> A proportion of funds that are earmarked for psychiatric research be directed towards research into racial and cultural issues in psychiatry. Hospitals and research establishments to formulate a policy on research into cultural and racial issues. This policy to reflect the needs of the service and current concerns in the community on the basis of 'equal opportunity'. All ethical committees to have a race adviser with a brief to advise on all research projects and on general ethical matters.

If the strategies outlined above work out, a research body to direct and formulate research into racial and cultural issues in psychiatry may become feasible. Such a body should be independent of professional organisations and independent of university departments; it should concentrate on matters that are identified as important to black and ethnic minorities and should contain a major input of staff from these communities.

Publications

The system used for selecting papers for publication is ostensibly fair, but in practice tends to be highly biased. Therefore, the editors of important journals wield a (hidden) power through a form of censorship. The type of publication accepted for a particular journal is often based on tradition but also influenced by the choice (made by the editor) of the referee to whom the paper is sent for an opinion and, indirectly, the status of its author. Very few papers on cultural and racial issues are published in British psychiatric journals. This may reflect the traditions of the journals, the dearth of black editors, or a general lack of papers on racial and cultural issues. Furthermore, some of the papers that have been published recently are racist and misleading, although written by eminent authors. Therefore:

175

Each major psychiatric journal, in particular the *British Journal of Psychiatry* to solicit papers on racial and cultural issues in psychiatry. The editor to specify a policy of rejecting papers with racist views and to instruct referees to examine papers from this angle. Each journal to take positive action to recruit referees interested in racial and cultural issues in psychiatry, drawing on members of organisations that represent the views of ethnic minorities. Finally (as noted later) all psychiatric journals to stop publication of papers submitted from South Africa unless they are statements criticising the system of apartheid psychiatry in that country.

Professional appointments

Racism within the profession of psychiatry has not yet been condemned by its professional body the Royal College of Psychiatrists. When one of its members, Dr J. E. Olive, was found by an Industrial Tribunal to have made racist remarks about another member of the college at an appointments committee held in Cambridge in October, 1984 (Anwar and Ali, 1987), the College took no action. Reports of racism in the appointments of nurses (Agbolegbe, 1984) and the selection of medical students (Veitch, 1986) are merely the tips of icebergs in all the major professions that are concerned with psychiatric services. Although many health authorities have agreed to an equal opportunities policy, there is little evidence of their effectiveness with regard to appointments to senior posts in any of the professions within psychiatry. It has been noted that very few senior staff in districts served by London teaching hospitals are from ethnic minorities (possibly because these posts are highly sought after), although the populations served by them have a relatively large proportion of ethnic minorities. Therefore:

The Royal College of Psychiatrists to establish a policy on race, instruct its representatives on appointments committees to take positive action in pursuing anti-racist policies, and combine with other professional bodies in formulating a course of action to eradicate racism in the admission to training courses and to professional appointments in the psychiatric services. Meanwhile, health authorities to examine their current policies on equal opportunity in employment, monitor the effectiveness of the policies, and make changes in the light of deficiencies. Further, health authorities servicing areas with a significant proportion of black and ethnic minority communities to devise a policy on employment to ensure that the ethnic mix of senior psychiatric staff are similar to that in the population they serve.

The establishment of non-racist employment policies for senior staff appointments in the psychiatric services would have far-reaching effects. The resulting anti-racist stance of psychiatry would result in changes occurring naturally to take account of cultural differences in patients and racist pressures on them. Once there is recognition of the importance of racism in the lives of black people and the strong policies necessary to combat it in practice, the need to have black people in senior staff positions in order to present psychiatry as a service that is credible to black people, will be obvious.

Schizophrenia

The over-diagnosis of schizophrenia among black and ethnic minorities is well established (Chapter 3). The ways in which this may come about were discussed in Chapter 5. It is one possible explanation for the over-representation of black patients among compulsory admissions to hospital (Harrison *et al.*, 1984). The diagnosis of schizophrenia implies a loss of contact with reality if not a state of 'madness'. Discussion of racist perceptions (of professionals) that contribute to this diagnosis often hinges on the question of 'mis-diagnosis'; the implication is that, if 'mistakes' arising from cultural misunderstanding are rectified and the correct principles of diagnosis are applied, the diagnosis is justified. However, this is not necessarily the true picture; while a diagnosis of schizophrenia may be a correct application of normal (psychiatric) practice, it may be inappropriate, or even unjust, in certain circumstances. The question therefore is not only about the correctness of the diagnosis but about the way its application to black people often does them harm. The diagnosis may both cover up and legitimise the (social) extrusion of black people from society by psychiatrising their problems—just as the legal system does so by criminalising them. Strategies to deal with the over-diagnosis of schizophrenia must confront the question of racist (mis)perceptions of black people as well as the wider issue of the use that is made of the diagnosis. Therefore:

The diagnosis of schizophrenia to be unacceptable unless the person making the diagnosis demonstrates clearly that adequate weight has been given, during the process of assessment, to the effects of racism in society and to cultural background of the patient; if cultural difference is recognised as significant and/or racism is deemed to play a part in the life situation of the prospective patient, a full account is given of possible social and cultural interpretations of his/her behaviour, emotional reactions and thinking. The diagnosis of schizophrenia to be used as a medical designation but not as a reason for estimating 'dangerousness' or as a reason for compulsory admission to hospital.

Pressure on psychiatrists to justify the diagnosis of schizophrenia and to make socio-cultural evaluations would result in a general questioning of the meaning of diagnosis and a highlighting of possible social explanations for 'illness'. In separating diagnosis from the consequences of diagnosis in terms of compulsory treatment, some protection is given to black and ethnic minorities who may suffer from the effects of inappropriate diagnoses. Strategies aimed at further protection from a misuse of psychiatry are suggested in the next section.

Compulsory detention

In a recent book on psychiatric institutions, Gostin (1986) states the view that the diagnosis of mental disorder alone is not sufficient justification for admission to hospital: 'There must be reasonable certainty that the individual will not simply receive custodial care in hospital but active treatment and rehabilitation.' He argues the need to prevent society from 'using psychiatry as a form of benign or preventive confinement that is, detention which is based, not on what a person has done, but what he *might* do in the future.' In the case of black and ethnic minorities, society goes further; the psychiatric service seems to be used as a means of covering up the control of black people as an adjunct to the prison service. Therefore, Gostin's suggestion that the treatability criterion for compulsory detention as set out in Section 37(2) of the Mental Health Act (1983), which, at present, applies to psychopathic disorder, and should apply to all types of mental illness, is insufficient to protect black people. Therefore:

The treatability criterion to apply to all compulsory admissions, supplemented by a 'suitability' criterion which takes into consideration the cultural characteristics of the patient, the total environment of the hospital including its staffing structure, and racism in society. Thus, compulsory admission to hospital to be possible only if the hospital is considered suitable for a patient whose diagnosed illness is considered treatable. The Mental Health Act Commission to draft guidelines for the evaluation of 'suitability' in consultation with organisations concerned with black and ethnic minorities. Each health district to monitor 'suitability' of establishments in its own district and ensure equal access to services in keeping with race relations legislation.

If the criteria of 'treatability' (of illness) and 'suitability' of institution providing the treatment are introduced into The Mental Health Act (1983), society's 'soft-option' of using psychiatry, and psychiatrists, to conceal the predicament of black people in a racist society will be eroded. This may result initially in further 'criminalisation' of blacks, but will benefit everyone in the long term because it is likely to increase the credibility of psychiatry and enable it to join hands with social forces striving for justice and fairplay.

Dangerousness

Assessments of dangerousness by psychiatrists are critical concomitants of compulsory hospitalisation and medical reports on offenders for the courts. The decision to impose secure conditions as a part of a hospital order for treatment (of someone diagnosed as mentally ill) is largely dependent on psychiatric assessment of his/her dangerousness. However, the accuracy of 'clinical' judgement (of dangerousness) by a psychiatrist is doubtful (Steadman, 1983) — probably no better than the judgement of a layman (Bowden, 1985)—even without taking account of racial and cultural issues that may affect it. Gostin (1986) quotes the observation of (British) lawyers dealing with mental health cases that 'doctors working in closed establishments such as prisons or special hospitals, are much more likely to recommend secure conditions as part of a custodial sentence than would, say, a general practitioner or a psychiatrist in a district general hospital or in a local mental hospital'. He makes the point that 'dangerousness is not a constant, fixed personal characteristic'. People may 'pose a risk at certain times and in response to certain situations but not in others.' In one of the very few studies on the use of dangerousness as a concept, Harding and Adserballe (1983) found that the reliability of the assessment (of dangerousness) was as low among psychiatrists as that among professionals other than psychiatrists; the overall level of agreement being under 50 per cent for

179

three-quarters of the cases considered. Moreover, psychiatrists tended to rate patients as more dangerous than did the non-psychiatrists. Thus, it is all too likely that psychiatric assessments of dangerousness merely reflect 'commonsense', possibly over-estimating the level of dangerousness; commonsense is based inevitably on images of violence current in society and reflected, or fostered, by the media, educational materials etc. Stereotypes described in Chapters 1 and 2 come into play catching black people in their web. A strategy to break it is crucial if psychiatry is to develop any credibility among black and ethnic minorities:

> Dangerousness to be assessed on the basis of a body of information (about the person being assessed) in which a general psychiatric view is only one part; this information to include episodes of observed violence, rather than assumptions about behaviour, and a full knowledge of the person's life circumstances (particularly those at the time when violence occurs) and culture, evaluated against a background of social conditions including racism. Questions of 'mental disorder' to be considered as a separate issue from dangerousness. Specialists to be appointed to advise courts on questions of dangerousness, while multidisciplinary research on the topic is fostered as a matter of urgency.

Once the assessment of dangerousness is separated from psychiatric evaluation, there is some chance for society to develop objective measures of dangerousness for particular purposes. Psychiatry too may eventually gain in objectivity.

South Africa

Psychiatric services for black people in South Africa were documented by an official delegation from the American Psychiatric Association (Stone *et al.*, 1978):

> Our investigations convinced us that there is good reason for international concern about black psychiatric patients in South Africa. We found unacceptable medical practices that resulted in needless deaths of black South Africans. Medical and psychiatric care for blacks was grossly inferior to that for whites. We found that apartheid has a destructive impact on the families, social institutions and the mental health of black South Africans. We believe that these findings substantiate allegations of social and political abuse of psychiatry in South Africa.

Action by British psychiatry against the Society of Psychiatrists of South Africa (SPSA), which colludes with racist psychiatry, would not only bring pressure for change in that country (Jewkes, 1984), but also indicate to black people in Britain where they stand. Therefore:

> The Royal College of Psychiatrists to establish and then implement an immediate and firm policy of breaking all cultural and professional links with the SPSA until such time as the SPSA takes positive action to discipline its members who condone torture, collaborate with apartheid and fail to speak out against the persecution of blacks. The policy to entail the refusal of papers from South Africa submitted to the *British Journal of Psychiatry* except for those attacking the racist system of psychiatry there, and a call on its members to desist from visiting that country except for campaigns against apartheid.

If the action on South Africa is taken resolutely, the credibility of the profession among black people within Britain is likely to be enhanced. If, on the other hand, it is half-hearted or absent, the profession will continue to be suspect of itself harbouring racist leanings.

Institutional psychiatry

Changes within the profession of psychiatry are likely to take time to implement. It is therefore important to devise strategies to influence psychiatry at an institutional level. Equal opportunity policies in employment have been accepted by many District Health Authorities but their implementation is often not monitored. In focusing on service provision, it is necessary to highlight the deficiencies of the psychiatric services in providing for the needs of black and ethnic minorities. Therefore:

> Adequate monitoring of equal opportunity policies be instituted in line with the recommendations issued by the Commission for Racial Equality (CRE). Each health district to examine the suitability of its services in terms of ability to provide for the needs of ethnic minorities in its catchment area. In so doing, a consumer survey be undertaken, an appraisal be made of the training of professionals, and a measure taken of the ethnic

181

balance of its workforce. Further, each health district to monitor the use of psychiatric services in terms of the ethnicity of its users. Any discrepancies in uptake of services be investigated in conjunction with the monitoring of ethnic suitability (of services).

The ethnic monitoring of compulsory admission to hospital and the provision of second opinions for compulsory treatment necessary under the Mental Health Act (1983), is being pursued currently by the Mental Health Act Commission (MHAC). A directive from the Department of Health and Social Services (DHSS) to District Health Authorities to cooperate in this matter would ensure progress. A Health Advisory Service (HAS), reconstituted in the way suggested earlier (in the previous section of this chapter) should be in a position to supervise monitoring of the services as a whole, if backed by a directive from the DHSS.

Monitoring alone is obviously insufficient to ensure that black and ethnic minorities achieve equality of access to services that are suitable for their needs. Therefore:

The Service Manager for psychiatric services in each District to report on the provisions for ethnic minorities and be personally responsible for correcting any discrepancies that are evident. Further, the head of each professional group in each District to report on the action taken to ensure cultural sensitivity of professional practice and to exclude racist practices.

The combination of strategies to change professional practice and to bring pressure to bear on institutional psychiatry should point psychiatry in an anti-racist direction. Cultural issues may then be addressed.

INCORPORATION OF CULTURE

Some of the practical lessons of cross-cultural research, and the resistance of psychiatry to incorporating these, were discussed in Chapter 3. But there is some chance of these lessons being assimilated into psychiatric practice once racism is confronted by the profession and the institution of psychiatry. The incorporation of the cultural dimension requires, first and foremost, a new approach to the concept of diagnosis. A way of disentangling psychiatry from its involvement with social control, thereby enabling psychiatry to function to the benefit of all racial and cultural groups, may then become evident.

Psychiatry cannot function without a diagnostic process but it does not need to adhere to its traditional approach in regarding psychiatric diagnoses as equivalent to diagnoses of medical illnesses. A psychiatric diagnosis should be seen as a part of a statement about a patient in a social context rather than a designation for an attribute or peculiarity within the patient. Used in this way, the value and use of a diagnostic label must vary according to the particular circumstances of the case. It will always say something about the person making the diagnostic statement (the psychiatrist), the person about whom the statement is made (the patient), and the social context in which their interaction occurs. The balance may tilt in any direction: if totally 'objective', it would be a valid description of some aspects of the patient; if completely 'biased', it would be an expression of the psychiatrist's prejudice(s); if it is essentially a reflection of social context, it would be a statement about the conditions in the person's family and /or society at large. In most instances, a diagnosis is influenced from all these directions. In this light, the nosology of the diagnostic system is a matter of convenience rather than a question of correctness. The use of the various diagnostic terms have to be agreed upon; research into the 'existence' (or otherwise) of entities, such as depression, schizophrenia and personality disorder, becomes redundant. The nomenclature is a sort of language or aid to communication. The patient does not 'have' depression, schizophrenia or personality disorder; he/she may appear to someone in a particular place and at a specific time as a schizophrenic, depressive or personality-disordered individual. But, to another person, at another place or time, in different circumstances, he/she may be entirely different.

Once the diagnostic process is loosened in this way, the practice ✗ of psychiatry will change: instead of looking for illnesses in individuals, psychiatrists will concentrate on the needs and problems of their patients; a problem-orientated approach to patient assessment will emerge. The issues in psychiatry too will change: for example, arguments about 'somatisation' will disappear since the main focus of attention in assessment will be on the estimation of distress rather than the discovery of symptoms to designate as illness. The 'detection' of schizophrenia will no longer be important and the use of psychiatric terms, such as 'schizophrenic', as adjectives to describe people will be clarified. In such a setting, cultural considerations will enter into psychiatric evaluation quite naturally–not as 'cultural factors' or as questions of normality, but as a part of describing people. The need for cultural and social clarification, including an appraisal of racism in the community, will become obvious very naturally. Moreover, the cultural problem will be evident as a dissonance that involves both psychiatrist and the patient in an environment that does not differentiate cultures in terms of worth. This differs from the cultural clarification that is sought after at present in a traditional psychiatric approach; for example, a diagnosis of the presence of (the 'entity' called) depression in an Asian patient may be examined in terms of the 'presentation' of illness, i.e. symptoms, and 'cultural factors' affecting the way 'it' (the illness) may have 'developed'. In highlighting the context in which the diagnostic statement is made, a loose and non-medical approach to diagnosis will bring to the fore the importance of the overall culture of each individual and the social pressures that influence the person's life. Thus, once a new approach to diagnosis is established, a need to understand cultural and social issues, including racism, will enter psychiatry without any pushing.

By converting (psychiatric) diagnoses into a non-technical descriptive terminology, the mystery that surrounds them at present will be dissipated. The social effects of diagnoses, when applied to people, will then be very different. For example, if a (schizophrenic) person is no longer perceived as having something pathological within the mind called 'schizophrenia' (which, distorts, or renders 'abnormal' various aspects of functioning and personality), his/her thinking, behaviour and emotions are not invalidated; personal integrity and social status are maintained. An anti-racist psychiatry that is open in its diagnostic position will become a force for reform in society. It will be able to identify with the needs of the individual irrespective of race or culture, disregarding the *mores* of the society at large, which are likely to continue to be racist. The role of psychiatry as an institution for helping, rather than controlling, people wi!l be established. It will then be in a position to break its present alliance with the state in maintaining social control, to challenge the power structure in society and to become a truly 'helping' profession and agency.

CONCLUSIONS

The blueprint for change is presented as a practical proposition. It is a broad outline of aims, strategies and expectations that are feasible and reasonable to expect from a profession that claims to deal with human suffering and a society that has accepted into its statutes, legislation to combat racism and provide equality of opportunity to its citizens irrespective of race. The recommendations arise naturally from the subject matter of the first six chapters of the book which dealt with issues of race and culture as they impinge on the theory and practice of psychiatry in contemporary British society. Three stages are described in the process of change. The freeing of the profession of psychiatry and its institutional counterpart from its present subservience to general forces in society is a necessary first step. The strategies for 'pushing' psychiatry into taking an anti-racist stance are designed to break down some of its traditional conservatism, so that psychiatry could synchronise its activities with the needs of society as a whole and its consumers in particular. Finally a new approach to diagnosis will enable psychiatry to absorb naturally the lessons of cross-cultural research and become sensitive to social issues, including racism.

The changes envisaged in this chapter would strengthen the profession and institution (of psychiatry) bringing it into the nineteen-eighties. But, since the struggle against racism in British society may well continue for a long time, psychiatry must continue to be sensitive to racial issues. It must take seriously the social realities of life in Britain for black and ethnic minorities. Theoretical models for dealing with racism must emerge from practical experience of confronting it. Psychiatry must establish a dialogue with black and ethnic minorities, seeing them as individuals and families in their own right, speaking their language, learning their customs and meeting their needs. The details of doing so is for the profession and the institution to work out. But clearly, psychiatric education and training will have to change, theory and practice will need to incorporate the social experiences of all sections of the community, and not just that of white Westerners, and treatment will have to be geared to the new concept of diagnosis. In all this, once psychiatry is established to practise independently of social forces that oppress minority groups, this independence must be jealously guarded.

References

Abse, D. W. (1966) *Hysteria and related mental disorders*, John Wright, London

Ackerknecht, E. H. (1943) 'Psychopathology, primitive medicine and primitive culture.' *Bulletin of the History of Medicine, 14*, 30–67

Agbolegbe, G. (1984) 'Fighting the racist disease.' *Nursing Times, 18*, April, 18–20

Ahmed, S. (1985) 'Cultural racism in work with women and girls.' In S. Fernando (ed.), *Women: Cultural Perspectives*. Report of Conference organised by the Transcultural Psychiatry Society (UK), TCPS (UK), London, pp. 3–13

Allport, G. (1954) *The nature of prejudice*, Doubleday, New York

Althusser, L. (1965) *For Marx*, Verso, London, (Quoted by Banton, *et al.*, 1985)

Altschule, M. D. (1965) *Roots of modern psychiatry. Essays in the history of psychiatry*, Grune and Stratton, New York

Amdur, M. K. (1944) 'The dawn of psychiatric journalism.' *American Journal of Psychiary, 100*, 205–16

American Psychiatric Association (1980) *Diagnostic and statistical manual of mental disorders, DSM-III*, 3rd edn, APA, Washington DC

Anastasi, A. (1976) *Psychological testing*, 4th edn, Allyn and Bacon, London

Andreou, M. (1986) 'Mental health and the Cypriot minority in Enfield', Dissertation for BA (Hons.) Degree, Middlesex Polytechnic, Enfield, Middlesex

Anwar, M. and Ali, A. (1987) *Overseas doctors: experience and expectations. A research study*, Commission for Racial Equality, London

Arthur, R. J. (1973) 'Social psychiatry: an overview.' *American Journal of Psychiatry, 130*, 841–9

Babcock, J. W. (1895) 'The colored insane.' *Alienist and Neurologist, 16*, 423–47

Bagley, C. (1971) 'Mental illness in immigrant minorities in London.' *Journal of Biosocial Science, 3*, 449–59

Banton, M. and Harwood, J. (1975) *The race concept*, David and Charles, London. (Quoted by Husband, 1982)

Banton, R., Clifford, P., Frosh, S., Lousada, L. and Rosenthal, J. (1985) *The politics of mental health*, MacMillan, London

Barker, M. (1981) *The new racism*, Junction Books, London. (Quoted by Ben-Tovim *et al.*, 1986)

Bavington, J. and Majid, A. (1986) 'Psychiatric services for ethnic minority groups.' In J. Cox (ed.), *Transcultural psychiatry*, Ch. 7, Croom Helm, London, pp. 87–106

Bean, R. B. (1906) 'Some racial peculiarities of the Negro brain.' *American Journal of Anatomy, 5*, 353–415

Bebbington, P. E. (1978) 'The epidemiology of depressive disorder.' *Culture, Medicine and Psychiatry, 2*, 297–341

——Hurry, J. and Tennant, C. (1981) 'Psychiatric disorders in selected immigrant groups in Camberwell.' *Social Psychiatry, 16,* 43–51

Beiser, M., Winthrob, A. B., Ravel, J. and Collomb, H. (1973) 'Illness of the spirit among the Serer of Senegal.' *American Journal of Psychiatry, 130,* 881–6

Ben-Tovim, G., Gabriel, J., Law, I. and Stredder, K. (1986) *The local politics of race,* MacMillan Education, Basingstoke, Hampshire

Benedict, R. (1935) *Patterns of culture,* Routledge and Kegan Paul, London

——(1942) *Race and racism,* Routledge and Kegan Paul, London

Bernal, M. (1987) *Black Athena. The Afroasiatic roots of classical civilisation,* Vol. 1, Free Association, London

Bernard, J. (1966) *Marriage and family among Negroes,* Prentice-Hall, Englewood Cliffs, New Jersey

Bethlehem, D. W. (1985) *The social psychology of prejudice,* Croom Helm, London

Bevis, W. M. (1921) 'Psychological traits of the southern Negro with observations as to some of his psychoses.' *American Journal of Psychiatry, 1,* 69–78

Bhate, S., Sagovsky, R. and Cox, J. (1986) 'Career survey of overseas psychiatrists successful in the MRCPsych Examination.' *Bulletin of the a Royal College of Psychiatrists, 10,* 121–3

Billig, M. (1979) *Psychology, racism and fascism,* A.F. and R. Publications, Birmingham

——(1982) *Ideology and social policy,* Blackwell, Oxford

Black Health Workers and Patients Group (1984) 'Psychiatry and the Corporate State.' *Race and Class, 25,* 49–64

Bolton, P. (1984) 'Management of compulsorily admitted patients to a high security unit.' *International Journal of Social Psychiatry, 30,* 77–84

Book, J. A. (1953) 'A genetic and neuropsychiatric investigation of a north-Swedish population.' *Acta Genetica (Basel), 4,* 1–189

Bowden, P. (1985) 'Psychiatry and dangerousness: a counter renaissance?' In L. Gostin (ed.), *Secure Provision* Ch. 9, Tavistock, London, pp. 265–87

Brandon, S. (1970) 'Crisis theory and possibilities of therapeutic intervention.' *British Journal of Psychiatry, 117,* 627–33

Brent Community Health Council (1981) *Black people and the Health Service,* Russell Press, Nottingham

Brewin, C. (1980) 'Explaining the lower rates of psychiatric treatment among Asian immigrants to the United Kingdom: A preliminary study.' *Social Psychiatry, 15,* 17–19

Bright, T. (1586) *A treatise of melancholy,* Vautrolier, London

Brittan, A. and Maynard, M. (1984) *Sexism, racism and oppression,* Blackwell, Oxford

Brody, E. B. (1964) 'Society, culture and mental illness.' *Journal of Nervous and Mental Diseases, 139,* 62–73

Brown, D. and Pedder, J. (1979) *Introduction to psychotherapy. An outline of psychodynamic principles and practice,* Tavistock, London

Bucknill, J. C. and Tuke, D. H. (1858) *A manual of psychological medicine, containing the history, nosology, description, statistics, diagnosis, pathology, and treatment of insanity; with Appendix of cases,* Blanchard and Lea, Philadelphia

Burke, A. W. (1976a) 'Attempted suicide among Asian immigrants in Birmingham.' *British Journal of Psychiatry, 128,* 528–33

——(1976b) 'Socio-cultural determinants of attempted suicide among West Indians in Birmingham: ethnic origin and immigrant status.' *British Journal of Psychiatry, 129,* 261–6

——(1984) 'Racism and psychological disturbance among West Indians in Britain.' *International Journal of Social Psychiatry, 30,* 50–68

——(1986) 'Racism, prejudice and mental illness.' In J. Cox (ed.), *Transcultural psychiatry* Ch. 9, Croom Helm, London, pp.139–57

Burnham, P. (1972) 'Racial classification and ideology in the Meiganga Region, North Cameroon.' In P. Baxter and B. Sansom (eds), *Race and social difference,* Penguin, Harmondsworth

Burton, R. (1621) *The anatomy of melancholy,* 11th edn. 1806, Hodson, London

Cannon, W. (1963) *The wisdom of the body,* Norton, London

Capra, F. (1982) *The Turning point. Science, society, and the rising culture,* Wildwood House, London

Carothers, J. C. (1951) 'Frontal lobe function and the African.' *Journal of Mental Science, 97,* 12–48

——(1953) *The African mind in health and disease. A study in ethnopsychiatry,* WHO Monograph Series No. 17, World Health Organisation, Geneva

——(1972) *The mind of man in Africa,* Stacey, London. (Quoted by Littlewood and Lipsedge, 1982)

Carpenter, L. and Brockington, I. F. (1980) 'A study of mental illness in Asians, West Indians and Africans living in Manchester.' *British Journal of Psychiatry, 137,* 201–5

Carstairs, G. M. (1965) 'Group Discussion.' In A. V. S. De Reuck and R. Porter (eds), *Transcultural psychiatry. A Ciba Foundation symposium,* Churchill, London, pp. 357–83

——and Kapur, R. C. (1976) *The great universe of Kota: Stress change and mental disorder in an Indian village,* Hogarth Press, London

Cashmore, E. (1979) *Rastaman. The Rastafarian movement in England,* Allen and Unwin, London

——and Troyna, B. (1983) *Introduction to race relations,* Routledge and Kegan Paul, London

Castel, R. (1985) 'Moral treatment; mental therapy and social control in the nineteenth century.' In S. Cohen and A. Scull (eds), *Social control and the state,* Paperback edn, Ch. 10, Blackwell, Oxford, pp. 246–66

Centre for Contemporary Cultural Studies (1983) *The Empire strikes back. Race and racism in the 70's Britain,* Hutchinson, London

Cheetham, J. (ed.) (1982) *Social work and ethnicity,* Allen and Unwin, London

Clare, A. (1976) *Psychiatry in dissent,* Tavistock, London

Claus, P. J. (1979) 'Spirit possession and spirit mediumship from the perspective of Tulu oral traditions.' *Culture, Medicine and Psychiatry, 3,* 29–52

Cobb, W. M. (1942) 'Physical anthropology of the American Negro.'
American Journal of Physical Anthropology, 29, 113–223

Cochrane, R. (1977) 'Mental illness in immigrants to England and
Wales: An analysis of mental hospital admissions, 1971.' *Social
Psychiatry, 12,* 23–35

——(1979) 'Psychological behaviour disturbance in West Indians, Indians and Pakistanis in Britian: A comparison of rates.' *British
Journal of Psychiatry, 134,* 201–10

——(1980) 'Mental illness in England, in Scotland and in Scots living
in England.' *Social Psychiatry, 15,* 9–15

——and Stopes-Roe, M. (1981) 'Psychological symptom levels in Indian immigrants to England — a comparison with native English.'
Psychological Medicine, 11, 319–27

——Hashmi, F. and Stopes-Roe, M. (1977) 'Measuring psychological
disturbance in Asian immigrants to Britain.' *Social Science and
Medicine, 11,* 157–64

Collomb, H. (1967) 'Aspectes de la Psychiatrie dans l'Ouest Africain
(Senegal).' *Aktuelle Fragen der Psychiatrie und Neurologie, 5,*
229–53. (Quoted by Draguns and Phillips, 1972)

Colville, Lord (1986) News Report. *Guardian,* October, 9, p. 6

Connolly, C. J. (1950) *External morphology of the primate brain,*
Springfield, Illinois. (Quoted by Carothers, 1953)

Cooper, J. E., Kendall, R. E., Garland, B. J., Sharpe, I., Copeland, J. R.
M. and Simon, R. (1972) *Psychiatric diagnosis in New York and
London,* Maudsley Monograph No. 20, Oxford University Press,
Oxford

——and Sartorius, N. (1977) 'Cultural and temporal variations in schizophrenia: A speculation on the importance of industrialization.'
British Journal of Psychiatry, 130, 50–5

Cox, J. L. (1986) 'Introduction.' In J. L. Cox (ed.), *Transcultural psychiatry,* Ch. 1, Croom Helm, London, pp. 1–6

Crammer, J. (1986) Letter to Editor. *Practical Reviews in
Psychiatry, 7,* 6

D'Andrade, R. G. (1984) 'Cultural meaning systems.' In R. A. Shweder
and R. A. Levine (eds), *Culture theory. Essays on mind, self and
emotion,* Cambridge University Press, Cambridge, Ch. 3, pp. 88–
119

Dahl, R. (1968) 'Power as the control of behaviour.' In D. L. Sills (ed.),
International encyclopedia of the Social Sciences, Vol. 12,
Crowell, Collier and MacMillan, pp. 405–15. (Reprinted 1986 in
S. Lukes (ed.), *Power,* Blackwell, London, Ch. 3, pp. 37–58)

Darwin, C. (1871) *The descent of man and selection in relation to sex*
Vol. 1, John Murray, London

——(1872) *The expression of the emotions in man and animals,*
Appleton, New York. (Reprinted 1965 University of Chicago
Press, London)

Davidson, B. (1974) *Africa in history,* Paladin Books, London

———(1984) *The story of Africa*, Mitchell Beazley, London

De Wet, J. S. Du T. (1957) 'Evaluation of a common method of convulsion therapy in Bantu schizophrenics.' *Journal of Mental Science, 103*, 739–57

Dean, G. Walsh, D., Downing, H. and Shelley, E. (1981) 'First admissions of native-born and immigrants to psychiatric hospitals in South-East England, 1970.' *British Journal of Psychiatry, 139*, 506–12

DiNicola, V. F. (1985a) 'Family therapy and transcultural psychiatry: An emerging synthesis. Part 1: The conceptual basis', *Transcultural Psychiatric Research Review, 22*, 81–113

———(1985b) 'Family therapy and transcultural psychiatry: An emerging synthesis. Part 2: Portability and culture change.' *Transcultural Psychiatric Research Review, 22*, 151–80

Dodson, J. (1981) 'Conceptualizations of black families.' In H. P. McAdoo (ed.), *Black families*, Sage Publications, Beverley Hill and London, Ch. 1, pp. 23–36

Donnelly, M. (1983) *Managing the mind. A study of medical psychology in early nineteenth-century Britain*, Tavistock, London

Donovan, J. L. (1984) 'Ethnicity and health: A research review.' *Social Science and Medicine, 19*, 663–70

Draguns, J. G. and Phillips, L. (1972) *Culture and psychopathology: The quest for a relationship*, General Learning Press, Morristown, New Jersey

Dressler, W. M. and Badger, L. W. (1982) 'Epidemiology of depressive symptoms in black communities. A comparative analysis.' *Journal of Nervous and Mental Disease, 173*, 212–20

Dube, K. C. (1970) 'A study of prevalence and biosocial variables in mental illness in a rural and an urban community in Uttar Pradesh, India.' *Acta Psychiatrica Scandinavica, 46*, 327–59

Eaton, J. and Weil, R. (1955) *Culture and mental disorders; A comparative study of the Hutterites and other populations*, The Free Press, Glencoe, Illinois

El-Islam, M. F. (1969) 'Depression and guilt: A study at an Arab psychiatric clinic.' *Social Psychiatry, 4*, 56–8

Ellenberger, H. F. (1974) 'Psychiatry from ancient to modern times.' In S. Arieti (ed.), *American handbook of psychiatry*, 2nd edn, Vol.1, Ch. 1, Basic Books, New York, pp. 3–27

Ellis, W. G. (1893) 'The Amok of the Malays.' *Journal of Mental Science, 39*, 325–38

Erickson, E. (1968) *Identity: Youth and Crisis*, Faber & Faber, London

Evarts, A. (1916) 'The ontogenetic vs the phylogenetic elements in the psychoses of the colored race.' *Psychoanalytic Review 3*, 272–87

Eysenck, H. J. (1971) *Race, intelligence and education*, Temple Smith, London

———(1973) *The inequality of man*, Maurice Temple Smith, London

Fabrega, H. (1970) 'On the specificity of folk illnesses.' *Southwest Journal of Anthropology, 26*, 305–14. (Quoted by Good and Good, 1984)

Fabrega, H. Jr. (1984) 'Culture and psychiatric illness: Biomedical and ethnomedical aspects.' In A. J. Marsella and G. M. White (eds.), *Cultural conceptions of mental health and therapy*, Ch. 2, Beidel, Dordrecht, Holland, pp. 29—68

Fanon, F. (1952) *Peau noire, masques blancs*, Editions de Seuil, Paris. Transl. C. L. Markmann, 1967, *Black skin, white masks*, Grove Press, New York

——(1964) *Pour la revolution Africaine, ecrits politiques*, Maspero, Paris. Transl. H. Chevalier, 1967, *Towards the African revolution*, Monthly Review Press, New York

Fernando, S. (1973) 'Sociocultural factors in depressive illness: A comparative study of Jewish and non-Jewish patients in East London', MD thesis, University of Cambridge

——(1975) 'A cross-cultural study of some familial and social factors in depressive illness.' *British Journal of Psychiatry, 127*, 46–53

——(1978) 'Aspects of depression in a Jewish minority group.' *Psychiatrica Clinica, 11*, 23–3

——(1986) 'Depression in Ethnic Minorities.' In J. L. Cox (ed.), *Transcultural Psychiatry*, Ch. 8, Croom Helm, London, pp. 107–38

——(ed.) (1985) *Women: Cultural perspectives. Report of conference organised by the Transcultural Psychiatry Society (UK)*, Transcultural Psychiatry Society (UK), London

Field, M. J. (1958) 'Mental disorder in rural Ghana.' *Journal of Mental Science, 104*, 1043–51

Fischer, J. (1969) 'Negroes and Whites and rates of mental illness: Reconsideration of a myth.' *Psychiatry, 32*, 428–46

Fitzpatrick, R. M. (1983) 'Cultural aspects of psychiatry.' In M. Weller (ed.), *The scientific basis of psychiatry* Ch. 27, Balliere Tindall, London, pp. 411–22

Foote, R. F. (1858) 'The condition of the insane and the treatment of nervous diseases in Turkey.' *Journal of Mental Science, 4*, 444–50

Foucault, M. (1967) *Madness and civilization*, Transl. R. Howard, Tavistock, London

Francis, E. (1985) 'Death at Broadmoor — the case of Michael Martin.' *Bulletin of the Transcultural Psychiatry Society (UK), 7*, 7–11

Freud, S. (1927) 'The future of an illusion.' Trans. 1961 W. Robson-Scott. In J. Strachey (ed.), *The standard edition of the complete works of Sigmund Freud*, Vol. 21, Hogarth, London, pp. 1–56

——(1930) 'Civilization and its discontents.' Trans. 1961 J. Riviere. In J. Strachey (ed.), *The standard edition of the complete works of Sigmund Freud*, Vol. 21, Hogarth, London, pp. 57–145

——(1950) *Totem and taboo. Some points of agreement between the mental lives of savages and neurotics*, Transl. J. Strachey, Routledge and Kegan Paul, London

Fried, M. H. (1968) 'The need to end the pseudoscientific investigation of race.' In M. Mead *et al.* (eds), *Science and the concept of race*, Columbia University Press, New York. (Quoted by Thomas and Sillen, 1972)

191

Frijda, N. and Jahoda, G. (1966) 'On the scope and methods of cross-cultural research.' *International Journal of Psychology, 1*, 110–27

Fromm, E. (1960) 'Psychoanalysis and Zen Buddhism.' In D. T. Suzuki, E. Fromm and R. De Martino (eds), *Zen Buddhism and Psychoanalysis*, Allen and Unwin, London, pp. 77–141

Fryer, P. (1984) *Staying power. The history of black people in Britain*, Pluto Press, London

Galton, F. (1865) 'Hereditary talent and character', *MacMillan Magazine*, 157–66 (Quoted by Billig, 1982)

Gillie, O. (1976) *Who do you think you are? Man or superman: The genetic controversy*, Hart-Davis, MacGibbon, London

Glick, I. D. and Kessler, D. R. (1974) *Marital and family therapy*, Grune and Stratton, London

Gold, J. (1985) 'Cartesian dualism and the current crisis in Medicine — a plan for a philosophical approach: Discussion paper.' *Journal of the Royal Society of Medicine, 78*, 663–6

Goldman, A. I. (1972) 'Towards a theory of social power.' *Philosophical Studies 23*, 221-68. (Reprinted 1986 in S. Lukes (ed.), *Power*, Ch. 8, Blackwell, London, pp. 156–202,

Good, B. J. (1987) 'Editorial.' *Culture, Medicine and Psychiatry, 11*, 1–2
——and Good, M. D. (1984) 'Toward a meaning-centred analysis of popular illness categories: "Fright illness" and "Heart distress" in Iran.' In A. J. Marsella and G. M. White (eds), *Cultural conceptions of mental health and therapy*, Reidel, Dordrecht, pp. 141–66

Gostin, L. (1986) *Institutions observed: Towards a new concept of provision in mental health*, Kings Fund, London

Green, E. M. (1914) 'Psychoses among Negroes — a comparative study.' *Journal of Nervous and Mental Disorder, 41*, 697–708

Griesinger, W. (1845) *Die Pathologie und Therapie der Psychischen Krankheiten fur Aerzte und Studirende*, Adolph Krabbe Verlag, Stuttgart. (Quoted by Altschule, 1965)

Gynther, M. D. and Green, S. B. (1980) 'Accuracy may make a difference, but does a difference make for accuracy? : A response to Pritchard and Rosenblatt.' *Journal of Consulting and Clinical Psychology, 48*, 268–72

Haeckel, E. (1876) *The history of creation*, Vol. 1, Transl. E. R. Lankester, Henry S. King, London
——(1901) *The riddle of the universe at the close of the nineteenth century*, Watts, London. (Quoted by Billig, 1982)

Haldipur, C. V. (1984) 'Madness in ancient India: Concept of insanity in Charaka Samhita (1st Century A.D.).' *Comprehensive Psychiatry, 25*, 335–43

Haley, J. (1963) 'Marriage therapy.' *Archives of General Psychiatry, 8*, 213–34

Hall, G. S. (1904) *Adolescence: its psychology and its relations to physiology, anthropology, sociology, sex, crime, religion and education*, Vol. II, D. Appleton, New York

Hall, S. (1978) 'Racism and reaction.' In Commission for Racial Equality, *Five views of multi-racial Britain*, CRE, London, pp. 23–35

——Critcher, C., Jefferson, T., Clarke, J. and Roberts, B. (1978) *Policing the crisis. mugging, the state, and law and order*, MacMillan, London

Harding, T. W. and Adserballe, H. (1983) 'Assessments of dangerousness: observations in six countries. A summary of results from a WHO co-ordinated study.' *International Journal of Law and Psychiatry, 6*, 391–8

Harrison, G., Ineichen, B., Smith, J. and Morgan, H. G. (1984) 'Psychiatric hospital admissions in Bristol. 2. Social and clinical aspects of compulsory admission.' *British Journal of Psychiatry, 145*, 605–11

Hemsi, L. K. (1967) 'Psychiatric morbidity of West Indian immigrants.' *Social Psychiatry, 2*, 95–100

Herberg, W. (1960) *Protestant — Catholic — Jew. An essay in American religious sociology*, Anchor Books, New York

Hes, J. P. (1960) 'Manic-depressive illness in Israel.' *American Journal of Psychiatry, 116*, 1082–6

Hill, P., Murray, R. and Thorley, A. (1986) *Essentials of postgraduate psychiatry*, 2nd edn, Grune and Stratton, London

Hodge, J. L. and Struckmann, D. K. (1975) 'Some components of the Western dualist tradition.' In J. L. Hodge, D. K. Struckmann and L. D. Trost (eds), *Cultural bases of racism and group oppression*, Pt. 4, Two Riders Press, Berkeley, pp. 122–95

Home Office Statistical Bulletin (1986) *The ethnic origin of prisoners: The prison population on 30 June 1985 and persons received July 1984 to March 1985*, Statistical Bulletin No. 17/86, Issue No. 17/86, Government Statistical Service, Surbiton, Surrey

Hospital Doctor (1985) 'Career ruined by race ruling.' *Hospital Doctor 28*, November, 1

Howells, J. (ed.) (1975) *World history of psychiatry*, Balliere Tindall, London

Husband, C. (1982) '"Race", the continuity of a concept.' In C. Husband (ed.), *Race in Britain. Continuity and change*, Introduction, Hutchinson, London, pp. 11–23

Imlah, N. (1985) 'Silverman enquiry on Handsworth riots', unpublished transcript

Ineichen, B., Harrison, G. and Morgan, H. G. (1984) 'Psychiatric hospital admissions in Bristol. 1. Geographical and ethnic factors.' *British Journal of Psychiatry, 145*, 600–4

Ingelby, D. (1985) 'Mental health and social order.' In S. Cohen and A. Scull (eds), *Social control and the state*, Ch. 7, Blackwell, Oxford, pp. 141–8

Institute of Race Relations (1982a) *Roots of racism*, IRR, London

——(1982b) *Patterns of racism*, IRR, London

International Congress on Transcultural Psychiatry (1976) Organised by The University of Bradford and The World Federation for Mental Health, 27–31 July 1976, at The University of Bradford, UK

Irvine, S. (1973) 'Tests on inadvertent sources of discrimination in personnel decisions.' In P. Watson (ed.), *Psychology and Race*, Ch. 23, Penguin, Harmondsworth, pp. 453–66,

193

Jenkins, D., Kemmis, S., MacDonald, B. and Verma, G. K. (1979) 'Racism and educational evaluation.' In G. K. Verma and C. Bagley (eds), *Race, education and identity*, Ch. 7, MacMillan, London, pp. 107–32

Jensen, A. R. (1969) 'How much can we boost IQ and scholastic achievement?', *Harvard Educational Review, 39*, 1–123

——(1984) 'Obstacles, problems and pitfalls in differential psychology.' In S. Scarr (ed.), *Race, social class and individual differences in I. Q.*, Part 5.2, Lawrence Erlbaum Associates, Hillside, New Jersey, pp. 483–514

Jewkes, R. (1984) *United Nations Centre against apartheid. Notes and documents*, United Nations, New York

Jones, J. S. (1981) 'How different are human races?' *Nature, 293*, 188–90

Jones, R. (ed.) (1985) *Mental Health Act manual*, Sweet and Maxwell, London

Jordan, W. D. (1968) *White over Black. American attitudes towards the Negro 1550 - 1812*, Penguin, Baltimore. (Quoted by Fryer, 1984)

Jung, C. G. (1945) 'Nach der Katastrophe.' *Neue Schweizer Rundschau (Zurich), n.s. 13*, reprinted 1970 in C. G. Jung *Civilization in transition. The collected works of C. G. Jung*, 2nd edn, Trans. R. F. C. Hull, Routledge and Kegan Paul, London

——(1964) *Civilization in transition. The collected works of C. G. Jung*, Vol. 10, Transl. R. F. C. Hull, Routledge and Kegan Paul, London

——(1930) 'Your Negroid and Indian behaviour.' *Forum, 83*, 4, 193–9

Kabbani, R. (1986) *Europe's myths of Orient. Devise and rule*, MacMillan, London

Kallarackal, A. M. and Herbert, M. (1976) 'The happiness of Indian children', *New Society*, 26 February, 422–4

Kamin, L. J. (1974) *The science and politics of IQ*, Wiley, New York

Kapo, R. (1981) *A savage culture*, Quartet Books, London

Kardiner, A. (1939) *The individual and his society. The psychodynamics of primitive social organisation*, Columbia University Press, New York

——and Ovesey, L. (1951) *The mark of oppression. A psychosocial study of the American Negro*, Paperback edn., Norton, New York

Katz, I. (1973) 'Negro performance in interracial situations.' In P. Watson (ed.), *Psychology and race*, Ch. 11, Penguin, Harmondsworth, pp. 256–66

Kenny, M. G. (1978) 'Latah, the symbolism of a putative mental disorder.' *Culture, Medicine and Psychiatry, 2*, 209–301

Kessel, N. (1965) 'Are international comparisons timely?' *Millbank Memorial Foundation Quarterly, 53*, 2, 199–204

Kettle, M. (1982) 'The racial numbers game in our prisons.' *New Society*, 30 September, 535–7

Kiev, A. (1963) 'Beliefs and delusions of West Indian immigrants to London.' *British Journal of Psychiatry, 109*, 356–63

——(1964) *Magic, faith and healing. Studies in primitive psychiatry today*, The Free Press, Glencoe, New York

——(1972) *Transcultural psychiatry*, The Free Press, Glencoe, New York

Kimura, Van B. (1965) 'Vergleichende Untersuchungen uber depressive Erkrankungen in Japan und in Deutschland.' *Fortschritte de Neurologie-Psychiatrie, 33*, 202–15

Kleinman, A. (1977) 'Depression, somatization and the "New Cross-Cultural Psychiatry".' *Social Science and Medicine, 11*, 3–10

——(1980a) 'Major conceptual and research issues for cultural (anthropological) psychiatry.' *Culture, Medicine and Psychiatry, 4*, 3–13

——(1980b) *Patients and healers in the context of culture. An exploration of the border between anthropology, medicine and psychiatry*, University of California Press, Berkeley

Kluckholm, C. (1944) *Mirror for man*, McGraw Hill, New York

Kraepelin, E. (1913) *Manic depressive insanity and paranoia*, translation of *Lehrbuch der Psychiatrie*, by R. M. Barclay, 8th edn, Vols 3 and 4, Livingstone, Edinburgh

——(1920) 'Die Erscheinungsformen des Irreseins.' *Zeitschrift fur die gesamte Neurologie und Psychiatrie 62*, 1–29. Transl. H. Marshall, reprinted 1974 in S. Hirsch and M. Shepherd (eds), *Themes and variations in European psychiatry. An anthology*, John Wright, Bristol

Kulhara, P. and Wig, N. N. (1978) 'The chronicity of schizophrenia in North West India: Results of a follow-up study.' *British Journal of Psychiatry, 132*, 186–90

Lambo, T. A. (1965) 'Psychiatry in the tropics.' *Lancet, ii*, 1119–21

Lau, A. (1986) 'Family therapy across cultures.' In J. L. Cox (ed.), *Transcultural psychiatry*, Ch. 14, Croom Helm, London, pp. 234-52

Lawrence, E. (1982a) 'Just plain common sense: the roots of racism.' In Centre for Contemporary Studies (ed.), *The Empire strikes back*, Ch. 2, Hutchinson, London, pp. 47–94

——(1982b) 'In the abundance of water the fool is thirsty: Sociology and black "pathology".' In Centre for Contemporary Cultural Studies (ed.), *The Empire Strikes Back*, Ch. 3, Hutchinson, London, pp. 95–142

Leff, J. (1973) 'Culture and the differentiation of emotional states.' *British Journal of Psychiatry, 123*, 299–306

——(1974) 'Transcultural influences on psychiatrists' rating of verbally expressed emotion.' *British Journal of Psychiatry, 125*, 336–40

——(1975) '"Exotic" treatments and Western psychiatry.' *Psychological Medicine, 5*, 125–8

——(1977) 'The cross-cultural study of emotions.' *Culture, Medicine and Psychiatry, 1*, 317–50

——(1981) *Psychiatry around the globe*, Dekker, New York

——(1986a) 'The epidemiology of mental illness across cultures.' In J. L. Cox (ed.), *Transcultural psychiatry*, Ch. 3, Croom Helm, London, pp. 23-36

——(1986b) 'Planning a community psychiatric service: from theory to practice.' In G. Wilkinson and H. Freeman (eds), *The provision of Mental Health Services in Britain: The way ahead*, Ch. 7, Gaskell/ Royal College of Psychiatrists, London, pp. 49–60

REFERENCES

Leighton, A. H. (1959) *My name is legion: The Stirling County study of psychiatric disorder and sociocultural environment*, Vol. 1, Basic Books, New York

——and Hughes, J. M. (1961) 'Culture as causative of mental disorder.' *Millbank Memorial Fund Quarterly, 39*, 3, 446–70

——Lambo, T. A., Hughes, C. C., Leighton, D. C., Murphy, J. M. and Macklin, D. M. (1963a) *Psychiatric disorder among the Yoruba*, Cornell University Press, New York

Leighton, D. C., Harding, J. S., Macklin, D. B., MacMillan, A. M. and Leighton, A. H. (1963b) *The character of danger: The Stirling County study of psychiatric disorder and sociocultural environment*, Vol. 3, Basic Books, New York

Leng, G. A. (1971) 'Traditional Chinese methods of mental treatment.' In N. N. Wagner and E. S. Tan (eds), *Psychological problems and treatment in Malaysia*, University of Malaya Press, Kuala Lumpur, pp. 102–14

Lewins, R. and Lewontin, R. (1985) *The dialectical biologist*, Harvard University Press, Cambridge Massachusetts. (Quoted by Rabkin, 1986)

Lewis, A. (1951) 'The twenty-fifth Maudsley lecture — Henry Maudsley: his work and influence.' *Journal of Mental Science, 97*, 259–77

——(1965) 'Chairman's opening remarks.' In A. V. S. De Rueck and R. Porter (eds), *Transcultural psychiatry. A Ciba Foundation symposium*, Churchill, London, pp. 1–3

Lind, J. (1914) 'The color complex of the Negro.' *Psychoanalytic Review, 1*, 404–14

Linnaeus, C. (1758–9) *Systema Naturae per Regina Tria Naturae* 10th edn., Laurentius Saluis, Stockholm. (Quoted by Fryer, 1984)

Linton, R. (1956) *Culture and mental disorders*, Thomas, Illinois

Littlewood, R. (1986a) 'Russian dolls and Chinese boxes: An anthropological approach to the implicit models of comparative psychiatry.' In J. L. Cox (ed.), *Transcultural psychiatry*, Ch. 4, Croom Helm, London, pp. 37–58

——(1986b) 'Ethnic minorities and the Mental Health Act.' *Bulletin of The Royal College of Psychiatrists, 10*, 306–8

——and Cross, S. (1980) 'Ethnic minorities and psychiatric services.' *Sociology of Health and Illness, 2*, 194–201

——and Lipsedge, M. (1981a) 'Some social and phenomenological characteristics of psychotic immigrants.' *Psychological Medicine, 11*, 289–302

——and ——(1981b) 'Acute psychotic reactions in Caribbean-born patients.' *Psychological Medicine, 11*, 303–18

——and ——(1982) *Aliens and alienists*, Penguin, Harmondsworth

——and ——(1986) 'The "Culture-bound Syndromes" of the dominant culture: culture, psychopathology and biomedicine.' In J. L. Cox (ed.), *Transcultural psychiatry*, Ch. 15, Croom Helm, London, pp. 253–73

Lloyd, G. and Bebbington, P. (1986) 'Social and transcultural psychiatry.' In P. Hill, R. Murray and A. Thorley (eds), *Essentials of postgraduate psychiatry*, Ch. 18, Grune and Stratton, London, pp. 547–69

Lo, W. H. and Lo, T. (1977) 'A ten year follow-up study of Chinese schizophrenics in Hong Kong.' *British Journal of Psychiatry, 131*, 63–6

Logan, M. H. (1979) 'Variations regarding Susto causality among the Cakchiquel of Guatemala.' *Culture, Medicine and Psychiatry, 3*, 153–66

Long, J. K. (1973) 'Jamaican medicine: choices between folk healing and modern medicine', PhD. Dissertation, Dept. Anthropology, University of North Carolina, USA. (Quoted by Wedenoja, 1983)

Lubchansky, I., Egri, G. and Stokes, J. (1970) 'Puerto Rican spiritualists view mental illness. The faith healer as a paraprofessional.' *American Journal of Psychiatry, 127*, 312–20

MacAndrew, C. (1965) 'The differentiation of male alcoholic outpatients from non-alcoholic psychiatric outpatients by means of the MMPI.' *Quarterly Journal of Studies on Alcohol*, 26, 238–46

Mall, F. P. (1909) 'On several anatomical characters of the human brain, said to vary according to race and sex.' *American Journal of Anatomy, 9*, 1–32

Malt, U. (1986) 'Philosophy of science and DSM-III. Philosophical, idea-historical and sociological perspectives on diagnosis.' *Acta Psychiatrica Scandinavica, 73*, Supplementum 328, 10–17

Marsella, A. J. (1978) 'Thoughts on cross-cultural studies on the epidemiology of depression.' *Culture, Medicine and Psychiatry, 2*, 343–57

——(1984) 'Culture and mental health: an overview.' In A. J. Marsella and G. M. White (eds), *Cultural conceptions of mental health and therapy*, Ch. 16, Reidel, Dordrecht, pp. 359–88

Maudsley, H. (1867) *The physiology and pathology of mind*, D. Appleton, New York

——(1879) *The Pathology of mind*, Macmillan, London

Mazrui, A. A. (1986) *The Africans. A triple heritage*, BBC Publications, London

McAdoo, H. P. (1981) 'Preface.' In H. P. McAdoo (ed.), *Black Families*, Sage Publications, London, pp. 9–17

McDougall, W. (1908) *Social psychology*, Luce, New York

——(1921) *Is America safe for democracy?*, Scribner, New York

McGovern, D. and Cope, R. (1985) 'Ethnicity — compulsory detention — offender patients.' Paper presented at Conference *Transcultural Psychiatry, Forensic Dimensions*, organised by The Transcultural Psychiatry Society (UK), 10–12 May 1985, Northampton, England

——and ——(1987a)'The compulsory detention of males of different ethnic groups, with special reference to offender patients.' *British Journal of Psychiatry, 150*, 505–12

——and ——(1987b) 'First psychiatric admission rates of first and second generation Afro-Caribbeans.' *Social Psychiatry, 122*, 139–49

Mental Health Act (1983) Her Majesty's Stationery Office, London

Minuchin, S. (1974) *Families and family therapy*, Tavistock, London

Molnar, S. (1983) *Human variation. Races, types and ethnic groups*, 2nd edn, Prentice-Hall, New Jersey

Moorhouse, G. (1983) *India Britannica*, Harvill Press, London

Mora, G. (1961) 'Historiographic and cultural trends in psychiatry: a survey.' *Bulletin of the History of Medicine, 35,* 26–36

———(1970) 'The psychiatrist's approach to the history of psychiatry.' In G. Mora (ed.), *Psychiatry and its history. Methodological problems in research*, Ch. 1, Charles C. Thomas, Springfield, pp. 3–25

Moynihan, D. (1965) *The Negro family in the United States: the case for national action*, US Governmental Printing Office, Washington

Murphy, H. B. M. (1969) 'Ethnic variations in drug response.' *Transcultural Psychiatric Research Review, 6,* 5–23

———(1973) 'Current trends in transcultural psychiatry.' *Proceedings of the Royal Society of Medicine, 66,* 711–16

———(1974) 'Differences between mental disorders of French Canadians and British Canadians.' *Canadian Psychiatric Association Journal, 19,* 247–57

———(1977) 'Migration, culture and mental health.' *Psychological Medicine, 7,* 677–84

———(1983) 'In Memorium Eric D. Wittkower 1899 – 1983.' *Transcultural Psychiatric Research Review, 20,* 1, 81–6

———(1986) 'The mental health impact of British cultural traditions.' In J. Cox (ed.), *Transcultural psychiatry*, Ch. 11, Croom Helm, London, pp. 179–95

———and Raman, A. C. (1971) 'The chronicity of schizophrenia in indigenous tropical peoples.' *British Journal of Psychiatry, 118,* 489–97

Nash, M. (1972) 'Race and the ideology of race.' In P. Baxter and B. Sansom (eds), *Race and social differences*, Ch. 9, Penguin, Harmondsworth, pp. 111–22

Norris, M. (1984) *Integration of special hospital patients into the community*, Gower, Aldershot

Obeyesekere, G. (1977) 'The theory and practice of psychological medicine in the Ayurvedic tradition.' *Culture, Medicine and Psychiatry, 1,* 155–81

Odegaard, O. (1970) 'Epidemiology of the psychoses.' *Acta Psychiatrica Scandinavica*, Supplement No. 217, 14–5

Okasha, A. and Ashour, A. (1981) 'Psycho-demographic study of anxiety in Egypt: the PSE in its Arabic version.' *British Journal of Psychiatry, 139,* 70–3

O'Malley, M. (1914) 'Psychoses in the colored race.' *American Journal of Insanity, 71,* 309–37

Orley, J. and Wing, J. (1979) 'Psychiatric disorders in two African villages.' *Archives of General Psychiatry, 36,* 513–20

Oxford Paperback Dictionary (1979) Oxford University Press, Oxford

Palazzoli, M. S. (1986) Letter to Editor, *Transcultural Psychiatric Research Review, 23,* 83–4

Panikkar, K. M. (1959) *Asia and Western dominance*, George Allen, London. Reprinted 1969 Collier, USA

Parker, S. (1960) 'The Wiitiko psychosis in the context of Ojibwa personality and culture.' *American Anthropology*, *62*, 603–23

Parkinson, W. (1978) *'This gilded African' Toussaint L'Ouverture'*, Quartet Books, London

Pasamanick, B. (1963) 'Some misconceptions concerning differences in the racial prevalence of mental disease.' *American Journal of Orthopsychiatry*, *33*, 72–86

Pattison, E. M. (1977) 'Psychosocial interpretation of exorcism.' *Journal of Operational Psychiatry*, *8*, 5–21

——Lapins, N. A. and Doerr, H. A. (1973) 'Faith healing. A study of personality and function.' *Journal of Nervous and Mental Disease*, *157*, 397–409

Pearson, K. (1901) *National life from the standpoint of science*, Adam and Charles Black, London. (Quoted by Fryer, 1984)

Pertold, O. (1930) 'Yakum-Natima.' In O. Pertold (ed.), *Ceremonial Dances of the Sinhalese*, Pt. 4, Tisara Press, Dehiwala, Sri Lanka, pp. 99–138

Pettigrew, T. F. (1964) *A profile of the Negro American*, Van Norstrand, Princeton. (Quoted by Erickson, 1968)

Pinel, P. (1809) *Traite Medico-Philosophique sur l'Alienation Mentale*, 2nd edn, Brosson, Paris. (Quoted by Woods and Carlson, 1961)

Powell, T. O. (1896) 'The increase in insanity and tuberculosis in the Southern Negro since 1800 and its alliance and some of its supposed causes.' *Journal of the American Medical Association*, *27*, 1185–8

Prince, R. (1968) 'The changing picture of depressive syndromes in Africa.' *Canadian Journal of African Studies*, *1*, 177–92

——(1983) 'Is anorexia nervosa a culture-bound syndrome?' *Transcultural Psychiatric Research Review*, *20*, 299–300

—and Tcheng-Larouche, F. (1987) 'Culture-bound syndromes and international disease classifications.' *Culture, Medicine and Psychiatry*, *11*, 3–19

Pritchard, D. A. and Rosenblatt, A. (1980) 'Racial bias in the MMPI: A methodological review.' *Journal of Consulting and Clinical Psychology*, *48*, 263–7

Pryce, K. (1979) *Endless pressure*, Penguin, Harmondsworth. (Quoted by Richardson and Lambert, 1985)

Rabkin, R. (1986) 'The Tower of Babble: the sociology of body and mind.' *Family Process*, *25*, 153–63

Rack, P. (1982) *Race, culture and mental disorder*, Tavistock, London

Rainwater, L. (1968) 'Crucible of identity: The Negro lower class family.' *Daedalus*, *95*, 258–64. (Quoted by Dodson, 1981)

Ratnavale, D. N. (1973) 'Psychiatry in Shanghai, China: observations in 1973.' *American Journal of Psychiatry*, *130*, 1082–7

Rendon, M. (1984) 'Myths and stereotypes in minority groups.' *International Journal of Social Psychiatry*, *30*, 297–309

Rex, J. (1972) 'Nature vs nurture: the significance of the revived debate.' In K. Richardson and D. Spears (eds), *Race, culture and intelligence*, Ch. 9, Penguin, Harmondsworth, pp. 167–78

Richardson, J. and Lambert, J. (1985) *The sociology of race*, Causeway Press, Lancashire

Rogers, A. (1987) Paper given at Conference, *Better Mental Health care for ethnic minorities*, organised by The Mental Health Act Commission, 6 April 1987, London

Rosaldo, M. Z. (1984) 'Toward an anthropology of self and feeling.' In R. A. Shweder and R. A. LeVine (eds), *Culture theory. Essays on mind, self and emotions*, Ch. 5, Cambridge University Press, Cambridge, pp. 137–57

Rosen, G. (1946) 'The philosophy of ideology and the emergence of modern medicine in France.' *Bulletin of the History of Medicine, 20*, 328–39

Rushdie, S. (1982) 'The new Empire within Britain.' *New Society*, 9 December, 417–20

Rutter, M., Yule, W., Berger, M., Yule, B., Morton, J. and Bagley, C. (1974) 'Children of West Indian immigrants. 1. Rates of behavioural deviance and of psychiatric disorder.' *Journal of Child Psychology and Psychiatry, 15*, 241–62

Ryan, J. (1972) 'IQ — The illusion of objectivity.' In K. Richardson and D. Spears (eds), *Race, culture and intelligence*, Ch. 2, Penguin, Harmondsworth, pp. 36–55

Sabshin, M., Diesenhaus, H. and Wilkerson, R. (1970) 'Dimensions of institutional racism in psychiatry.' *American Journal of Psychiatry, 127*, 787–93

Saifullah Khan, V. (1979) *Minority families in Britain: support and stress*, MacMillan, London

Sashidharan, S. P. (1986) 'Ideology and politics in transcultural psychiatry.' in J. Cox (ed.), *Transcultural Psychiatry*, Ch. 10, Croom Helm, London, pp. 158–78

Scarman, Lord (1981) *The Brixton Disorders 10–12 April 1981*, Her Majesty's Stationery Office, London

Scarr, S. (ed.) (1984) *Race, social class and individual differences in I. Q.*, Lawrence Erlbaum Associates, Hillside, New Jersey

Schon, D. A. (1971) *Beyond the stable state. Public and private learning in a changing society*, Temple Smith, London

Schwartz, M. A. and Wiggins, O. P. (1987) 'Typifications. The first step for clinical diagnosis in psychiatry.' *Journal of Nervous and Mental Disease, 175*, 65–77

Scull, A. (1979) *Museums of madness. The social organization of insanity in nineteenth-century England*, Allen Lane, London

——(1981) 'The social history of psychiatry in the Victorian era.' In A. Scull (ed.), *Madhouses, mad-doctors and madmen. The social history of psychiatry in the Victorian era*, Ch. 1, Athlone Press, London, pp. 5–32

Select Committee on Race Relations and Immigration (1977) *The West Indian community*, Her Majesty's Stationery Office, London

Sethi, B. B., Gupta, S. C., Mahendru, R. K. and Kumari, P. (1974) 'Mental health and urban life: A study of 850 families.' *British Journal of Psychiatry, 124*, 243–6

Shaikh, A. (1985) 'Cross-cultural comparison: psychiatric admission of Asian and Indigenous patients in Leicestershire.' *International Journal of Social Psychiatry, 31*, 3–11

Shelley, D. and Cohen, D. (1986) *Testing psychological tests*, Croom Helm, London

Showalter, E. (1987) *The female malady. Women, madness, and the English culture, 1830–1980*, Virago, London

Shweder, R. A. and Bourne, E. J. (1984) 'Does the concept of the person vary cross-culturally?' In A. J. Marsella and G. M. White (eds), *Cultural concepts of mental health and therapy*, Ch. 4, Reidel, Dordrecht, Holland, pp. 97–137

——and Bourne, E. J. (1984) 'Does the concept of the person vary cross culturally?' In R. A. Shweder and R. A. LeVine (eds), *Culture theory. Essays on mind, self and emotions*, Ch. 6, Cambridge University Press, Cambridge, pp. 158–99

——and LeVine, R. A. (eds) (1984) *Culture theory. Essays on mind, self, and emotion*, Cambridge University Press, Cambridge

Siegler, M. and Osmond, H. (1974) *Models of madness, models of medicine*, MacMillan, New York

Simon, B. (1978) *Mind and madness in ancient Greece. The classical roots of modern psychiatry*, Cornell University Press, London

Singer, K. (1975) 'Depressive disorders from a transcultural perspective.' *Social Science and Medicine, 9*, 289–301

Singer, P., Aarons, L. and Aronetta, E. (1967) 'Integration and indigenous practices of the Kali cult and Western psychiatric modalities in British Guiana.' *Interamerican Journal of Psychology, 1*, 103–14. (Quoted by Draguns and Phillips, 1972)

Skultans, V. (1979) *English madness. Ideas on insanity 1580–1890*, Routledge and Kegan Paul, London

Slater, E. and Roth, M. (1960) *Clinical psychiatry*, 3rd edn, Balliere Tindall and Cassell, London

Spuhler, J. N. and Lindzey, G. (1967) 'Racial differences in behaviour.' In J. Hirsch (ed.), *Behaviour-genetic analysis*, Ch. 19, McGraw-Hill, New York, pp. 367–414

Steadman, H. J. (1983) 'Predicting dangerousness among the mentally ill: art, magic, science.' *International Journal of Law and Psychiatry, 6*, 381–90

Stone, A., Pinderhughes, C., Spurlock, J. and Weinberg, M. D. (1978) 'Report of the committee to visit South Africa.' *American Journal of Psychiatry, 136*, 1498–1506

Stone, M. (1981) *The education of the black child*, Fontana, London

Stott, D. H. (1983) *Issues in the intelligence debate*, NFER-Nelson Publishing, Windsor, Berkshire

Strecker, E. A., Appel, K. E., Eyman, E. V., Farr, C. B., Lamar, N. C., Palmer, H. D. and Smith, L. H. (1931) 'The prognosis in manic-depressive psychosis.' In W. A. White, T. K. Davis and A. M. Frantz (eds), *Manic-depressive psychosis. An investigation of the most recent advances*, Williams and Wilkins, Baltimore

Street, B. (1975) *The savage in literature*, Routledge and Kegan Paul, London. (Quoted by Littlewood and Lipsedge, 1982)

Suzuki, T. and Suzuki, R. (1977) 'Morita Therapy.' In E. D. Wittkower and H. Warner (eds), *Psychosomatic medicine. Its clinical applications*, Ch 18, Harper and Row, London, pp. 180–9

Swartz, L., Ben-Arie, O. and Teggin, A.F. (1985) 'Subcultural delusions and hallucinations. Comments on the Present State Examination in a multi-cultural context.' *British Journal of Psychiatry, 146,* 391–4

Sykes, J. B. (ed.) (1982) *The concise Oxford dictionary of current English*, 7th edn., Clarendon Press, Oxford

Sypher, W. (1942) *Guinea's captive kings*, Chapel Hill. (Quoted by Lawrence, 1982a)

Szasz, T. S. (1960) 'The myth of mental illness.' *American Psychologist 15*, 113–8. (Reprinted 1967 in T. J. Scheff (ed.), *Mental illness and social processes*, Harper and Row, London, pp. 242–54)

Terman, L. M. (1916) *The measurement of intelligence*, Houghton, Boston

Therborn, G. (1980) *The ideology of power and the power of ideology*, New Left Books, London

Thomas, A. and Sillen, S. (1972) *Racism and psychiatry*, Brunner/Mazel, New York

Thomas, C. S. and Comer, J. P. (1973) 'Racism and mental health services.' In C. V. Willie, B. M. Kramer and B. S. Brown (eds), *Racism and mental health. Essays* Ch. 6, University of Pittsburgh Press, USA, pp. 165–81

Thomas, W. I. (1904) 'The psychology of race prejudice.' *American Journal of Sociology 9*, 593–611

Thornicroft, G. and Moodley, P. (1986) 'Profile of compulsory admissions to a psychiatric hospital: A prospective study.' Paper given at Conference, *Mental health services and ethnic minorities,* organised by The Royal College of Psychiatrists and The Transcultural Psychiatry Society (UK), 12 November, 1986, London

Torrey, E. F. (1980) *Schizophrenia and civilization*, Jason Aronson, New York

Transcultural Psychiatry Society (1985) The Constitution of the TCPS (UK), TCPS, London

Trevor-Roper, H. (1963) 'The rise of Christian Europe.' *Listener, 70,* 1809, 871–5

Triseliotis, J. (1986) 'Transcultural social work.' In J. Cox (ed.), *Transcultural psychiatry*, Ch. 12, Croom Helm, London, pp. 196–217

Tuke, D. H. (1858) 'Does civilization favour the generation of mental disease?' *Journal of Mental Science, 4*, 94–110

Van Brero, P. C. Z. (1895) 'Latah.' *Journal of Mental Science, 41,* 537–8

Veitch, A. (1986) 'Medical schools to face discrimination enquiry.' *Guardian*, December 8, p. 4,

Veith, I. (1970) 'Reflections on comparative methods in the history of psychiatry.' In G. Mora (ed.), *Psychiatry and its history. Methodological problems in research*, Ch. 7, Charles C. Thomas, Springfield, Illinois, pp. 149–58,

Vernon, P. E. (1969) 'Intelligence and cultural environment.' Summary from end of book, *Intelligence and cultural environment*, Methuen, London. (Reprinted 1972 in H. J. Butcher and D. E. Lomax (eds), *Readings in human intelligence*, Ch. 21, Methuen, London, pp. 353–72)

Vint, F. W. (1934) 'The brain of the Kenya native.' *Journal of Anatomy, 68*, 216–23

Visram, R. (1986) *Ayahs, lascars and princes*, Pluto Press, London

Walters, G. D., Greene, R. L., Jeffrey, T. B., Kruzich, D. J. and Haskin, J. J. (1983) 'Racial variations on the Mac Andrew alcoholism scale of the MMPI.' *Journal of Consulting and Clinical Psychology, 51*, 947–8

Walwin, J. (1973) *Black and white: Negro and English society, 1555– 1945*, Allen Lane, London

Warner, R. (1983) 'Recovery from schizophrenia in the Third World.' *Psychiatry, 46*, 197–212

Watson, P. (1973a) 'Some Mechanics of Racial Etiquette.' In P. Watson (ed.), *Psychology and Race*, Ch. 12, Penguin, Harmondsworth, pp. 267–85

——(1973b) 'Race and intelligence through the looking glass.' In P. Watson (ed.), *Psychology and race*, Ch. 17, Penguin, Harmondsworth, pp. 360–76

Watts, A. W. (1961) *Psychotherapy East and West*, Mentor Books, New York

Waxler, N. E. (1977) 'Is mental illness cured in traditional societies? A theoretical analysis.' *Culture, Medicine and Psychiatry, 1*, 233–53

——(1979) 'Is outcome for schizophrenia better in non-industrial societies? The case of Sri Lanka.' *Journal of Nervous and Mental Disease, 167*, 144–58

Wedenoja, W. (1983) 'Jamaican psychiatry.' *Transcultural Psychiatric Research Review, 20*, 233–58

Weller, M. (1983) *The scientific basis of psychiatry*, Balliere Tindall, London

Wellman, D. (1977) *Portraits of white racism*, Cambridge University Press, Cambridge

West, M. (1979) 'Meditation.' *British Journal of Psychiatry, 135*, 457–67

White, G. M. and Marsella, A. J. (1984) 'Introduction: Cultural conceptions in mental health research and practice.' In A. J. Marsella and G. M. White (eds), *Cultural conceptions of mental health and therapy*, Ch. 1, Reidel, Dordrecht, Holland, pp. 1–38

Wijesinghe, C. P., Dassanayake, S. A. W. and Dassanayake, P. V. L. N. (1978) 'Survey of psychiatric morbidity in a semi-urban population of Sri Lanka.' *Acta Psychiatrica Scandinavica, 58*, 413–41

——Dissanayake, S. A. W. and Mendis, N. (1976) 'Possession trance in a semi-urban community in Sri Lanka.' *Australian and New Zealand Journal of Psychiatry, 10*, 135–9

Wilkinson, C. B. (1970) 'The destructiveness of myths.' *American Journal of Psychiatry, 126*, 1087–92

Williams, A. H. (1950) 'A psychiatric study of Indian soldiers in the Arakan.' *British Journal of Medical Psychology, 23,* 130–81

Wing, J. K. (1978) *Reasoning about madness,* Oxford University Press, Oxford

——(1985) 'The PSE in different cultures.' *British Journal of Psychiatry, 147,* 325–6

——Cooper, J. E. and Sartorius, N. (1974) *The measurement and classification of psychiatric symptoms,* Cambridge University Press, London

Wise, T. A. (1845) *Commentary on the Hindu system of medicine,* Smith Elder, London

Wittkower, E. D. (1965) 'Recent developments in transcultural psychiatry.' In A. V. S. De Reuck and R. Porter (eds), *Transcultural psychiatry. A Ciba Foundation symposium,* Churchill, London

——(1968) 'Transcultural psychiatry.' In J. Howells (ed.), *Modern perspectives in world psychiatry,* Ch. 26, Oliver Boyd, Edinburgh, pp. 697–712

——and Dubreuil, G. (1971) 'Reflections on the interface between psychiatry and anthropology.' In I. Galdston (ed.), *The interface between psychiatry and anthropology,* Brunner/Mazel, New York, pp. 1–27

Woods, E. A. and Carlson, E. T. (1961) 'The psychiatry of Philippe Pinel.' *Bulletin of the History of Medicine, 35,* 14–25

World Health Organisation (1973) *Report of the international pilot study of schizophrenia,* Vol. 1, WHO, Geneva

——(1978) *Mental disorders: glossary and guide to classification in accordance with the ninth revision of the international classification of diseases,* WHO, Geneva

——(1979) *Schizophrenia: An international follow-up study,* Wiley, London

Worsley, P. (1972) 'Colonialism and categories.' In P. Baxter and B. Sansom (eds), *Race and social difference,* Ch. 7, Penguin, Harmondsworth, pp. 98–101

Wynne, L. C., Ryckoff, I. M., Day, J. and Hersch, S. I. (1958) 'Pseudo-mutuality in the family relations of schizophrenics.' *Psychiatry, 21,* 205–20

Yap, P. M. (1965) 'Phenomenology of affective disorders in Chinese and other cultures.' In A. V. S. de Rueck and R. Porter (eds), *Transcultural psychiatry,* Churchill, London, pp 84–108

——(1974) *Comparative psychiatry: a theoretical framework,* University of Toronto Press, Toronto

Yerkes, R. M. (ed.) (1921) *Psychological examining in the United States Army. Memoirs of the National Academy of Sciences,* Vol. 15 Government Printing Office, Washington

INDEX

Siegler, M. 5
Sillen, S. 21, 23, 24, 34
Simon, Bennett 4
Singer, K. 69
Singer, P. 88
Skultans, V. 8, 19
Slater, E. 138, 153, 154
slavery 9–10, 35
    legitimised by psychiatry
    23–4
    see also colonialism
social control
    and psychiatry
    49–50, 97, 145, 184
social psychiatry 39, 41, 46, 56,
    101–2 *passim*
Social Psychiatry Research Unit
    41, 54, 98
social sciences 14
social system
    defined 1–2
social therapy 121
social worker(s)
    137, 149, 159, 166
    power 128, 129
    role 108
    training 116
sociology 17
somatisation
    and communication
    110, 113, 183
    and racism
    31, 98, 130, 140, 166
    see also emotional
    differentation; mind-body
    dualism
somato-psychic model of illness
    89, 93
    see also mind-body dualism
South Africa
    policy on 56, 174, 181
    services for Blacks 68, 180–1
Soviet Union
    concept of schizophrenia xiv
    dissenters 140
spirit possession 90
Spuhler, J.N. xv
Sri Lanka
    community survey 84
    depression 66

possession states 87
schizophrenia 68
Steadman, H.J. 43, 164, 179
stereotypes
    and categories 29, 44–8
    passim, 45
    and 'maladjustment' 81
    defined 47
    in psychiatry
    17, 42, 105, 109, 149
    of Afro-Caribbeans/West
    Indians 56, 138, 147
    of Asians 29, 56, 138, 147
    of Blacks 25, 48
    see also Afro-Caribbean
    families; Asian families
Stone, A. 56, 68, 180
Stone, M. 30
Stopes-Roe, M. 75
Strecker, E.A. xiv
Street, B. 25
student selection
    racism 146, 176
suicide rates 80, 85
susto
    see also culture-bound
    syndromes
Suzuki, T. 88
Swartz, L. 68
Sweden
    occurrence of schizophrenia
    xiv
Sykes, J.B. 47, 131, 149
Sypher, W. 18

'tangle of pathology'
    see black families
Terman, Lewis 20–1
Thatcher, Margaret 130
Therborn, G. 1
Thomas, A. 21, 23, 24, 34
Thomas, W.I. 20
Thornicroft, G. 78
training 115–16, 144–5
'transference' 119
transcultural psychiatry xi,
    xiii-xiv, 55
    American xi-xii
    and family therapy 103–4
    British xii-xiii